REFORMING THE REPUBLIC

REAL POLITICS IN AMERICA

Series Editor: Paul S. Herrnson, *University of Maryland*

The books in this series bridge the gap between academic scholarship and the popular demand for knowledge about politics. They illustrate empirically supported generalizations from original research and the academic literature using examples taken from the legislative process, executive branch decision making, court rulings, lobbying efforts, election campaigns, political movements, and other areas of American politics. The goal of the series is to convey the best contemporary political science research has to offer in ways that will engage individuals who want to know about real politics in America.

REFORMING THE REPUBLIC

DEMOCRATIC INSTITUTIONS FOR THE NEW AMERICA

Todd Donovan
Western Washington University

Shaun Bowler
University of California, Riverside

PEARSON

Prentice
Hall

UPPER SADDLE RIVER, NEW JERSEY 07458

Library of Congress Cataloging-in-Publication Data

Donovan, Todd.
  Reforming the republic: democratic institutions for the new America/Todd
Donovan, Shaun Bowler.
    p. cm.—(Real politics in America)
Includes bibliographical references and index.
  ISBN 0-13-099455-3
  1. Elections—United States.   2. Political campaigns—United States.
3. Proportional representation—United States.   4. Representative government
and representation—United States.   I. Bowler, Shaun.   II. Title.   III. Series.
  JK1976.D66   2004
    324.6'0973—dc22

                                                              2003015484

Editorial Director: Charlyce Jones Owen
Acquisitions Editor: Glenn Johnston
Assistant Editor: John Ragozzine
Editorial Assistant: Suzanne Remore
Director of Marketing: Beth Mejia
Marketing Assistant: Jennifer Bryant
Prepress and Manufacturing Buyer: Sherry Lewis
Interior Design: John P. Mazzola
Cover Design: Kiwi Design
Cover Art: The Studio Dog/Getty Images, Inc.
Composition/Full-Service Project Management: Kari C. Mazzola and John P. Mazzola
Printer/Binder: RR Donnelley & Sons Company
Cover Printer: Phoenix Color Corp.

This book was set in 10/12 Palatino.

Real Politics in America
Series Editor: Paul S. Herrnson

Pearson Education LTD.   Pearson Education North Asia Ltd
Pearson Education Singapore, Pte. Ltd   Pearson Educación de Mexico, S.A. de C.V.
Pearson Education, Canada, Ltd   Pearson Education Malaysia, Pte. Ltd
Pearson Education–Japan   Pearson Education, Upper Saddle River, NJ
Pearson Education Australia PTY, Limited

10 9 8 7 6 5 4 3
ISBN 0-13-099455-3

CONTENTS

PREFACE

For those of us who vote, our direct experience with elections is fairly simple. We figure out whom to vote for, and then later we hear who won. After any election, however, pundits take things much further. Their election post-mortems are filled with reasons why certain candidates won or lost. Winners are credited with having better ideas, great debate performances, the ability to "sell their message" or connect with the electorate's "mood." In retrospect, winners had the better "handlers" and consultants, produced killer television commercials, had the "electoral tides" in their favor, and so forth. Losses are explained by the opposites of these.

For the most part, neither the average voter nor the average pundit spends much time reflecting on how institutional rules determine electoral outcomes. This is not typically the stuff of heated exchanges on television shows such as "Crossfire" or "O'Reily Factor."

From our perspective, however, rules that shape elections have critical effects on election outcomes—and are far more important than most of the things we usually hear about. Most of these rules deal with things that are seemingly mundane but their consequences are huge.

Consider voting in any general election. Myriad rules shape what our choices look like each November. Thousands of people might want to be president or a member of Congress, but few have a credible chance of ever being elected. But that's the point—the rules predetermine who will have a chance. These rules—our election laws—determine the sort of person who will become a party's candidate. Rules determine if candidates run with party labels or not, and determine the number of candidates or parties who have any credible chance of winning.

The purpose of this book is to illustrate the importance of such rules, and to encourage readers to think about changing America's electoral rules. We examine rules that affect how congressional districts are drawn and rules that limit how many people are elected per district. We examine rules about how votes are cast in elections and rules governing how they are counted. The

Electoral College, campaign finance regulations, court rulings about who gets to participate in primary elections, laws defining the number of members of Congress—each of these has tremendous implications for who wins and loses elections. Democracy in the American republic has evolved as these rules are updated and reformed.

For a moment, the 2000 presidential election had the public focused on how institutional rules determine outcomes. If the national popular vote total had been used, Gore would have been president. With the electoral college vote used, Bush won. But the effects of rules run much deeper than this. Had voters in Florida and elsewhere been able to rank-order their preferences as Irish voters do when electing their president, Gore may have won the electoral college as well. Even using our traditional voting methods, different vote-counting machines may have helped one candidate more than the other. The issue goes even deeper. Another set of nomination rules or campaign finance rules might have produced completely different Democratic and Republican candidates. Likewise, another set of rules regulating congressional elections affected which party won control of the U.S. House in 2000.

Our point is not that the 2000 election was any more flawed than previous elections. It probably was not. It does, however, provide a compelling illustration of how rules matter. It is also a compelling demonstration of how big the stakes can be for those who win and lose. The trajectory of American history was changed in September 2001—yet the government that presided over that crisis was as much a product of election rules as it was a clear expression of what voters wanted when they cast their ballots in November of 2000.

Most of the time, citizens probably do not notice how election rules shape who wins or loses. We argue that they do sense that something is seriously wrong with how elections work in this nation. We begin from the premise that something is wrong with the American electoral process. Cynicism about elections is high, and participation is low. We admit that the symptoms are more easily identified than the cure—nonetheless, the problem is real. Americans express little confidence in the utility of their electoral process, and this predated the 2000 election.

This book examines some of the most important rules that shape America's electoral landscape. We direct attention to some major reform proposals that have received attention in the United States over the past decade: proportional representation, term limits for Congress, reforming the electoral college, direct election of the president, campaign finance reforms, Internet voting, and more. We make no explicit recommendations for reform. Rather, we seek to assemble the best evidence available to anticipate what might happen if certain rules were changed.

Many of the major electoral reform proposals that reach our nation's agenda have been adopted in some of our states, or in other established democratic nations. This allows us a comparative perspective from which to draw inferences about how such reforms might change American politics. This gives readers the ability to see that there are alternatives to the status quo U.S. electoral system that are used in the "real world." We hope that this book will help readers think critically about how election results are structured by rules that define how elections are conducted.

Todd Donovan
Shaun Bowler

ELECTORAL REFORM AND AMERICAN POLITICS

Most of the world's established democracies have adopted electoral arrangements very different from those found in America. Some take comfort from American exceptionalism and independence. To others, electoral politics in America looks a bit old-fashioned. America retains a form of party competition and representation that, compared to other advanced democratic societies, can seem a little limited. When the world's newest democracies search the globe for models of how to be a democracy, very few select the "winner-take-all" rules that the United States adopted in the eighteenth century. Even Britain has begun to use election rules that provide for more proportional representation.[1] The United States also stands as one of the only advanced democracies never to have allowed its citizens to vote directly on a major policy or constitutional question.[2] Many other democracies also have regulations on campaign finance that make illegal anything resembling America's free-wheeling campaign contribution system. In this book we consider some possibilities for reforms to America's system of representation. We do this with an eye toward more practical or politically possible kinds of reforms. There seems little point in suggesting a wholesale rewriting of the Constitution to provide, for example, for parliamentary government or an end to federalism. The reforms we examine, then, are in many ways incremental changes but ones that, nevertheless, may be worth making. By and large the reforms we consider concern the core of a democratic polity—its system of elections and representation.

It is always difficult to begin considering changes to a series of institutions that many think have served us well for over 200 years now.

Sometimes the impression is given that the Constitution was an act of inspiration drafted by prescient men with a broad faith in democracy. The Founders were wise, we learn, and apart from minor tinkering, the Constitution they drafted in Philadelphia was (wisely and intentionally) written broadly enough to endure for centuries. From this perspective, the document contained the embryo of an enduring democratic society, and the flexibility of its institutional arrangements provided for our nation's future democratic expansion. Thus, it is not surprising that when proposals are made to change basic elements of our democratic arrangements and electoral processes, we hear resistance made in the name of the Founders' intent.

Such a view does disservice to the Constitution and, for that matter, to the Founders by seeing it as unchanging and—for some at least—therefore unchangeable. But as one of America's greatest jurists—Thurgood Marshall—noted on the occasion of the Bicentennial of the Constitution in 1987:

> I do not believe that the meaning of the Constitution was forever "fixed" at the Philadelphia Convention. Nor do I find the wisdom, foresight, and sense of justice exhibited by the framers particularly profound. To the contrary, the government they devised was defective from the start, requiring several amendments, a civil war, and momentous social transformation to attain the system of constitutional government, and its respect for the individual freedoms and human rights, that we hold as fundamental today. When contemporary Americans cite "The Constitution," they invoke a concept that is vastly different from what the framers barely began to construct two centuries ago.[3]

This book is premised on the idea that resistance to change in America's basic democratic institutions, whether that resistance is grounded in appeals to our constitutional tradition or to the Founders' intent, is flawed at many levels. For one thing, our Constitution provides much less guidance than standard civics courses might suggest. As Marshall noted, American democracy has always been in a process of evolution and reform. American political development reflects a history of democratic expansions that often conflicted with the original Constitution. Social movements seeking greater democracy have often had their greatest success when they were able to change the original document, perhaps the most graphic example being the expansion of civil rights. Indeed, American history can be well-understood in terms of struggles that flowed out of the democratic deficit of the original Constitution.

The preceding argument is not new. Nor is it universally accepted. And so before we can examine contemporary proposals to reform American electoral institutions, we must address one of the primary barriers to change: the near mystic and certainly romantic fascination that many have with the Philadelphia Constitution of 1789, and their assumption that the document and our election practices were not meant to be changed.

ELECTORAL REFORM AND AMERICAN HISTORY

Given the historical context, the Philadelphia document was a remarkably progressive achievement. It was also a product of bargaining, deal-making and compromise growing out of often quite bitter fights. Many of these fights stemmed from the dismal failure of the first American constitutional experiment—the Articles of Confederation. The Constitution was a deal brokered between the rich and powerful states and the smaller and poorer ones, between farmers and nonfarmers, and even many of the Framers acknowledged that it left fundamental issues—such as slavery—unresolved.[4] Attempts to change the deal began even as early as the first Congress. Over twenty amendments were proposed, and ten known collectively as the Bill of Rights were adopted.

Despite amendment, ambiguity inherent in the document has continually shaped political conflict in the nation. The Supreme Court, for example, left unspecified in the original Constitution and its subsequent amendments, struggled for decades to define its mission. In the nineteenth century the relationship between states and the federal government was also ill-defined and the definition of many fundamental rights of citizens was left to the whims of state legislatures.

The "flexibility" that is often said to mitigate the need for any further amendment to the "living constitution" quickly proved unworkable. Americans fought the horrifically bloody Civil War (1860–1865) over some of the constitutional questions that could not be resolved in Philadelphia—a mere seventy years after the founding of the republic. After that war, the substance of the Constitution was changed radically, particularly in the area of electoral laws. Citizenship was redefined in a more expansive manner via the Thirteenth Amendment (1865), which abolished slavery, and the "equal protection" Fourteenth Amendment (1868), that gave a statement of the definition of citizenship. Voting rights were redefined in a more expansive manner by the Fifteenth Amendment of 1870, which began the long process of extending voting rights to nonwhites.

Long after the Civil War, other constitutional amendments reflected the enduring need to address and re-address questions of electoral law. The Nineteenth Amendment of 1920 extended voting rights to women in all states. The twenty-fourth Amendment of 1964 continued attempts to extend voting rights to nonwhites by eliminating the poll tax in Federal elections. The twenty-sixth Amendment of 1971 also extended the right to vote to eighteen-year-olds.

These constitutional changes redefined relations between states and the federal government with a result that looks little like the Philadelphia document. The Fourteenth Amendment in particular led, albeit gradually, to the national government having a level of supremacy over the states that would have been unimaginable to the first Founders. To observers like Thurgood Marshall, however, the post–Civil War amendments finally established the prospect for national standards of democratic citizenship that reflect America's true founding as a republic. Without the amendments secured after the Civil War, the national government would be unable to protect all Americans from state governments that routinely abuse(d) the political and civil liberties of citizens. Without these amendments, there would have been no *Brown v. Board of Education* ending racial segregation in schools, no *Baker v. Carr* and *Reynolds v. Sims* establishment of the "one person, one vote" principle, and no Voting Rights Act to protect a citizen's right to register and vote.

We often overlook the magnitude of these changes and sometimes romanticize the Civil War as being something other than an ugly fight over competing visions of constitutional arrangements. This is easy to do, given that many elected officials and majorities on the Supreme Court ignored the spirit of the Fourteenth and Fifteenth Amendments until the middle of the twentieth century. Many also see the Civil War as having resolved many of the major disputes about the proper nature of America's democratic arrangements.

But others see the Civil War and the constitutional changes that it produced failing to resolve America's conflict with the limits on democracy that were embedded in the original Constitution. After that war, expectations about the citizen's proper role in a democracy continued to shape political conflict in the nation. Within two decades of its end, social movements pressed for granting legislative majorities the power to tax income and regulate corporations. They pressed for greater direct popular participation in selecting senators and presidents, for further expansion of the right to vote (to women), and for more direct citizen participation in writing legislation. By the 1890s, the Populists merged with the Democratic party, and by the early twentieth century, Populist, Progressive, and Prohibitionist reformers secured amendments to the U.S. Constitution that enshrined some (but not all) of these goals.

We see the results of this wave of democratic expansion in the U.S. Constitution in the period at the turn of the nineteenth century. The Seventeenth Amendment provided for the direct election of U.S. senators and, during the period between 1898 and 1918, nineteen states adopted provisions for direct citizen participation in drafting laws and voting on legislation.[5] Many states also began experiments with direct voter participation in the political parties' nomination process. These reforms marked the success of some, but not all, of the proposals of the Populists and Progressives whose hopes for further expansion of democratic practices were left unfulfilled. To this date, for example, the U.S. Constitution lacks provisions for direct democracy (e.g., referendum), and for direct popular election of the president.

Even without amending the Constitution, major changes in electoral arrangements continued through the twentieth century. Federal statutes such as the Voting Rights Act of 1965 made local voter registration procedures subject to federal regulation and Justice Department protection. This led to a dramatic rise in participation by African Americans, and redefined, in practice, who would pick governments and who would be represented. Between 1950 and 1970, moreover, several Supreme Court decisions eliminated barriers to voting such as whites-only primary elections and literacy tests. *Baker v. Carr* (1962) established that the malapportionment of state legislatures could be contested in federal courts. *Gray v. Sanders* (1963) and *Reynolds v. Sims* (1963) established that lightly populated rural areas could no longer be systematically overrepresented in state legislatures or state congressional delegations simply because state legislatures wanted to keep it that way. These decisions together established the principle of "one person, one vote" and radically changed the nature of representation in the United States.

Federal and state statutes and Supreme Court decisions also define the autonomy of political parties and regulate how (indeed, if) voters can participate in the selection of candidates who run under a party's label. Prior to 1972, few citizens were allowed to have any direct say in who would be the party's nominee for president. Today, all states require parties to let voters participate in primary elections that select these nominees but the Supreme Court continues to grapple with the parties' rights to exclude certain voters from participating in their nomination process.[6]

The point of this discussion is to underscore the fact that basic laws and rules, including constitutional ones, that define democratic practice in the United States have changed both frequently and substantially over the years. The original deal has been restruck and renegotiated when people have felt the need to do so. Since the founding of the republic, one of the major motivating forces for change, we suggest, has been demands for greater expansion of democratic practice in terms of rights of citizens, access to the political process, and citizen influence over government. So there has been change, considerable change, in core aspects of the democratic process concerning the electoral system over the years. As society changes, as it becomes more educated and more diverse and as information technology expands, it seems reasonable to suppose that citizens would like to see more institutional changes in response

In Chapter 2 we investigate what Americans think about representation and democracy. Polling evidence suggests that many Americans are unhappy with some aspects of their political process, and that this unhappiness is based on a sense that they are not represented in government, and can't influence what it does. Our analysis of contemporary elections in subsequent chapters illustrates that there are valid reasons for public concern about their lack of influence over their government. As we proceed through these chapters, we offer our assessment of various proposals designed to make Americans have more faith in their elections and representatives.

THE PRIMARY ROLE OF ELECTORAL RULES

There are a wide variety of political reforms—constitutional, statutory, and administrative—that we could consider in this book—reforms that might produce major changes in American politics. Our focus, however, is mainly on reforms that are directed at electoral processes—that is, the rules governing how elections are conducted. Although these matters might seem dry and uninspiring to many, electoral institutions are of primary importance partly because they help to define what a democracy is and also because they ultimately shape who serves in office, who has influence, and who has power in the political system.

Different electoral rules are likely to produce different winners and losers in contests for political office. Moreover, electoral rules shape the behavior of elected officials by shaping their sense of constituency. Who holds elected officials accountable, what they're held accountable for, and how they are held accountable are all aspects of electoral rules. Electoral rules affect how candidates campaign by shaping whether candidates need to win a small proportion of votes, or a plurality, or a majority. Campaign finance rules affect who candidates turn to for funding; districting rules can determine how competitive a reelection contest will be. Even with no change in voters' preferences, slight changes in how we draw district lines, how we cast ballots, or how we count votes can produce very different winners and losers.

As the simplest possible case, consider the following example. In a society there are three different kinds of people. Let's call them As, Bs, and Cs. These letters can reflect different party views or different issue positions (e.g., liberals, conservatives, and moderates). Assume they live in six precincts (P) in a city, and we have to draw boundaries to make two congressional seats.

Here are the six precincts with the three sorts of people in them. There are 50 As in two precincts (25 in each), forty Bs (20 voters in 2 precincts) and 20 Cs (10 x 2).

P1 (25 As)	P4 (25 As)
P2 (20 Bs)	P5 (20 Bs)
P3 (10 Cs)	P6 (10 Cs)

We represent the border between two districts by a thick line, like so:

DISTRICT 1	DISTRICT 2
P1 (25 As)	P4 (25 As)
P2 (20 Bs)	P5 (20 Bs)
P3 (10 Cs)	P6 (10 Cs)

If the As all vote for the same candidate, the As win both seats under this electoral rule. But we could have drawn the seats like this:

District 1	A: 25	A: 25
District 2	B: 20	B: 20
	C: 10	C: 10

In this case the As win one seat and the Bs win another. No voters changed their minds and the numbers of voters stayed the same but the outcome shifted. The *only* thing we altered was the boundary of the district or the rule of who is in which district. In the real world the distribution of populations are often not as neat and tidy as this example and so drawing district boundaries becomes a bit more complicated. But the simple example has made our point. Rules—even the ones in the U.S. Constitution—are not neutral. Rules shape outcomes and can decide who wins and who loses, and the Founding Fathers knew this.

The election rules we use allowed one party to win the House and presidency in 2000, even though their candidates failed to win a majority in either contest. Our current rules allowed the winning candidate in the 2000 presidential election to finish second in the popular vote. Even with no change in voters' preferences, slight changes in how we draw district lines, how we cast ballots, or how we count votes could have given a different party control of Congress *and* the presidency after the 2000 election. Different rules might have also given Republicans control of the presidency after the 1992 election. Of course, it is impossible to know how one party might have acted if they, rather than the other, controlled government after either election. It is safe to assume that history would have been different—whether tax cuts, court appointments, war against terrorism, or George W. Bush's invasion of Iraq were the issue.

If such results are very rare, there may be no immediate crisis of public opinion. As we shall see, however, these odd outcomes could become more common, given the present state of parties and our antiquated election rules. The legitimacy of public policies, court decisions, and governmental actions in general may suffer in the public's eyes if, over time, citizens see the electoral process as failed. Cynicism about the process is also likely to be higher among citizens who vote for the losers. What happens, then, when most citizens who bother to cast a ballot vote for candidates who lose? We will show that the prospects for this is greater than many might expect, and that our "winner-take-all" election rules are to blame.

Different rules also allow different voices to influence the political agenda and structure political debates. One way to show this is not simply to examine the rules that govern our elections but also to compare our process to those in other established democracies. As we will see in subsequent chapters, some reform proposals might not produce dramatic changes in who wins office; some rule changes may not make much of a difference. Electoral rules ultimately affect who gets what from government, but their effects can often be subtle or indirect. We hope to shed some light on how some contemporary electoral reform proposals might change things in the United States.

None of this is to say that court decisions, legislation, or administrative rules, are trivial matters. These are typically the "big issues" of politics that structure differences between candidates and parties. Indeed, over the last few decades, new public policies have altered the American political landscape. Policies on free trade, the death penalty, abortion, war powers, and the "war on terrorism," to name but a few of the current issues, touch upon the lives of nearly all Americans. But the actors who make the policies, we must not forget, are the products of particular laws that shape how elections are conducted. Different rules can produce different political parties, as well as different points of consensus and disagreement over policy.

ELECTION RULES: PROCESS AND OUTCOME

So far we have emphasized outcomes, but process also matters. Beyond their effects on policy outcomes, electoral rules are critically important because they spell out how politics will be conducted. Even if some rules changes make little difference in outcome, they may nevertheless bring about subtle but important changes in how winning candidates campaign and in whom they rely upon to win. As an obvious example of a concern for process over outcome, and one we will hear more about, consider the 2000 presidential election and the Florida vote. The fact that George Bush won did not offend people so much as the manner in which he was judged to be the winner. For many Americans, concerns about *process* loom as large as, if not larger than, concerns about the substance of what government does in many areas of policy. Mountains of survey research show that Americans are relatively inattentive to the details of specific public policies but perceptions of the political process nevertheless structure views about the legitimacy of government. Thus, to the extent that certain types of rules make elections more or less "fair", or more or less "competitive", we expect that they shape attitudes about government generally, and Congress specifically.[7]

A change in any of these electoral rules can not only affect *who* wins office, but also *how* someone wins. A different electoral process creates different incentives for politicians, and a different set of actors who influence them.[8] This means that changes in such rules should condition what elected officials do when they govern.

WHERE HAVE MAJORITIES GONE?

Besides these fundamental reasons for examining election rules and investigating how they might be improved, there are other issues that highlight the need to consider reforming American elections.

In the past decade alone, American national elections have consistently produced outcomes that were, at best, a poor expression of what the public asked for when they voted, and, at worst, an invitation to constitutional crisis. In 1992, for example, President Clinton was elected with only 43.01 percent of the vote. If we recall that just half of those who are eligible to vote actually do vote, then the percentage of American adults who actively supported President Clinton was even lower. Although this low vote proportion was not unprecedented for the United States (Nixon was elected in 1968 with just 43.4 percent), Clinton's 1992 vote was one of the lowest winning margins in the history of the republic. Since popular voting began for president in 1828, only two candidates were ever elected with margins lower than Clinton's.[9] Lincoln won the four-way 1860 election with just 39.8 percent of the votes cast, as the nation's political parties fragmented over the questions of secession and slavery. Wilson won in 1912 with 41.8 percent when T. Roosevelt bolted the Republican party to take up the mantle of Progressivism.

Other than these contests, most presidents have been elected with majorities, or with pluralities very close to 50 percent. In the last decade, however, nationwide electoral majorities have become quite elusive. No president has been elected since 1988 with the support of a majority of those who voted. This represented the first time in American history that three consecutive elections have failed to produce a president who could win a majority. The period from 1992–2000 produced some of the highest support for minor party presidential candidates over any three consecutive elections since the Civil War. The disappearance of electoral majorities is not limited to presidential elections. The Republican majority controlling the U.S. House of Representatives was elected with a mere 47.0 percent of the popular vote in 2000, while the Republican House majority in power after the 1998 election received only 48.4 percent.[10]

Results such as these have become more common in presidential races as minor party candidates like Ross Perot and Ralph Nader capture a measurable share of votes. These candidates take votes from regular supporters of the major parties *and* they bring new voters to the polls. In many state and local contests, candidates are also winning with smaller vote shares as independent candidates attract greater support. In Minnesota, for example, Jesse Ventura was elected governor with just 37 percent of the vote in a 3-candidate race, in an election where turnout was rather high. In many other places, even relatively modest showings by Libertarians and Greens can bring down winning margins.[11]

Similar results can be found in major state elections, particularly in the west. Support for minor party candidates reached an average of 7 percent by 1994 in a set of elections in western states. This leaves the major parties less of the vote to split, allowing candidates to win with less than 50 percent. In California's 1990 and 1994 elections several offices (including governor, two U.S. Senate races and a number of other state-wide offices) were won with margins well below 50 percent. Oregon's Senator Gordon Smith was also denied a majority in 1996. In 1997, New Jersey's Republican Governor Christie Todd Whitman was narrowly reelected with 47 percent support when a Libertarian candidate received 5 percent of the vote. In 2000, Maria Cantwell defeated incumbent Slade Gorton to win Washington's U.S. Senate race, with neither candidate receiving a majority.[12]

By mobilizing new voters who are not loyal to the major parties, and by collecting votes from traditional supporters of the two main parties, Perot, Nader, Buchanan, Ventura, the Libertarians, and other new political forces are making it difficult for winning candidates to claim majority support after an election. More voters have been supporting these "minor" candidates, as well as identifying with and registering with their parties, than at any point in the last several decades (although their numbers remain small). At the same time, support for the major parties is stagnant, if not in decline[13]

Disappearing electoral majorities are not a phenomena isolated to occasional elections. If Americans continue to flirt with minor candidates and support independents in 3- or 4-way races, interest in electoral reforms should accelerate. When voters begin to support more than two parties, our election rules may not only fail to produce clear winners, but they may also fail to produce winners supported by most voters. As we show in Chapter 3, "first-past-the-post," winner-take-all election rules used in nearly all U.S. elections already produce awkward results under the best of circumstances, when voters are choosing between just two candidates (or parties).

A TALE OF TWO ELECTIONS: 1996 AND 2000

The kinds of examples of declining majorities we noted above might be dismissed as simple nuisances were it not for the corrosive effects these election results can have on our nation over the long term. Recall, for example, that from the start of the Clinton administration the far-right considered his election illegitimate, and thus used "any means possible" to attack him.[14]

Despite public opinion that was decidedly supportive of him remaining president throughout the Monica Lewinsky scandal, President Clinton was impeached in 1998.

The U.S. House of Representatives thus nearly toppled a popular president over a matter that most Americans did not find to be a grave offense. How could this have happened? The Republican House majority presiding over the impeachment was elected in 1996 with just 48.9 percent of the national vote (of the 45 percent of eligible voters who voted in House races). Sizing up their reelection prospects, House members from both parties know that only about one-third of Americans bother to vote in midterm (non-presidential) elections. As we illustrate in Chapter 3, few members of Congress (Democrat or Republican) come from competitive districts—most are elected from seats that are nearly impossible for their party to lose. Many incumbents are easily reelected by activating their own core partisans who form a relatively small proportion of citizens in a district.[15]

Even if we think of elections to Congress as hundreds of individual contests, the sum result of all these elections need not produce a legislature that will have attitudes and concerns that reflect national public opinion. Candidates are responsive to forces inside their district. Very few districts look anything like a cross-section of the American public. Nearly all are designed to be "safe" for one party or the other. Nomination processes in many states (see Chapter 5), furthermore, tend to reward candidates from the ideologically extreme wings of the parties. Even if a district's electorate were somehow representative of voters generally, it might be faced with choices between candidates who have policy positions at odds with most voters in the district.[16]

Put simply, election rules reduce the number of moderate candidates and limit the places they could win. Candidates for Congress are elected by skewed subgroups of voters, many of whom find ideologically distinctive candidates appealing. Safe districts are designed to protect incumbents from any reversal their party might suffer nationally. Once elected, they hardly ever lose. This may leave many members of Congress with little incentive to consider the opinions of voters from outside the core of their own party. In 1998, most House Republicans had nothing to lose by ignoring polls that showed a large majority of Americans nationwide opposing impeachment and approving Clinton's job performance. After all, they were not accountable to national majorities but to their core constituencies who, small as they were, wanted impeachment, and would reelect incumbents who pursued Clinton.[17]

Indeed, after defying public opinion and impeaching Clinton in 1998, Republicans were able to retain control of the House, despite winning only 49 percent support nationally (of the 34 percent who voted). Republicans received slightly more votes than Democrats, but support for minor candidates prevented either big party from claiming a majority of votes. The president, we should not forget, was reelected in 1996 by only 49 percent of the 49 percent who bothered to vote. Although his standing in the polls was strong, his party's electoral position was weaker.

The handful of Republican senators and many Democrats who voted to acquit Clinton did not question that the charges against him may have been trivial or even false.[18] Rather, these senators acted on the concern that the charges had not been well-proven by the House's impeachment process. The contemporary electoral context and the impeachment of 1998 have thus redefined the range of matters that partisans now deem an impeachable offense. The range of offenses is now wide-open, public preferences be damned.

Is this an outcome we can pin on electoral rules rather than, say, the deep-seated commitment of many in Congress to high standards in public life? We answer that question with another: Had more members of Congress faced re-election in competitive districts, would history have been different? Perhaps if moderate candidates had better chances of being nominated, sitting Republicans may not have pursued impeachment. Would things have been different if voter turnout in congressional elections had been substantially higher than 33 percent in 1998? Furthermore, if the 1992 or 1996 elections had been conducted using voting methods that insured that winning candidates had at least a bare electoral majority (discussed in Chapter 5), would the president have been a target for impeachment at all? Of course, there are no easy answers to any of these questions. They are meant to illustrate how different electoral rules might not only change who is elected, but they also affect what elected officials might do (or not do) when in office.

The 1998 impeachment example suggests that America's election rules can produce awkward outcomes, as well as weak incentives for elected officials to heed opinion. The 2000 presidential and congressional elections represent a different type of democratic failure. The presidential contest produced a winner who lost the popular vote, and House elections gave majority control to a party that received fewer votes nationally than the opposition.[19]

It is important to remember that the 2000 election was incredibly close, but the election nevertheless illustrates the dangers of winner-take-all elections. In the best of circumstances, a victory under winner-take-all by even the slimmest of margins can give tremendous power to the winning party. In 2000, however, unified control of the House and the presidency was placed in the hands of a party that received fewer votes nationally than the Democrats. The presidential election result, ultimately decided by the Supreme Court (*Bush v. Gore*), also gave Republicans the tie-breaking vote in the Senate, and thus granted the party unified control of the House, Senate, and presidency. The defection of one Republican Senator—Jeffords—diluted this control somewhat, but election results produced a national government that failed to reflect the preferences voters cast when national vote totals are considered. While survey data provide no clear sense of public outcry about these results, our concern is what might happen if our elections continue to produce such outcomes. At what point does the legitimacy of elected officials suffer?

For President George W. Bush, the question is highly problematic. In late November 2000, as the Florida recounts dragged on, most Americans did not believe that either Bush or Gore could claim to have legitimately won the presidency, whatever the outcome. Rather, a majority were unsure, or they believed the eventual winner would be produced by whatever way votes were counted.[20] Although Bush enjoyed little or no public opinion "honeymoon" after his election, concerns about his legitimacy faded in the immediate aftermath of the attack on the World Trade Center. But the 2000 election outcomes produced ample opportunities to challenge the legitimacy of elected officials—something that is not healthy to the long-term health of a democratic system.

The 1998 impeachment and 2000 elections are but two recent examples of a near constitutional crisis that might have been averted had different election rules been in place. A House of Representatives more representative of, or responsive to, the American public would almost certainly not have impeached the president; and a different system of elections might have given the victorious presidential candidate greater legitimacy. But these are simply the most dramatic examples of how institutional reforms may be worth thinking about. As we will see, there are many other examples that receive less publicity and less attention.

The problems we consider in the following chapters are even larger than the disappearance of electoral majorities and occasional elections that produce governance that fails to reflect popular attitudes about matters such as impeachment. Our elections produce results by which candidates or parties with the most votes lose. In many elections, most voters vote against the eventual winner. As we see in Chapter 2, many American elections also lack competitiveness and fail to elect officials that represent the diversity of American life. To make matters worse, public perceptions about the relationship between politicians and their campaign donors breed cynicism about government and democracy. And, as we see in the next chapter, many Americans think elected officials are corrupt, that elections don't really matter, and they do not think that government is responsive to regular citizens.

Of course, reforms have their downsides. A wealth of studies suggests that earlier reforms and various social trends have had ill effects on U.S. elections. The development of personality rather than policy-centered campaigns, voter dealignment from political parties, the increased use of TV and its rising costs are all seen as ills, some of them stemming from earlier reform efforts. American elections have become less competitive, they mobilize fewer voters, and they (might) present voters with choices that fail to reflect the diversity of public preferences for representation. Perhaps it is time to consider some new changes?

THE RANGE OF REFORMS CONSIDERED IN THIS BOOK

We examine a set of contemporary proposals that aim to fix some of these problems by changing how Americans elect their government. In the chapters that follow, we examine what aspects of American elections need fixing, and some proposals that have been offered as fixes. We do this with an eye toward what is practical or politically possible rather than some fanciful attempt to rewrite the entire Constitution. Thus, we are not interested in assessing wholesale revising of America's Constitution. Fundamental changes in federalism, separation of powers, and checks and balances are not at issue here. For example, we do not consider proposals for parliamentary government to be a reform worth considering, since there is no chance that the U.S. Constitution would be scrapped to provide for such a chance.

Rather, we ask what the effects of more subtle rules changes might be. Many of the proposals we consider were selected because they are the pet ideas of various advocacy groups and think-tanks in the United States, or because the specific electoral reform, or concepts related to the reform, have received popular support in American opinion polls. Some would probably require amending the Constitution, although, as we have seen, it is possible to amend the Constitution. Others could be enacted with basic changes in statutory laws. For the record, we like some of these proposals, are neutral on some, and dislike others. Our goal, however, is to try to assess how these various rules might change the way elections work here. To do this, we draw on empirical studies of the effects of political reform and examine how these proposals have worked in other nations that have adopted them. We should also say that we are not intent on making a partisan argument. In our view no one party is better or worse than the other and the examples we use are drawn from both major parties.

In what follows, among the reforms we discuss are the direct election of the president, the adoption of a preferential electoral system for Congress, reforms in the campaign finance system, a national initiative proposal, and other reforms to the actual conduct of elections. All of these have been offered as solutions to what ails America's institutions. But before examining the solutions, we should ask if there is a problem in need of solution. As the phrase has it, "if it isn't broken don't fix it." Before we offer a whole range of fixes, let's see if America's institutions are broken. This we do in the next chapter.

NOTES

1. Elections to the regional Assemblies of Scotland, Wales, and N. Ireland, as well as elections for the European Parliament now use proportional representation, which provides seats for more than just 2 or 3 parties. The British Parliament is still elected by single-member

districts where the candidate with the most votes gets the seat. Tony Blair has promised a referendum on alternatives for electing Parliament, but no referendum was held in his first term.

2. Many European nation's legislatures have referred measures to their citizens for votes. Issues include abortion and divorce (in Ireland), joining NATO (Spain), terms of joining the European Union (in several continental nations), nuclear power (Norway), etc. Referendums have also been quite common in the new democracies of eastern Europe and states of the former Soviet Union. See Henry Brady, "Eastern Europe," in *Referendums around the World: The Growing Use of Direct Democracy*, ed. E. Butler and A. Ranney (Washington, D.C.: AEI Press, 1994).

3. Thurgood Marshall, "The Constitutions Past and Present," speech presented to the Annual Seminar of the San Francisco Patent and Trademark Law Association, May 6, 1987, San Francisco, CA.

4. John P. Roche, "The Founding Fathers: A Reform Caucus in Action," *American Political Science Review* 55 (1961).

5. David Magleby, *Direct Legislation: Voting on Ballot Propositions in the United States* (Baltimore, MD: Johns Hopkins University Press, 1984).

6. See U.S. Supreme Court decision, *California Democratic Party et al. v. Jones 2000*.

7. See John Hibbing and Elizabeth Theiss-Morse, *Congress as Public Enemy: Public Attitudes toward American Political Institutions* (New York: Cambridge University Press, 1995); M. Delli Carpini and S. Keeter, *What Americans Know about Politics and Why It Matters* (New Haven, CT: Yale University Press, 1996).

8. G. Cox, *Making Vote Count: Strategic Coordination in the World's Electoral Systems* (New York: Cambridge University Press, 1997).

9. In 1824, several states began allowing citizens to vote in contests that apportioned the state's presidential electors. In 1824, six states (of 22) continued to have electors appointed by their state legislature. By 1828, nearly all states allowed (white) males to vote in a general election for electors who were often affiliated with specific presidential candidates.

10. <http://www.fec.gov>.

11. S. Rosenstone, Roy L. Behr, Edward H. Lazarus, *Third Parties in America: Citizen Response to Major Party Failure* (Princeton, NJ: Princeton University Press, 1996); Dean Lacy and Barry C. Burden, "The Vote-Stealing and Turnout Effects of Ross Perot in the 1992 Presidential Election," *American Journal of Political Science* 43 (1999): 233–255; S. Frank and S. Wagner, *We Shocked the World! A Case Study of Jesse Ventura's Election as Governor of Minnesota* (New York: ITP, 1999); Barry Burden, "Did Ralph Nader Elect George Bush? Analysis of Minor Parties in the 2000 Presidential Election," paper presented at the American Political Science Association Meeting, 2001, San Francisco, CA.

12. C. Collet and J. Hansen, "The Rise of Third Parties in Western States," paper presented at the Western Political Science Association Meeting, 1995, Portland, OR.

13. See C. Collett, "Bye-Bye GOP, Ta-Ta Dems: California Voters Flee Traditional Parties," *California Journal* 24 (1993): 33–37; M. Wattenberg, *The Decline of American Political Parties, 1952–1994* (Cambridge, MA: Harvard University Press, 1996).

14. NRA members declared, for example, that "My President Is Charlton Heston." The failure to accept Clinton may have come, in part, from the sense that most Perot voters might have voted Republican if Perot had not run in 1992, and thus would have reelected George Bush (Sr.). Although there is no definitive academic answer to this question, there is some evidence that the Perot supporters and activists supported Republicans in subsequent elections. See Walter Stone and Ron Rapoport, "It's Perot, Stupid! The Legacy of the 1992 Perot Movement in the Major Party System, 1992–2000," *PS: Political Science and Politics* 34 (2001a): 49–58; Walter Stone and Ron Rapoport, "The Legacy of Ross Perot and the Reform Party: Third Party Politics and Change in the Major Party System," paper presented at the American Political Science Association Meeting, 2001b, San Francisco, CA.

15. Steven E. Schier, *By Invitation Only: The Rise of Exclusive Politics in the United States* (Pittsburg, PA: University of Pittsburg Press, 2000).

16. E. Gerber and R. Morton, "Primary Election Systems and Representation," *Journal of Law, Economics, and Organization* 14 (1998): 304–324.

17. From this perspective, the only Republicans with much to worry about under this scenario would be highly conservative members trying to hold a district where voters were

relatively moderate and equally likely to vote for Democrats or Republicans (e.g., James Rogan's 2000 election defeat in California's 27th District). But that's the point: There are hardly any of these sorts of districts left.

18. Ronald Dworkin, "The Wounded Constitution," *The New York Review of Books*, 18 March 1999.

19. Of 99,502,246 votes cast for House candidates, Republican candidates received 190,257 more than Democrats in 2000. Bernie Saunders (I-Vt.), who votes with Democrats, received 216,471 votes. His votes, combined with votes for Democrats, exceed votes for all Republican candidates. Data at <http://www.fec.gov>.

20. Pew Center Poll, "Many Question Bush or Gore as Legitimate Winner" (release date December 1, 2000).

2

IS AMERICA'S SYSTEM OF ELECTIONS BROKEN?
THE PUBLIC'S ATTITUDES

One of the indications that something *may* be wrong is that people are unhappy about their government. Americans today are less trusting of government than previous generations. In 1958 almost three-quarters of people surveyed said they trusted the federal government "to do what is right" most of the time or just about always. By 2002, after a modest upswing in trust, only 40 percent offered such responses. The trusting proportion of the population reached as low as 21 percent in 1994, and has been oscillating around 40 percent since the 1970s. This decline has been well documented, with substantial debate about what this distrust actually means and what its causes are.[1] Television, the Vietnam War, the Watergate scandal that brought down President Nixon, the Iran-Contra scandal of the 1980s, the Clinton impeachment, and various other scandals are all probably related to lower levels of trust in government.

The erosion of public trust has been quite steady, with only minor rebounds during the Reagan and Clinton years and, very briefly, after the terrorist attacks of September 11, 2001 (see Figure 2.1 on page 18). Any effects September 11 may have had in changing Americans' perspective on their federal government seems to have been short-lived—a temporary rally in a moment of crisis.[2] As we show below, trends in other opinions about the responsiveness of government suggest that the roots of public discontent with government may lie in something more than just episodic discontent associated with specific policies or with occasional scandals.

We believe these trends reflect, at least in part, that many Americans have lost faith in their electoral processes and, thus, simply do not feel that they are represented in the political system. Beneath the general distrust of government are specific perceptions that American government or, more specifically, elected officials, are no longer responsive to citizens. Data illustrating this are plotted in Figure 2.2 on page 18. By 2002, only 33 percent of Americans believed that government was run for the benefit of all rather than for the benefit of a few "big interests." This was a reversal from 1964, when 64

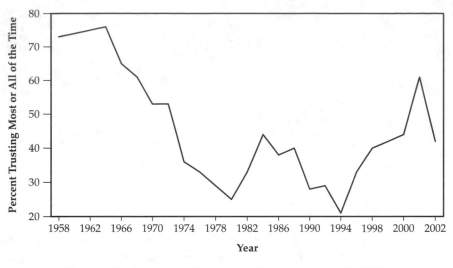

FIGURE 2.1   TRUST IN THE FEDERAL GOVERNMENT: 1958–2002

Source: National Election Study Data.

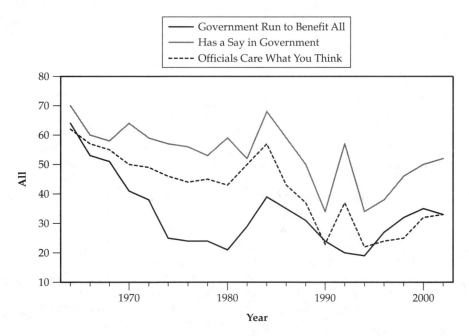

FIGURE 2.2   ATTITUDES ABOUT REPRESENTATION: 1964–2000

Source: National Election Study Data.

percent thought government benefited everyone. By 2002, moreover, only 33 percent of Americans thought that public officials cared about what "people like them" thought, down from 73 percent in 1960. Public discontent with elected officials continued to increase in the 1990s when, for the first time, most Americans began to agree with the statement, "people like me don't have any say in what government does." In the early 1960s, fewer than one-third of survey respondents agreed with this. Thus, for most Americans, the links between them and their elected officials seems broken.

Distrust of government is not limited to the United States, yet only one of the large European democracies—France—has higher levels of distrust (see Table 2.1). Table 2.2 (on page 20) presents data from another survey that offers further hints at what American distrust of government reflects. It is important to note that some of the most common reasons for distrusting government relate to perceptions of the political process, and how it fails. Large majorities are upset with how politicians campaign, how they behave in office, and who influences them. Far fewer cite concerns about actual government policies or the problems that government focuses on.

Thus, there has been a dramatic change in public opinion over the last three decades. People now see Congress largely influenced by "special" interests and increasingly see themselves as not represented. Public cynicism has reached such levels that by 1994, almost 90 percent believed that disagreement in Congress reflected political parties trying to "score political points," rather than honest disagreement about policies.[3] Partisan agendas, moreover, are seen as being something different from the concerns of most citizens. A 1999 study by the Center on Policy Attitudes concluded:

> The public's dissatisfaction with the U.S. government is largely due to the perception that elected officials, acting in their self-interest, give priority to special interests and partisan agendas over the interests of the public as a whole. Most Americans feel that they are marginalized from the decision making process, that elected officials neither pay attention to nor understand the public, and that most of the decisions the government makes are not the decisions the majority of Americans would make.[4]

TABLE 2.1   TRUST IN GOVERNMENT, EUROPE AND THE UNITED STATES

	DISTRUST	TRUST	DON'T KNOW
France	59%	33%	8%
United States	56	40	4
Italy	51	35	14
Spain	42	38	20
Germany	41	41	18
United Kingdom	32	57	11

Source: Pew Research Center for the People and Press, March 10, 1998 Survey Report

TABLE 2.2   REASONS FOR DISTRUSTING GOVERNMENT: 1999

	MAJOR REASON	MINOR REASON
Government leaders tell us what they think will get them elected, not what they really believe	80	14
The federal government is inefficient and wastes time	73	18
There is too much bickering between political parties	68	20
Special interests have too much influence on the federal government	65	24
Elected officials lack honesty and integrity	64	25
Federal taxes are too high	57	26
The federal government doesn't do enough to help people who really need it	56	27
People in government don't have high moral values	49	33
Federal government policies don't reflect your own beliefs and values	42	40
The federal government interferes too much in people's lives	42	37
The problems it focuses on cannot be solved by the federal government	39	39

Question wording: People give different reasons for NOT trusting the government. I'm going to read you a list of some of those reasons. Please tell me if each one is a major reason, a minor reason, or not a reason at all why YOU [often/sometimes] DON'T trust the federal government.

Source: NPR/Kaiser/Kennedy School survey, 1999.

THE ROOTS OF DISCONTENT

Can distrust of government be rooted in some failure in our electoral process-es that has unfolded at the same time that cynicism has increased? Is there something about contemporary elections that, in fact, leaves citizens under-represented in governments' decision-making processes? In the next chapter, we demonstrate that American elections have become far less competitive during the period that many more citizens began to feel marginalized. Before concluding that part of public discontent lies in the failures of our elections, however, we must assess other explanations for current public discontent with government.

Some of the decline in trust recorded in the opinion poll record is an ar-tifact of when polling began. It is likely that early opinion polls measured higher levels of trust as a result of the unique moment when this polling began. After World War II, trust in government may have been driven up by the ex-perience of overcoming the war and the preceding Great Depression. With the WW II generation starting from such a high level, a subsequent decline in trust was probably to be expected over time, as new citizens entered the electorate.[5] Once we add in the aggressive style of journalism associated with contemporary TV news, and events such as the Vietnam war, Watergate and, more recently, the set of scandals surrounding the Clinton impeachment, it should not be so surprising that popular faith in government was shaken.

Each of these major events also seemed to be surrounded by a series of well-publicized events such as Iran/Contra (1986), the House of Representative's check-bouncing scandal (1991–1992), two different scandals concerning Speakers of the House (Jim Wright [D] 1989 and Newt Gingrich [R] 1994), who entered into questionable book-royalty contracts, Clinton's Whitewater episode (1990s), Gary Condit's evasiveness about his relations with a missing intern (2001), and on and on. These events continue to show the country's political elite in a singularly unflattering light. Not surprisingly, public perceptions of dishonesty among politicians is one of the primary reasons for distrusting government (see Table 2.3).

TABLE 2.3 TOP REASONS PEOPLE GIVE FOR DISLIKING GOVERNMENT

Political Leadership/Political System (40 percent)
Politicians are dishonest/crooks
Only out for themselves/for own personal gain
Representatives say one thing and do another
Too partisan
Scandals

Critiques of Government (24 percent)
Too much spending/spend money frivolously
Fed. government can't get anything done
Government is too big/Too much government
Government interferes too much/too intrusive

Policy (15 percent)
Taxes too high
Dislike govt. policies in general/dislike specific policy
Spend too much on foreign countries
Government has the wrong priorities

Government doesn't care/Unresponsive (13 percent)
Government doesn't pay attention to/care about people
Needs/opinions of people not represented in government

Source: Pew Research Center for the People & Press, March 10, 1998 Survey Report.

Contemporary polls, then, may simply reflect that citizens now see more of the raw stuff of politics, and that while the basic nature of our politics has not changed, our awareness of the messy business of governing (and the way that groups influence government) is now greater. When surveys measured high levels of regard for government in the past, a less aggressive, less pervasive media may not have exposed potential scandals, nor displayed the messiness of politics as vividly as it does today.[6] Televisions' pursuit of political scandal, as a way to attract viewers, may drive some of the cynicism found in more recent polls. Television may also provide politicians with more visibility and, hence, more opportunities to be seen trying to score political points. Or, to put this differently, politics and politicians may have always been something that offended people, but before everyone had TV most people didn't see much of it.

This may explain part of the growing discontent with politics in the United States, but not all of it. Television became the nation's primary information medium after 1970, and it was not until 1980 that as many as 40 percent of Americans begin to list TV alone as their primary source of news.[7] Of course, the rise of TV predates the trends in the polls we are discussing, but our figures illustrate that discontent with government was on the rise well before TV became so ubiquitous as a conduit of political information.

It cannot be denied that the downward spiral of regard for government also has its roots in the action that politicians *want* the public to see. Democrats and Republicans alike, when in control of the House or Senate, attempt to use their majority status to pass bills they know a president may veto in order to weaken the president's standing with voters. In 1997, Clinton and House Republicans pushed such tactics to the point that budget appropriations were not passed, forcing a temporary shutdown of much of the federal government. For decades, the parties have fought bitter tactical fights over judicial appointments. Republican senators, for example, championed the idea of individual senators having the prerogative to secretly veto judicial appointments when Clinton was president, but attacked the idea when Bush was in office. Party leaders also use floor votes for the purpose of embarrassing the other side. Soon after the terrorist attack on the United States of September 11, 2001, Republicans ensured that a foreign operations bill was defeated in an attempt to bring attention to Senate Democrats' slow pace at confirming Bush's judicial appointments.[8] While Republicans stressed that confirmation was essential to fighting "the war on terrorism," Democrats stressed they were moving no slower than Republican senators had under Clinton. Both parties seemed to have missed the bigger picture.

These conflicts over the budget, judicial appointments, and foreign operations funding clearly reflect sincere policy differences between the parties. However, it is reasonable to expect that many disinterested observers might view partisan positioning in these battles as cynical and hypocritical "point scoring," and thus think less of government generally. This expectation seems more plausible than positing that voters who lack party attachments will suddenly rally to the side of whichever party leader "spins" the latest conflict in the best light.

Likewise, party leaders and representatives behave in ways they might hope the public fails to notice. Leaders in both parties block floor votes on popular bills they oppose if they fear the bill might somehow pass. Both parties place unpopular "rider" amendments on bills they know the president must sign because the amendment would never pass if put to a separate vote (e.g., the Democrat's Bolland Amendment blocking aid to the Contras in 1980, and Republican antienvironmental riders of the late 1990s). And parties take one position on popular policy matters when the costs to them are minimal, then later switch for strategic reasons. The evaporation of House Republican support for campaign finance reform (which it passed prior to 2000) is an example of this. House Republicans passed a version of the bill in 1999 when they knew the GOP-controlled Senate would kill it. After the bill passed the Democrat-controlled Senate in 2001, GOP House leaders' enthusiasm for campaign finance quickly waned. Similarly, House Republicans opposed fast-track trade powers for President Clinton, but found new sympathy for the concept after Bush took office. In late 2001, the public also witnessed the mysterious financial collapse of Enron, then one of the nation's largest corporations. Nearly every elected official involved with regulating or investigating the scandal had received major campaign contributions from the firm and its auditors.[9]

We suggest that Congress's record provides citizens with many reasons for responding, as we see in Table 2.3 on page 21, that "special interests have too much power," that leaders only "tell us what they think will get them elected," and that there is "too much bickering between political parties." In contrast, party leaders and many academics often seem to believe that voters make too much of such political posturing and conflicts of interest. After all, voters tend not to be very interested in politics and, hence, are not as well-informed as pundits and commentators, academics or professional politicians. Public criticism of those inside the beltway may thus be readily dismissed as the opinion of the untutored and unknowing. The disdain for government seen in these tables could, then, simply reflect a "misunderstanding" of how Congress works, rather than valid conclusions based on reasoning and observations. The previous, very simple history provides another plausible alternative: Voters see an endless series of politicians behaving badly. It should come as no surprise, then, that voter regard for politics and politicians is not as high as we might want.

With the political stakes so high, however, it is no surprise that parties often translate sincere policy disagreements into take-no-prisoners tactics. When control of government rests in the hopes of swinging just a few key congressional races, the "winner-take-all" nature of American politics takes on new meaning. Yet we must consider how all of this affects public attitudes about government over the long haul. Consider the effects over time of citizens observing this style of politics and seeing it presented by the media. When this is combined with recurring political scandals and messages about government as "the problem," it is no surprise that high levels of cynicism are found.

This goes some way toward resolving an old paradox. Typically, as individual voters become more educated, they are more likely to vote and take an interest in politics. Yet over the last few decades, increased education levels in American society have corresponded with increased levels of distrust of government, and a decline in voter turnout levels. Hence, a paradox exists. If anything, as aggregate levels of education have risen, aggregate levels of engagement with politics have decreased.[10] One way of reconciling this may be that as the public became more knowledgeable (at least superficially) about scandals, partisan tactics, interbranch struggles between parties, and about who funds campaigns, it became more critical of that government. Many probably see partisan battles for what they are: clear policy differences that are lost in strategic attempts to undercut public perceptions of the other party.

If this is the case, we may have moved some ways toward understanding why many Americans dislike elected officials, and why their explanations (in Tables 2.2 and 2.3, on pages 20 and 21) often focus on the political process as much as on policy outcomes. It is important to consider how (or if) such attitudes have roots in the current state of American elections. Some argue that politicians and Congress in particular get a bum rap. Partisan conflict, name-calling, dubious rider-amendments, corporate influence over legislation, and passing or torpedoing bills simply to embarrass one's opponents, are accepted by many as good old-fashioned politics. From this perspective, if citizens only had a better understanding of "political realities" they might be less cynical about their political system.[11]

Overly romantic portraits of a conflict-free politics, the sort of civics-class version of government many of us are taught in high school, may be to blame for some of the public's cynicism since they raise unrealistic expectations. When the real world of political conflict shatters this ideal, cynicism may result. However, assuming that discontent only reflects citizen misunderstanding is to neglect a very real disconnect between citizens and their government. The trends in opinion we presented above also correspond with a disturbing decline in the competitiveness of congressional elections and with increased party-line voting in Congress.

As we document in the next chapter, Congress has become more partisan in recent decades, while voters have become less so. Increased cynicism about politics also corresponds with the exploding use of huge "soft money" contributions in federal elections. We take up in this issue in Chapter 8. Although TV coverage of campaign finance and scandals may have shattered civic-class expectations about politicians, to blame the growing cynicism on the media is, in effect, directing blame at the messenger. The roots of public discontent, we believe, live in a growing disconnect between citizens and representative government. The problem is that our electoral process is failing.

A Portrait of the Disconnected: Independents and Moderates

The Center for Policy Attitudes (COPA) conducted interviews with small groups of citizens in 1999—focus groups—to identify why so many Americans are fed up with politics. They heard a number of complaints:

> It's not what the people want or think or care about. It's a political struggle for power up there: who's going to be in control, the Republicans, the Democrats? They're stepping on everybody along the way. They don't care.[12]

A very common complaint was that government no longer served the interests of "voters like me" and instead served the interests of well-organized, well-financed interests. For example, one man said that representatives should be

> more impartial to the money . . . and not necessarily let big business . . . govern how you make the law, but actually look to what's going to be best for the people.[13]

A woman in one of the COPA focus groups said she thought that "the things that I really want to see happen normally don't, because the individuals running the government are too self-serving." Another woman, nodding in agreement said, "very self-serving."[14]

These opinions expressed by people in the focus groups are shared by many in the public. Who are these discontented and disconnected Americans? We identify them by examining attitudes about representation within key subgroups of the electorate. By tracking such attitudes over time, we can see how changes in the American electoral context have conditioned perceptions about representation.

Scholars of political behavior have established that attachments to political parties are a key determinant of political attitudes and behavior. Decades of research have made it fairly clear that partisans are more engaged with politics, more interested in politics, and, not surprisingly, more likely to vote.[15] It is reasonable to expect that people who identify with either political party are less cynical about who government listens to, and about which interests are represented in government. Furthermore, partisan voters may see elected officials as reflecting an agenda they identify with, which makes them more likely than others to feel they have a say in government.

The proportion of Americans aligned with political parties, however, is in decline. Fewer Americans now identify with either the Democratic or Republican party. In 1958, 77 percent of Americans did, while just 63 percent did in 1998. Citizens who lack an attachment to either main party are categorized here as independents.

Since 1970, Americans generally have become more cynical about whom the government represents, and about how responsive the government was (see Figure 2.2 on page 18). Independents, however, posted the highest levels of cynicism. Figures 2.3 and 2.4 display the extent to which independents have become more cynical about representation, relative to self-identified partisans.[16] Each point reflects the difference between the percent of all independents and the percent of partisans giving the distrusting response to these survey questions, in a given year. The trends illustrate the degree to which independents were more (or less) cynical than Democrats (Figure 2.3) and Republicans (Figure 2.4).

Figure 2.3 illustrates that, since 1970, independents were more cynical about government than people who call themselves Democrats, based on two of these measures. By the late 1990s, they were 5 to 10 percent more cynical on all three measures. Likewise, Figure 2.4 demonstrates that, relative to Republicans, an independent was far more likely to believe she had no say, that

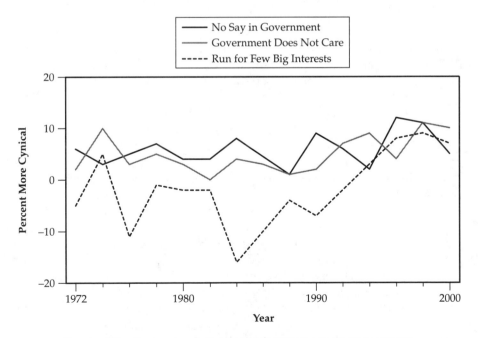

FIGURE 2.3   CYNICISM—INDEPENDENTS COMPARED TO DEMOCRATS

Source: National Election Study Data.

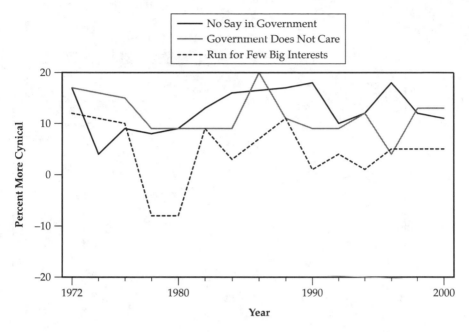

FIGURE 2.4   CYNICISM —INDEPENDENTS COMPARED TO REPUBLICANS

Source: National Election Study Data.

government was run by special interests, and that officials did not care about people like them. In some years, 10 to 15 percent more of the independents gave the cynical responses, compared to Republicans.

It should be no surprise that independents are more cynical about government than partisans, especially if those who lack attachments to parties are less likely to grow up seeing politics as meaningful.[17] A lack of partisanship probably comes hand-in-hand with low levels of efficacy. That being said, the magnitude of differences between independents and Republicans shown in Figure 2.4 are striking, and trends mask the fact that while everyone was becoming more cynical, independents have become even more cynical (particularly relative to Democrats) during the 1990s.

When we compare attitudes of self-identified moderates to those people who identify themselves as liberals and conservatives, we see a similar pattern. During this period when cynicism was increasing generally in the electorate, those who consider themselves political moderates (about one-fourth of all citizens) typically were more cynical than self-identified liberals or conservatives (see Figure 2.4 above and Figure 2.5 on page 28). Indeed, apart from 2000, moderates were nearly always more likely to respond that they believed they had no say in government, and to claim that government did not care about people like them.

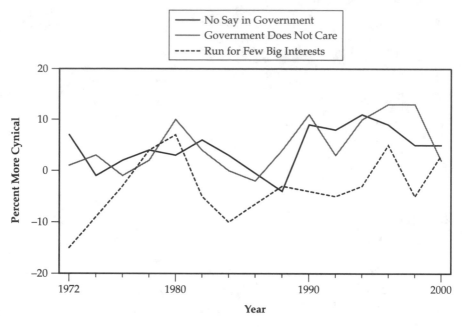

FIGURE 2.5   CYNICISM—MODERATES COMPARED TO LIBERALS

Source: National Election Study Data.

These data demonstrate that a sense of disconnect between people and their government is often most pronounced among citizens who see themselves in the political center, and those having no allegiance to the major parties. As we shall see in the next chapter, there may be some objective basis for such attitudes, grounded in how elections operate. At times in the last decade, parties in Congress were more polarized than at any point since 1957. Independents and moderates who may expect some "centrism" on policies might thus find themselves left out when it comes to representation. It is worth noting that although cynicism among independents and moderates has increased, other key demographic markers do not reveal heightened cynicism among social groups who are underrepresented in the political system. Cynicism among Blacks in 1996 was similar to levels observed in the 1950s. The gap between whites and blacks has closed, in fact, as cynicism among whites has increased. Likewise, levels of cynicism among the poor have changed very little since 1970, while a gap between rich and poor has closed.[18]

DOES CYNICISM ABOUT GOVERNMENT MATTER?

Does it matter that public regard for government has been declining? From our perspective, trust in government matters. Those citizens who trust the government are probably more likely to take part in politics, more likely to obey

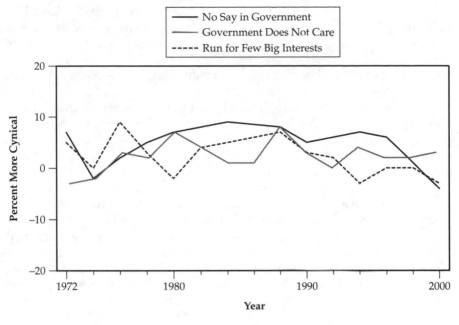

FIGURE 2.6   CYNICISM—MODERATES COMPARED TO CONSERVATIVES

Source: National Election Study Data.

the laws passed by institutions they trust and, hence, contribute to the overall stability of the political regime. Moreover, citizen regard for both politicians and the political system is reflected in trust.[19] Although political trust may represent an abstract concept, higher levels of trust are a reflection of many factors that are good for a political system. One of the things it helps to denote is support for the system as a whole.

Many voters like particular politicians and are willing to support them, but there is a difference between that and trusting the system as a whole. More accurately, there is a difference between disliking a particular politician—a president for example—and rejecting that president's legitimacy or distrusting America's system of government. We can dislike George W. Bush but still like how American democracy works, and go about our lives. But distrusting the process that produces our politicians can lead to questions about their having a legitimate claim to govern. In extreme cases, it can lead to violent rebellion. If, however, citizens are able to trust their electoral process, then the people who win elections are more likely to be seen as legitimate—even by those who opposed them. Trust, then, is tied to the legitimacy of a political system. High levels of cynicism and distrust like those we report above thus give reasons to be concerned about the health of the American political system.

Before moving on we should note that it is possible to make too much of the decline of trust and the rise of cynicism about government. The United States is nowhere near any of the more extreme kinds of scenarios that declining legitimacy may imply. We are not like Venezuela, Sri Lanka, Fiji, or many other places where those on the losing side of elections foment coups and civil wars against those who win. As a Pew Center investigation of distrust pointed out, Americans do not feel any less patriotic than before, nor are they more tolerant of those who break the law. Our decline of trust does not, then, foreshadow a massive rise in criminal activity.[20]

The sky may not be falling as a consequence of growing distrust and the new distance that people feel between themselves and government. Most Americans, furthermore, are at least "fairly" satisfied with how democracy works as a political system. They might also hate how Congress works, but they support the general concept of representative democracy.[21]

Nevertheless, distrust of government and perceptions of unresponsive public officials are important concepts to try to understand. After all, what these opinion polls seem to show is that people today feel less like the federal government is *their* government and more like it is simply *a* government. These attitudes "matter" in another way—they may be associated with the sense, among others, that electoral participation is not worth the effort. As we illustrate in Figure 2.7, most Americans now believe that elections do not make government "pay attention" to them. In the early 1960s, 65 percent believed

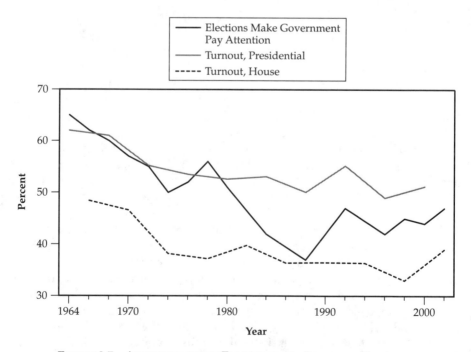

FIGURE 2.7   ATTITUDES ABOUT ELECTIONS AND LEVELS OF TURNOUT

Source: National Election Study Data.

that elections got the attention of public officials. By 2000, only 46 percent thought so. Figure 2.7 also demonstrates how the trend in attitudes about the value of elections corresponds with a decline in voter turnout. More Americans have come to believe that elections no longer really matter, and fewer vote. If participation continues to decline, the legitimacy of elected officials will suffer.

There is additional evidence that cynicism about elections is associated with citizens staying home on election day. The U.S. Census Bureau surveyed registered voters who did not vote in the 1996 election. Among registered nonvoters, over one-third explained their lack of participation as the product of logistical difficulties: They said they were out of town, couldn't get transportation, or were just too busy to vote. But another 30 percent said that they avoided the election because they felt their vote wouldn't make a difference, or they didn't like the candidates. To put this in perspective, Clinton beat Bob Dole by 8 million votes in 1996. More than 12 million people didn't vote that year because they didn't like the candidate choices and/or didn't think voting would make any difference.[22] The number of *registered* voters who didn't think voting mattered dwarfed the president's victory margin—his mandate to govern.

WHY INSTITUTIONS MATTER TO CITIZENS: EFFECTS ON ATTITUDES AND BEHAVIOR

The examples above demonstrate that trends in attitudes about representation correlate with a key benchmark of political behavior: trends in voter turnout. A major theme of this book is that attitudes about government, and behavior corresponding to such attitudes, have some grounding in objective reality. Attitudes and behavior are shaped by political institutions: If institutions can be changed, attitudes and behavior might also change.

There is a growing body of research demonstrating that attitudes about government—levels of trust, perceptions of representation, feelings that one's voice is heard—are conditioned by the election rules we live under. A succession of articles have found that voting for losing candidates can generate discontent among voters. If "your" candidate loses, then you aren't as satisfied with politics as people who voted for the winner.

On the face of it this may seem an obvious, even trite, point to make—except that this focus on voters who lose leads to a series of important questions: How many folks end up on the losing side of elections? How badly do they feel when their candidate loses? And how often, if ever, do they get to win? One of the features of democratic politics is that candidates lose and they are expected to do so in a peaceful and orderly manner. The loser's willingness to voluntarily forgo a position of power is one of the major features of democratic society.

But if some voters' candidates lose time after time, they may feel less satisfied with government and with how democracy works. Imagine how satisfaction with baseball might wane if, every year, only the New York Yankees and Atlanta Braves were allowed to play in the World Series. Of thirty teams, only two could be "winners" in this scenario. How long would fans of the perennially losing twenty-eight remain engaged with the sport?

We cannot answer the last question directly, but it relates to a second point: Some institutional arrangements, those that limit the losses felt by citizens, seem to generate less unhappiness among voters.[23] We can categorize election rules by how they treat winners and losers, by how many winners there might be, or by how easy it is to lose. Under "plurality" or "majoritarian" systems such as those in Australia, Britain, Canada, France, and the United States, a bare majority or less is enough to rule without much regard for anyone else's opinion: Single-party government is common. Losers might get nothing in the form of representation, while winners get everything.

On the other hand, in "consensus" systems, such as those in Scandinavian nations, coalition arrangements mean power is shared among several parties and the "out" parties limit their losses. A cross-national comparison of attitudes about democracy found that voters who supported "losers" felt better if they lived in nations that use more "consensual" election rules (e.g., proportional representation).[24]

This is but one empirical demonstration of an important point: Rules that define elections and representation shape how citizens feel about their government and their representatives. At least some of the attitudes that we describe in this chapter—such as trust, or feeling that one has a say—reflect the rules that define how our political system operates.

There are other examples of this. Research has found that people who live in states that let citizens vote directly on legislation tend to have higher levels of political efficacy, and higher voter turnout. Efficacy refers to the individual's beliefs about their capacity to engage in politics—to understand politics and feel that their participation makes a difference. We posit that the process of asking voters to decide directly on major policy questions forces some to seek out more information. This ballot initiative process also leads many to sense that they can actually affect what their state's government does. The difference in efficacy levels holds up even after controlling for a whole set of other factors such as education.[25]

Studies of election rules that facilitate ethnic and minority representation in the United States make a similar point. African Americans often feel better represented and have greater levels of efficacy if they have an African American representative. African Americans living in congressional districts represented by an African American may also be more likely to vote, other things being equal.[26]

It is important to underscore that these effects need not be confined to racial minorities. We also know how electoral institutions shape attitudes and behavior of political minorities from observing a nation that changed from one set of rules to another. In 1996 New Zealand changed its electoral system from a U.S.-style winner-take-all system to proportional representation (PR). PR allows smaller parties a chance to win seats in the legislature. Polls tracking citizen opinions before and after the change revealed that supporters of smaller parties (who "lost" under the old rules) were more likely to think they had a say, and that voting mattered, under the new rules. After all, if institutions are important in shaping opinions and behavior, then new institutions should generate new opinions and behavior.[27] Taking these studies together, they provide evidence that citizen responses to institutions are in part a product of the institutions themselves.

WHAT TO DO: MORE DEMOCRACY OR LESS?

If it is the case that many voters no longer feel connected to government, this raises a number of questions: Why do voters feel this way? And what can be done about it?

Given public opinion data presented here, it should come as no surprise that Americans may prefer to see different kinds of electoral institutions, particularly new ones that may allow them a greater say in affecting what government does. Evidence for this comes again from public opinion data. The COPA survey asked people about the kinds of things that could be done to fix the political system. The overwhelming answer was to give the public more of a say in government.

The COPA poll asked respondents to consider "how much influence the views of the majority of Americans" have on "the decisions of elected officials in Washington," and told them to answer on a scale of 0 to 10, with 0 meaning not at all influential and 10 meaning extremely influential. The average answer was 4.6. Respondents were then asked how much influence they thought the views of the majority of Americans *should* have on the decisions of elected officials in Washington. The average response was 8.4. Thus, the average difference between the actual and preferred level of influence was 3.8 (COPA, 1999, *Expecting More Say*). Majorities of around 80 percent believed that things would be better if the government followed the views of the public more closely and an even larger majority thought the public should have more say than it does now.

Part of the reason for these patterns is that citizens believe that the underlying principles of democracy require that the will of the majority be discovered and put into practice. As we see in a subsequent chapter, these views are especially important when it comes to the question of direct democracy. But for the time being it is worth noting that these figures build to a quite subtle picture of what democratic politics should be about in the eyes of voters. As the COPA study noted:

> When an elected official makes decisions, a strong majority feels the views of the majority of the public should have more influence than the views of the [elected] official. At the same time, most Americans do feel that elected officials have an important role to play: that elected officials should not simply follow ill-informed majority opinion, but try to determine what the majority would favor if it had more complete information; and that elected officials should consult their own sense of what is right and, ideally, find policies that integrate their values as well as those of the majority.[28]

Some evidence, then, suggests that new institutional arrangements could help address at least some of the problems we outlined at the beginning of the chapter. Not all analysts necessarily agree. Some argue that the public really does not demand more of a say in politics, rather what they lack is an appreciation for the "ugliness of democracy."[29] To borrow a phrase, democratic politics is like sausage making—the more we know about how sausages are made and what goes in them, the less we feel like eating them. The whole business of making and cutting deals seems to characterize what modern politics is about and underpins the way in which some people use the word "politics" more as a swear word than anything else.

The distrusting public may be convinced that, in essence, they can have their cake and eat it. That is, many believe that we can have a democracy without conflicting opinions and partisan rancor. This argument leads to a very different interpretation of the data we presented above. Rather than seeing complaints about politicians as a reasonable response to the behavior and actions of politicians, the opinion data presented above can be seen to reflect the fact that voters have unreasonable expectations of politicians because they (voters) are too naïve to understand the innate nature of the democratic process.[30]

It is hard to sort out which of the two arguments is correct—that citizens are naïve, or that they need "more" democracy. Although the argument that "citizens don't understand" is a plausible one, so too is the converse: Citizens do not like current democratic processes because they understand all too well how they work.

Some institutional changes could, at least in principle, restrain politicians from engaging in unpalatable behaviors or push them toward more desirable behaviors. One institution that does generate lots of support among citizens is that of direct democracy. Repeated surveys, both within states that have the initiative process and nationwide, show large majorities in favor of the process.[31] Support for this institution is far from surprising, if we are willing to allow voters to hold even moderately consistent views. If citizens think the problem is that politicians do not listen to voters enough and that things would be better if ordinary people were listened to more often (see Figure 2.8 on page 35 and Figure 2.9 on page 36) then it is not surprising that citizens strongly support an institution that gives the people a bigger voice in politics.

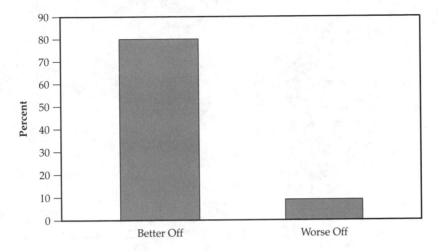

**FIGURE 2.8   PUBLIC VIEWS ON EFFECTS
OF GREATER PUBLIC INFLUENCE OVER GOVERNMENT**

Question: If the leaders of the nation followed the views of the public more closely, do you think the nation would be better off or worse off than it is today?
Source: COPA Survey, January 1999, 1,204 respondents.

If the kinds of complaints we saw voters expressing in Tables 2.2 and 2.3 were unreasonable, or the complaints simply reflected some kind of general grumbling or discontent, then we might expect to see institutional reforms having next to no effect: People will still keep on grumbling about the new institutions. Yet, studies on majoritarian and consensus institutions suggest people can and do respond to institutional changes. Institutional reform may thus be one way to address the criticisms we saw above and also to encourage greater participation. Institutional reform can do this because citizens—and elected officials—respond to institutional changes.

It is not likely that any set of institutional reforms will do away with all complaints about the process for all time. Institutional reform is no magic bullet and the claims of many activists who see different reforms as panaceas should be discounted accordingly. Indeed, in the following chapters, we seek to hold up the claims of reform proponents to the harsh light of empirical analysis.

We should note, furthermore, that citizens may be more attentive to political issues when asked about them in surveys than they are in real life. For the vast majority of citizens, politics is a distinctly part-time concern. The demands of job and family, not to mention the appeal of sports, movies, TV, and a host of other things that compete with politics for the public's attention, all tend to make politics a fairly low priority for the average voter. This is yet another reason why we should not overstate the impact of declining trust in government, or the promise of electoral reform.

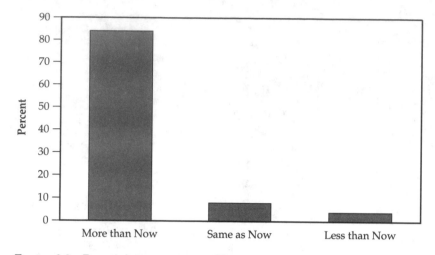

FIGURE 2.9   PUBLIC ATTITUDES ABOUT HOW MUCH SAY PEOPLE SHOULD HAVE

Question: How much more say should people have?
Source: COPA Survey, January 1999, 1,204 respondents.

Nevertheless, the survey evidence we have shown above is consistent with a simple pattern: Citizens, when asked, register a great deal of dissatisfaction with the performance of current institutions and they support institutional changes that give them a greater say over what politicians do. To the extent that the trends in Figure 2.1 (page 18) are a problem, institutional reform offers some way of making that problem a little less bad.

NOTES

1. Stephen C. Craig, ed., *Broken Contract: Changing Relationships between Americans and Their Government* (Boulder, CO: Westview Press, 1996); Joseph S. Nye, Philip Zelikow, and David King, eds., *Why People Don't Trust Government* (Cambridge, MA: Harvard University Press, 1997); Joseph Cooper, ed., *Congress and the Decline of Public Trust* (Boulder, CO: Westview, 1999).
2. The trends we discuss are based on National Election Study Data. Gallup uses the same trust in government question as NES. The Gallup time series is much shorter, but results tend to match the NES data shown in Figure 2.1. Gallup data show lower levels of trust during Clinton's second term than NES data. Gallup data are used in Figure 2.1 to illustrate the post-September 11 level of trust. See Brian Gaines, "Where's the Rally? Approval and Trust of the President, Cabinet, Congress, and Government since September 11," *PS: Political Science and Politics*, 2002.

   Gallup's poll soon after the terrorist attack had 64 percent in the trusting categories. By September 2002, 40 percent were in the trusting categories. The 2000 Gallup data are from a *Washington Post* poll conducted 9/25–9/27/01 by TNS Intersearch; 1,215 adults surveyed;

with a margin of error ± 3% (release, 9/28). The 2002 Gallup data point is from a *Washington Post* poll conducted 9/3–9/6/02 that surveyed 1,003 adults, with margin of error ± 3% (release, 9/8). Both results were found at <nationaljournal.com>.

3. *ABC News Poll*, 1994.
4. Center on Policy Attitudes, "Expecting More Say: The American Public on Its Role in Government Decisionmaking, 1999," on-line report accessed on November 15, 2002, at <http://www.policyattitudes.org>.
5. Just as September 11, 2001, prompted huge spikes in regard for current levels of trust in government.
6. E. J. Dionne, *Why Americans Hate Politics* (New York: Touchstone Books, 1992).
7. Stephen Ansolabehere, Roy Behr, and Shanto Iyengar, *The Media Game* (New York: Macmillan, 1993).
8. *New York Times*, 21 October 2001.
9. *New York Times*, 20 January 2002.
10. This is known as the Brody paradox, after Richard Brody, a Stanford professor who first pointed out the paradox.
11. See Hibbing and Theiss-Morse, 1995; Roger Davidson, "Congress and the Public Trust: Is Congress Its Own Worst Enemy?" in Nye et al., eds. (1999).
12. See Center on Policy Attitudes, "Expecting More Say," <http://www.policyattitudes.org/ems2.htm#1>.
13. See Center on Policy Attitudes, "Expecting More Say," <http://www.policyattitudes.org/ems2.htm#1>.
14. See Center on Policy Attitudes, "Expecting More Say," <http://www.policyattitudes.org/ems2.htm#1>.
15. For reviews see Russell Dalton, *Citizen Politics: Public Opinion and Political Parties in Advanced Industrial Democracies* (Chatham, NJ: Chatham House, 1996); W. Flanigan and N. Zingale, *Political Behavior of the American Electorate* (Washington, D.C.: CQ Press, 2002).
16. The data here are drawn from the American National Election Study, Cumulative Data File.
17. Campbell Angus et al., *The American Voter* (Chicago, IL: University of Chicago Press, 1960).
18. American National Election Study, Cumulative Date File.
19. Pippa Norris, *Critical Citizens: Global Support for Democratic Governance* (New York: Oxford University Press, 1999); Marc Hetherington, *Why Trust Matters: Declining Political Trust and the Demise of American Liberalism*, book manuscript, Bowdoin College, Dept. of Political Science.
20. Pew Research Center, *How Americans View Government: Deconstructing Distrust*, 1998 <http://people-press.org/reports/display.php3?PageID=596>, accessed November 15, 2002.
21. John Hibbing and E. Theiss-Morse, "Process Preferences and American Politics: What People Want Their Government to Be," *American Political Science Review* 95 (March 2001).
22. 143 million voters were registered in 1996. 72 percent of those *registered* voted, leaving 40 million nonvoting registered. If 30 percent of these had the attitudes found in the Census sample, 40 million* .30 = 12 million.
23. For consequences of losing in elections, see C. Anderson and C. Guillory, "Political Institutions and Satisfaction with Democracy," *American Political Science Review* 91 (1997): 66–81; A. Lijphart, *Patterns of Democracy* (New Haven, CT: Yale University Press, 1999); S. Bowler and T. Donovan, "Democracy, Institutions, and Attitudes about Citizen Influence on Government," *British Journal of Political Science* 32 (2002): 371–390; O. Listhaug, "The Dynamics of Trust in Politicians," in *Citizens and the State*, ed. H. D. Klingemann and D. Fuchs (Oxford: Oxford University Press, 1995); Andre Blais and Richard Nadeau, "Accepting the Election Outcome: The Effect of Participation on Losers' Consent," *British Journal of Political Science* 23 (1993): 553–563.
24. See Anderson and Guillory, 1997. Losers were voters who supported parties that did not form government.
25. Shaun Bowler and Todd Donovan, "Democracy, Institutions, and Attitudes about Citizen Influence on Government," *British Journal of Political Science* 32 (2002): 371–390. See Chapter 7 in this volume for a broader discussion of the effects of direct democracy.
26. Lawrance Bobo and Frank Gilliam, "Race, Sociopolitical Participation, and Black Empowerment," *American Political Science Review* 84 (1990): 377–397; Claudine Gay, "The Impact of Black Congressional Representation on the Behavior of Constituents," paper presented at the Midwest Political Science Association meeting, 1996, Chicago, IL; S.

Banducci, T. Donovan, and J. Karp, "Minority Representation, Empowerment, and Participation, *Journal of Politics* (forthcoming).

27. S. Banducci, T. Donovan, and J. Karp, "Proportional Representation and Attitudes about Politics: Results from New Zealand," *Electoral Studies* 18, no.4 (1999): 533–555.

28. Center on Policy Attitudes, *Expecting More Say*.

29. Hibbing and Theiss-Morse (1995), 155.

30. Hibbing and Theiss-Morse (1995), 157. We have a somewhat different interpretation of how citizens relate to institutions.

31. Hibbing and Theiss Morse (2001), 145, claim the opposite, without data measuring public attitudes about direct democracy. A selection of polls showing favorable evaluations may be found on the Web site of a group promoting the use of the initiative process: <http://www.iandrinstitute.org>.

3

Pathologies of Congressional Elections

America's first founders intended the legislative branch to dominate the president and courts in most matters. In *The Federalist* Nos. 67 and 69, for example, Hamilton stressed this by arguing that the president could do little without congressional approval. Madison noted that most major governmental powers—taxation, spending, and declaring war—were placed in the hands of the Congress. Congress, particularly the House of Representatives, was designed to be close to the people. Elections for the House gave the U.S. Constitution a key element of its "republican" character. Madison also argued (in *The Federalist* Nos. 47 and 51) that separation of powers, combined with a highly diverse, representative Congress, would protect citizens against tyrannical majorities and any antidemocratic excess that might be committed.

This close relationship between citizens and the "energetic" new national government was institutionalized by requiring that elections for the entire House of Representatives would be held every two years. As recorded in *The Federalist* No. 52:

> It is essential to liberty that the government in general should have a common interest with the people, so it is particularly essential that [the House of Representatives] should have an immediate dependence on, and an intimate sympathy with, the people. Frequent elections are unquestionably the only policy by which this dependence and sympathy can be effectually secured.

To this date, this remains one of the shortest election cycles in any established democracy. Much of the Federalists' argument about the republican character of the government was based on the idea that House elections would be the primary "ties that bind the representative to his constituents." The Federalists assumed that House elections would be vigorous, competitive affairs that would keep self-interested members of Congress from exercising power in a manner that runs counter to the public interest. In *The Federalist* No. 57, they wrote that the House, via elections,

> is so constituted as to support in the members a habitual recollection of their dependence on the people. Before the sentiments impressed on their minds by the mode of their elevation can be effaced by the exercise of power, they will be compelled to anticipate the moment when their power is to cease, when their exercise of it is to be reviewed, and when they must descend to the level from which they were raised.

Despite this vision, and the goal of legislative preeminence, American national politics is now centered around the executive branch: the president, as well as legions of appointed and career administrative officials who run the vast web of federal agencies. By the end of the twentieth century, very few legislators need worry about descent "to the level from which they were raised" (that is, losing), and the sheer size of House districts means that they have grown more distant from the public. Perhaps as a result of this, most Americans have little interest in congressional elections. In recent "off years"— congressional races held two years after the presidential election—fewer than 37 percent of eligible voters participate. The trend, moreover, appears to be downward. Less than one-third of eligible Americans voted in the 1998 congressional elections. Despite the fact that the Constitution provides for the election of the U.S. House every two years, few contests are competitive, as we illustrate below. It is hardly a surprise, then, that few Americans care enough about these contests to bother to vote.

PROBLEMS WITH CONTEMPORARY CONGRESSIONAL ELECTIONS

FEW SEATS ARE COMPETITIVE

One problem is that the vast majority of House races are rather meaningless to most voters. Elections to the U.S. House no longer connect most citizens with the institution. The frequent complaint that members of Congress are "out of touch" reflects just part of the problem. Due to uncompetitive and uncontested races, most citizens are not touched by congressional elections in even the most minimal fashion.[1] Perceptions of elections, we believe, can affect citizen's attitudes about their ability to influence government, and their perceptions about the operation of democracy generally. These attitudes are important, as we have shown elsewhere, because they affect how much people are willing to consider changing the rules that structure institutions such as Congress.[2]

By many standards, the process of electing the U.S. House of Representatives looks worrisome. At the end of the twentieth century, many House races displayed levels of electoral competitiveness equal to the sham contests held to elect the former Soviet Union's People's Assembly. This lack of competitiveness has been growing, and can be seen on several levels. In fact, outcomes in U.S. House elections have become so predictable that one Washington D.C.-based advocacy group, the Center for Voting and Democracy, draws attention to the issue by releasing predictions for most House races a full year prior to each election (titled *Monopoly Politics*). In 2000, they had a 99 percent accuracy rate.

These highly accurate predictions are not hard to make. Since many voters tend to retain their partisan loyalties over time and vote for candidates of the same party year after year, general election results are easily predicted. Districts with more Republicans almost always elect a Republican just as districts with more Democrats almost always elect a Democrat. Incumbents rarely lose. In recent years, 98 percent of House incumbents have been reelected. Even when incumbents retire, predictions of results of "open seat" contests are usually not very difficult. In any House district a disproportionate number of voters usually support one of the two major parties, so if an incumbent might retire (just under 10 percent of incumbents die or retire every two years, on average, since 1994), the result in November is still largely predetermined.[3] By guessing that nearly all incumbents will win, and by looking at which voters have been placed in a district, in most years it is not very hard to predict House election outcomes, even while having no information about the candidates or the campaigns they wage.[4]

The declining competitiveness of House races is illustrated in Figure 3.1, which plots the proportion of all races each year (since 1898) where a major party candidate defeated the second-place challenger by less than 5 percent.

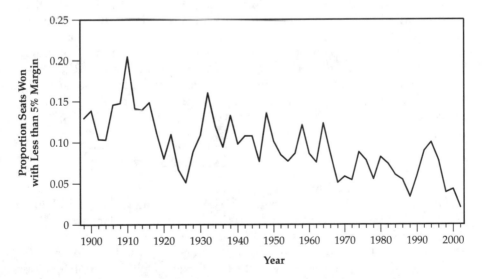

FIGURE 3.1   COMPETITIVE SEATS: U.S. HOUSE ELECTIONS, 1898–2000

Sources: 1898–1992, U.S. House of Representatives Electoral Data, Gary King, Department of Political Science, Harvard University; 1994–2002, author's calculations.

In the early decades of the twentieth century, it was not rare for races in at least 15 percent of all districts to be competitive, in the sense that the winner beat the second-place finisher by a relatively narrow margin.[5] At midcentury, the proportion of all races that were competitive oscillated around 10 percent, even though these data include results from the one-party south where nearly all Democrats ran unchallenged. By the end of the twentieth century, however, we have reached a new equilibrium in which it is rare for an election to have 10 percent of all 435 House contests decided by margins that might be seen as leaving the incumbent vulnerable to future electoral challenge. This means that in years like 1998 and 2000, fewer than two dozen districts might have had campaigns where voters made decisions that might actually have had the slightest effect on which party controls Congress.

By contrast, there are now far more races in any year that are predetermined to be so lopsided that one of the major parties simply gives up, without bothering to run a candidate. In the 1998 election, 94 districts (22 percent of the U.S. House) were so safe for their incumbents that the other major party did not present a challenger. Roughly 50,000,000 Americans lived in these districts. In 2000, 15 percent of seats were contested by one candidate from either of the two major parties. This problem is much worse in some states than others: 78 percent of Florida's U.S. House races found incumbent candidates running without opposition in 1998. In 2000, 50 percent of Massachusetts's U.S. House seats and 30 percent of Texas's seats were uncontested. In 2002, only one incumbent House member lost to a nonincumbent challenger. Hundreds of millions of dollars in soft money and "outside money" are spent by parties and groups to try to swing a handful of key seats, while most races lack meaningful competition.[6] At the ground level, in most years few Americans will ever be touched by a meaningful, competitive general election campaign for the U.S. House. Sadly, it now probably takes a major scandal, economic recession, or rare electoral realignment to mobilize enough candidates and resources to make at least 10 percent of U.S. House seats competitive. A long research tradition suggests that electoral competition *within* a jurisdiction is a prime force that leads representatives to be responsive to the preferences of larger numbers of voters.[7]

INCUMBENTS, MARGINS, AND MONEY

But this is only part of the story. As the proportion of competitive seats has shrunk, incumbent House members have been winning by larger and larger margins. Figure 3.2 illustrates this striking aspect of U.S. House elections. Throughout the first two-thirds of the twentieth century, incumbent House members defeated their challengers by margins that varied considerably between the majority and minority party. Democratic House incumbents (outside of the South) and Republican House incumbents, on average, won with victory margins that ranged between 20 percent and 30 percent. Much of the time, incumbents' average victory margins were much lower than 20 percent,

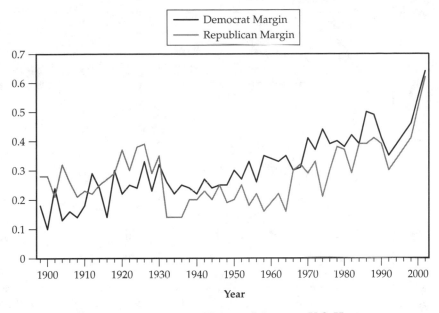

FIGURE 3.2 INCUMBENT VICTORY MARGINS, U.S. HOUSE

Source: 1898–1992, U.S. House of Representatives Electoral Data, Gary King, Department of Political Science, Harvard University; 1994–2002, author's calculations.

particularly for Democrats when they were the minority party prior to the New Deal, and Republicans when they were relegated to minority status after that. In a two-candidate race, a 20 percent margin means an incumbent might defeat her challenger 60 percent to 40 percent. Although such margins were probably healthy enough to make incumbents of a previous era seem rather safe, they pale in comparison to margins that contemporary incumbents roll up against their hapless challengers. By 1998, Democratic incumbents average victory margin was 44 percent, while Republican margins averaged 41 percent. That translates into the average Democratic incumbent winning 72 percent to 28 percent. These margins might not exactly lead winners "to anticipate the moment when their power is to cease."

In the past, competition between the parties within House districts was more likely to put pressure on winners from a broader section of the electorate in their district. This was particularly so for incumbents of the minority party prior to the 1980s.[8] Winning by smaller margins, in theory, should cause an incumbent to accommodate voters who could support an opponent with a plausible chance of winning the next election. The trends in Figures 3.1 and 3.2, however, suggest diminished incentives for either party to field candidates who might accommodate voters who do not support their party. One paradoxical result of this may be that while the national electoral strength of the major parties was closely balanced through the 1990s, by 1995 there

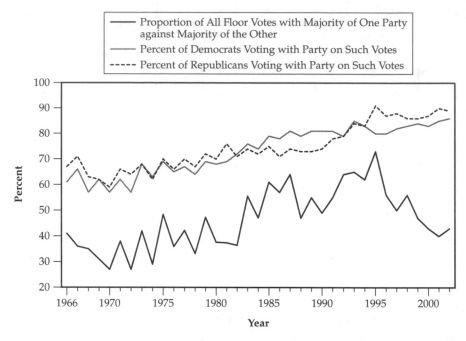

FIGURE 3.3   PARTY UNITY IN U.S. HOUSE, 1960–2000

Source: Congressional Quarterly, Annual Reports.

was less bi-partisan voting on bills in Congress than at any time since *Congressional Quarterly* began recording such data.

Figure 3.3 plots the proportion of floor votes in the House where a majority of one party votes together on a bill against a majority of another party. In the 1970s, only about 30–40 percent of bills had this sort of party-line "unity" vote. Moreover, unity was less ironclad then; about two-thirds of Democrats would oppose about two-thirds of Republicans. By 1995, however, 73 percent of all House votes were clearly partisan divisions. Even as partisan votes decreased a bit as a proportion of all floor votes after 1995, when they do occur, over 80 percent of Democratic and Republican representatives vote in synch with their respective parties.

Thus, as individual House districts have become less competitive over time, they are more likely to produce representatives who have no need to accommodate minority party voters in their district. Representatives are less inclined to cross party lines to support legislation.[9] Party-line voting in the House reached a modern high by 1995, in an era when the proportion of voters with firm allegiances to the parties was in decline. Put differently, as the force and unity of *party-as-organization* (the fundraising arms of the parties—the DCCC, RNCC, etc.) and *party-in-government* (party-line voting among representatives in Congress) were as strong as ever, *party-in-the-electorate* (voters' allegiances with parties) was weak. Although parties may be less useful to voters, they have become stronger as organizational vehicles for candidates and as a means of organizing government. As voter regard for parties drops, the importance of parties in government has risen. It is not surprising, then, that public confidence in Congress, and in utility of elections, has plunged.[10]

The lack of competitiveness in House races—and the corresponding failure of the U.S. House to represent many (moderate) voters—reflects the growing number of incumbents who run without any meaningful opposition, and the fact that few areas of the United States contain House districts with similar numbers of Democratic and Republican voters. There is a large political science literature that debates why incumbents of both parties began to win with much larger margins after 1970. One answer is that gerrymandered districts pack like-minded partisans together, and thus reduce inter-party competition within the House district. Partisan gerrymandering, although surely an aid to incumbents, was around long before incumbent victory margins shot upward after 1970. Other scholars note that the modern Congress—largely a product of institutional reforms that occurred during the early 1970s—provides members with new opportunities to advertise themselves for free and to direct services and resources to their constituents. The combined effect of these forces increases public awareness (name recognition) of incumbents, mutes the electoral effects of national partisan trends, and discourages strong challengers.[11]

In addition, contemporary incumbents have tremendous advantages in raising campaign funds, particularly from Political Action Committees (PACs). These advantages have always been large and have increased since 1974, when Congress established the regulatory framework that created a legal mechanism (PACs) for organized groups, unions, and businesses to contribute to federal candidates. In the 1999–2000 election cycle, PACs contributed $162 million to House candidates, providing about one-third of all contributions directed to these candidates. Over 80 percent of the PAC contributions directed to House candidates went to incumbents. By 2000, even though few incumbents ran in competitive districts (see Figure 3.1 on page 41), the average House incumbent raised over $893,000 for their reelection campaigns—with 42 percent of all incumbent campaign funds coming from PACs. The average challenger raised $362,000, but this figure is distorted upward by a small handful of challengers who were relatively well-funded. Incumbents in relatively uncompetitive districts still have incentives to raise large amounts of cash. By raising money well in advance of their next elections, their campaign bank accounts can deter "quality" challengers.[12]

When election results are considered, the effects of this disparity in raising campaign resources are clear, albeit somewhat indirect. Incumbent spending may be driven upward if a strong challenger is present, which explains why studies of the direct effects of campaign expenditures find that incumbent spending is not necessarily associated with higher incumbent vote margins.

If challengers can ever match or exceed an incumbent's level of spending, then the challenger's vote share does increase substantially, and a race can become quite competitive.[13] However, if a strong challenger might occasionally make a race close, incumbents respond by raising more money.

As members of influential congressional committees who regulate the interests that PACs lobby on behalf of, incumbents are far better situated to raise money than congressional outsiders. Incumbents thus rarely face a situation where a challenger can match their campaign resources. Overall, less than one-third of all incumbents (124 out of 401 seeking reelection) had challengers who were capable of raising more than $100,000 in 2000 (FEC data). Although this may seem like a good deal of money, the average winning candidate raised $931,000 in 2000. Only 16 percent of all the money raised by challengers came from PACs. Since PAC contributions, by law, can be given in amounts five times larger than individual contributions, challengers must round up a greater number of small individual contributions, and/or lend money to their campaigns.[14]

When these forces are considered, incumbency advantages now structure House election outcomes, rather than the ebb and flow of national support for the political parties. Turnover in the House, as with the Supreme Court, is largely driven by incumbent deaths and retirements, rather than competitive elections.

HOUSE ELECTION OUTCOMES FAIL TO REPRESENT MANY (MOST?) VOTERS

In addition to this lack of competitiveness, House elections fail at another level. They do a fairly poor job of translating the preferences that voters express on their ballots into seats in the House. At times, these elections don't even allow voters to express their true preference for representation. Consider the plight of millions of voters living in uncompetitive districts who might object to an incumbent or her party. These citizens have the option to stay home at election time, or if they vote, to skip the House race, or "protest" by supporting a minor party candidate who may have reached the ballot. In fact, minor candidates do much better, other things being equal, when only one major candidate is on the ballot. In either case, these votes are wasted—it does not contribute to electing a representative that the voter agrees with.[15]

Even when voters are presented with choices between major party candidates, those supporting the losing candidate in a district that elects just one representative receive nothing in return for their vote, in some respects. That is, whether supporters of a losing candidate amount to just 20 percent of the district vote, or 49.9 percent, their votes do nothing to elect a candidate from their party since only one representative is elected per district, and votes can't be delivered to another candidate or another district. In short, second place, no matter how close, gets nothing. This is a fundamental principle of winner-take-all elections. The wasted vote problem for voters supporting losers also works in reverse. If Party A wins many districts by large margins but loses narrowly in many competitive districts, surplus votes cast by supporters of Party A in uncompetitive districts were "wasted" in the sense that, under a different electoral system, they could have helped elect more candidates for Party A and made a party's share of seats in the legislature look more like its share of the national vote.

When these forces are considered across all 435 districts, it means that a party can assume control of a relatively large share of seats in the U.S. House while receiving proportionately fewer popular votes. That is, if a party loses by large margins in some districts, yet wins by narrow margins in many others, it can capture a clear majority of seats without collecting a proportionate margin of the vote. Results are also distorted when a third or fourth party starts capturing more votes. This problem tends to give an advantage to large parties under any electoral arrangements, but it is magnified in winner-take-all systems that elect only one representative per district.[16]

Returning to the same kind of made-up example as the ones we saw in Chapter 1 where society has three opinion divisions (As Bs and Cs), here is another that illustrates the point. Here are two districts and their composition: District 1 has 25 As, 20 Bs, and 5 Cs. District 2 has 25 Cs, 20Bs, and 5 As. Assume that the As and Cs in each district all vote for the same candidates.

DISTRICT 1	DISTRICT 2	TOTAL VOTES	SEATS WON
A: 25	A: 5	30	1
B: 20	B: 20	40	0
C: 5	C: 25	30	1

Simple pluralities within each district win a seat: even though the Bs have quite a few votes, they win no seats because of where they are located relative to others. In fact in the example, they have the most votes of any bloc (40) but because they are distributed poorly the Bs win no seats. Britain's Liberal Democratic party is often in the position of bloc B: It comes second in many districts but wins seats far more rarely.

Figure 3.4 (on page 48) illustrates this kind of example with real trends in popular votes for the majority party in Congress since 1954, and the seats received by the majority party.

In every election, the majority party received a bonus of seats, relative to their share of the national popular vote. In the 1976 election, for example, Democratic candidates won 66 percent of all U.S. House seats while receiving 56 percent of the popular vote.

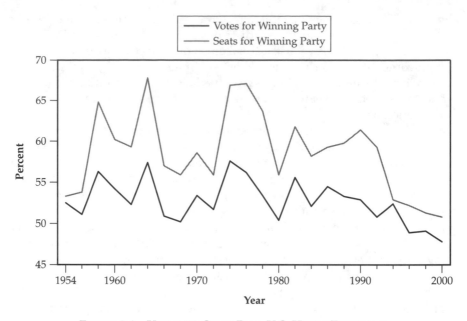

FIGURE 3.4   VOTES-TO-SEATS BIAS: U.S. HOUSE ELECTIONS

Table 3.1 presents two extreme, real-world examples of the disjuncture between votes and seats from recent elections of the Texas and Washington state U.S. House delegations. Democratic candidates for Washington's nine U.S. House seats won well over 50 percent of the popular vote statewide in 1996, but they won only one-third of the states' seats. Why? Washington's redistricting was done by a bipartisan commission that, while protecting some incumbents, also created a number of districts that contained roughly similar numbers of Democrat and Republican voters. When the electoral tide shifted in 1994 to give Republicans a narrow 51–49 popular vote advantage in the state, the GOP won the competitive seats by narrow margins and was rewarded with seven of nine seats. The party managed to hold on to some of these seats as the electoral tide shifted back to favor Democrats by 2000. Republicans might have seen this lag effect as justice, given that 41 percent of the statewide vote gave them only one of nine seats in 1992.

The Washington results illustrate that even competitive single member districts can produce large deviations from proportionate outcomes, while also distorting the effect of swings in popular support for the parties. Provincial elections using FPTP in Canada's Prince Edward Island (P.E.I.) produce dramatic examples of this. In 1993 the Liberal Party won control of 97 percent of seats in the provincial legislature, despite 40 percent of the province-wide vote going to the opposition Progressive Conservatives (PC). The PC opposition was "represented" by a single member. In 1996, a relatively modest 7.7

TABLE 3.1 EXAMPLES OF VOTES-TO-SEATS BIAS FROM FIRST-PAST-THE-POST ELECTIONS

	1992	1994	1996	1998	2000
Texas					
percent votes D/percent seats D	50/70	42/63	44/57	44/57	47/57
percent votes R/percent seats R	48/30	56/37	54/43	52/43	49/43
percent votes other	2	2	2	4	4
Washington					
percent votes D/percent seats D	56/89	49/22	52/33	53/56	53/67
percent votes R/percent seats R	41/11	51/78	47/67	44/44	37/33
percent votes other	3	0.4	1	3	7

percent vote swing toward the PC gave it 67 percent of seats, despite the Liberals 45 percent vote share. Results in P.E.I. have become particularly unstable since 1993, when a small party began to receive 5 percent of the popular vote in the province.[17]

The Texas example in Table 3.1 illustrates a different problem with winner-take-all, FPTP elections. In 1992, Texas Democrats controlled the districting process, and packed many Republican voters into just eight of the state's thirty districts. Democratic voters were strategically distributed across the remaining districts, allowing Democrats to win large majorities of the state's seats for a decade, even as their statewide vote totals dropped under 45 percent. The Texas examples demonstrate how FPTP election results can be predetermined and biased by the way that district boundaries are drawn.

The examples of Texas and Washington should not detract from the fact that the bias associated with FPTP elections nearly always advantages the party that wins the most popular votes nationally. Since 1954, the average bias, or bonus in seats over votes received, has been about 6 percent in the United States. National outcomes from recent House elections provide other twists to this, however. By 2000, for example, the party finishing second in the popular vote nonetheless won control of the House. Republicans formed a majority in the U.S. House even though their candidates received fewer votes nationally than Democrats. This is because their voters were better distributed geographically in most states than were Democrats. In effect, control of Congress in 2000 was not simply decided by voters, but by the cartographers who determined which districts voters would cast their ballots in. Another outcome worth noting is that both Democrats and Republicans are advantaged relative to smaller parties. This results from minor parties and independents now winning a small share of votes, as can be seen in both the Washington and Texas examples. Since these candidates can gain no seats, their vote share further distorts how House elections translate voter preferences into seats in Congress.[18]

In many nations, the distortion created by FPTP frequently allows a party to win a majority of seats in the legislature without having an outright majority of votes. In nations like Britain, Canada, and (prior to 1996) New Zealand, where small parties often win a sizable share of votes in many districts, no large party can win a popular vote majority. By making sure that second, third, and lower-placed candidates get nothing, winner-take-all, FPTP elections "manufacture" legislative majorities where there are no popular vote majorities. To many observers—particularly the supporters of large parties, this is one of the virtues of FPTP elections. In 2000, for example, Republican candidates won 51 percent of U.S. House seats with just 47.8 percent of the popular vote. Had results been proportionate to votes, one of the large parties would have to control the House in coalition with members of another party, or govern as a minority. In many nations, this is normal. In the United States, however, elections produce legislative majorities despite how votes are cast.

At some point, however, it might be difficult for America's FPTP system to continue to manufacture majorities. Minor party candidates have received enough support to deny either party a popular vote majority in the three House elections since 1996. If small parties and independents continue to gain popular support in the United States, then the distorted translation of votes into congressional seats will become a bigger problem in the years to come. In thirteen other FPTP nations where minor candidates gain modest support but few seats (UK, Canada, India), the votes-to-seats bias averaged 25 percent.[19] This means that large parties received 25 percent more seats in these nations' legislatures than they would have if seats were allocated proportionate to the votes a party received.

In Canada and Britain, where no large party commands the loyalties of a majority of voters nationally, results under FPTP can seem perverse from the perspective of Americans accustomed to U.S. election results of past decades. For example, the Canadian Liberal party won 60 percent of seats in parliament in 1993 with just 41 percent of the vote. In 1979, the British Conservative party won 53 percent of seats in the House of Commons with only 44 percent of the vote. Each of these elections, it is worth noting, established a governing majority party that would dominate their nations for years while the party's electoral support eroded. If the 2000 election is any indication, and if American voters continue to grow less loyal to the two main parties, then Americans might not see such results as rare events in the future.

Although somewhat more rare, it is not completely uncommon for parties to finish second in the popular vote in FPTP legislative elections and nevertheless win a majority of seats, as occurred in the United States in 2000. Again, if votes continue to go to minor party candidates, there is a greater likelihood of this happening in America again.

First-past-the-post rules, combined with a campaign finance structure that advantages incumbents, create House elections that fail to engage voters, and produce results that fail to reflect the votes they cast. We should stress

TABLE 3.2 NET CHANGE IN MAJORITY PARTY SHARE
OF LEGISLATIVE SEATS AFTER ELECTIONS

Australia	9.3%	1990–1998 (4 elections)
Canada	23.2	1993–2000 (3 elections)
United Kingdom	11.7	1992–2001 (3 elections)
United States	3.3	1992–2000 (5 elections)

Note: Values are the absolute value of the majority party's net change (gain or loss) in the percent of seats they held in the legislature after an election. Values are averaged.
Source: Authors' calculations.

that while many of these problems may be attributed to winner-take-all elections that rely on single-member districts, these election rules are only part of the problem. Incumbent advantages associated with campaign finance (see the chapter on campaign finance) may make America's FPTP elections even less competitive than FPTP elections in other nations. As Table 3.2 demonstrates, recent U.S. House elections produced little change in the majority party's share of seats, when compared to recent elections in other nations using FPTP election rules. Incumbent politicians in America, it would seem, have less need to worry about elections than representatives in other nations using similar election rules.

MAJORITARIAN POLITICS IN AN ERA OF SOCIAL DIVERSITY

FPTP election rules that exist in the United States, Canada, Britain, and a handful of other democracies are often described as *"majoritarian."* In these nations, elections tend to produce legislative majorities and to kill off small parties, while political institutions utilize other rules (such as giving all executive power to a single party) that give majorities substantial ability to dictate the political agenda. In these systems, political and social minorities must cast their lot with a larger political party and hope for the best. In contrast, many other established democracies are structured on *consensus* models of politics[20] where legislatures and political decision processes are designed to incorporate a wide range of social interests. Since legislatures in these nations are elected by rules that allow many parties to gain representation, it is rare for a single party to reach majority status. Decisions must be made on the basis of a formed consensus, rather than on majority strength.

FPTP elections are also majoritarian in another, related manner. By limiting representation to two large parties, and by rewarding only individual candidates who finish first in a district, these elections might produce legislatures that are socially homogeneous. That is, the vast majority of representatives are upper-middle-class white men, since they have, historically, benefited from all the advantages of incumbency. Despite the fact that many other social groups desire representatives who look like them, winner-take-all elections do a poor job of providing for the *descriptive* representation of society. Descriptive representation is valued not just because it produces a legislature that looks like a cross-section of society, but because many members of cohesive social groups believe that their substantive political interests are best represented by legislators who are "like" them.[21] That is, we have discussed the patterns of election results mostly in terms of party blocs. But party blocs reflect social groups, and so instead of thinking of As, Bs and Cs as liberals, moderates, and conservatives, we could think of them as groups such as women or Latinos. Here the distortions of FPTP may have even more serious consequences.

Many scholars find it no coincidence that nations using FPTP elections tend to have fewer women as representatives than nations that use PR elections. After the "Year of the Woman" in 1992, when a record number of women were elected to the U.S. House, women still held only 11 percent of House seats. By 2002, the proportion of women in the House had only reached 14 percent. In contrast, Scandinavian nations that use PR election rules have had one-fourth to one-third of seats in national legislatures held by women over the last few decades.[22] Racial and ethnic diversity in representation may also be constrained by winner-take-all rules. It is rare, for example, for African American, Asian, and Latino/Latina candidates to be elected to the U.S. House unless they run in "majority-minority" districts that contain relatively large proportions of voters that are the same race/ethnicity of the candidate.[23] For minority groups who live in spatially compact areas (i.e., they are largely segregated from whites), FPTP is not necessarily a barrier to representation if districts can be drawn that contain large proportions of voters from the relevant group. This is why African Americans have achieved representation in the U.S. House in rough proportion to their share of the U.S. population.[24]

If citizens interested in descriptive representation were limited to those living in spatially concentrated groups, FPTP and aggressive use of majority-minority districts might be able to produce a legislature that reflects the social composition of society. One problem for America, however, is that many cohesive groups are not easily placed in a district. Women, for example, are distributed fairly evenly across the nation and cannot form an overwhelming majority in any district. Most minority populations are less segregated than African Americans and thus less likely to form a majority in a district. In the 1990s, for example, although Latinos/Latinas/Hispanics comprised over 12 percent of the U.S. population, less than 4 percent of members of Congress were Latino/Latina/Hispanic.[25] Latino citizens are underrepresented (descriptively) because they vote at lower rates than others, and because it is difficult to create districts where Latino/Hispanic voters can form a majority. Since many white voters tend to vote only for white candidates, minority candidates often have little chance of being elected in districts where members of their race/ethnic group do not form a majority.[26]

Census Bureau projections illustrate that American society will become even more diverse in coming decades as Latinos, Asians, and other groups who are relatively geographically dispersed (relative to African Americans) claim a larger share of the U.S. population. In an era when nearly 40 percent of the U.S. population will soon be nonwhite (see Table 3.3), and it is safe to assume that many minority citizens value descriptive representation, how can maps be carved up so that substantial numbers of majority Black, majority Hispanic/Latino, and majority Asian districts might be created?

Prospects for further minority representation in Congress have been dampened since the U.S. Supreme Court has shown that it is now less sympathetic to districts designed to assure the election of minority candidates. In years to come, the creation of winner-take-all, majority-minority districts may become even more of a zero-sum game. Since minority groups often live in close proximity to each other in urban areas, it is difficult, under the best of circumstances, to draw districts that favor a single group without denying other groups descriptive representation. Given the Court's lack of tolerance of race as a criterion for districting, cartographers may be limited in what they can do. African Americans, Asians, and Latino political groups may be left to fight over the design of a relatively finite number of potential majority-minority districts. Whites may thus remain a majority or bare plurality in enough districts to maintain a disproportionate share of seats in the House.

PUBLIC CONTEMPT FOR CONGRESS

Although no change in the way we elect Congress will be likely to reestablish legislative preeminence (we address one proposal that might do this in Chapter 5), there are reasons to expect that changes in how we elect the House could reinvigorate interest in congressional elections and, perhaps, restore the public's sense that they are represented in Congress. The disconnect between the American people and Congress is much more serious than lack of

TABLE 3.3   DEMOGRAPHICS AND DESCRIPTIVE REPRESENTATION IN CONGRESS—2002

	PERCENT OF U.S., 2000	PERCENT SEATS IN U.S. HOUSE, 2002	ESTIMATED PERCENT OF U.S. POPULATION, 2020
White	70.9	86.0	63.8
Hispanic or Latino	12.4	3.9	17.0
African American	12.3	9.1	12.8
Asian/Pacific Isl	3.7	1.0	5.7
Native American	0.7	n/a	0.8

Source: U.S. Census Bureau, Projections of the Resident Population by Race, Hispanic Origin, and Nativity: Middle Series, 2016 to 2020 (NP-T5-E).

interest in congressional elections. People have a deep-seated contempt for the U.S. Congress. Studies of attitudes about Congress find that hostility to Congress stems not so much from objections about public policies as from perceptions of the legislative process itself. Recurring scandals that gain media attention also harm the institution's reputation, and affect opinions about House members.[27]

By the late 1990s, opinion polls indicated that Americans rated Congress lower than any other public or private institution, including domestic and foreign organizations. Gallup studies of public opinion find that fewer people reported having confidence in Congress than in the federal government, the president, the courts, the media, the military, organized labor, major corporations, and "foreign organizations." In 1996, only 3.4 percent expressed "a great deal" of confidence in Congress.[28] The trend in the Gallup measure of attitudes about Congress has been in decline since the mid-1980s, while public confidence in many other institutions has remained fairly steady. In 1980, the NES began asking respondents "Do you approve or disapprove of the way the U.S. Congress has been handling its job?" every two years. In most surveys since then, barely a third responded that they approved. Only twice (1984 and 1988) did Congress's approval ratings exceed 50 percent in NES surveys. It remained below 50 percent in Gallup measures after the 2002 election, having moved above 70 percent for a few weeks immediately after September 11, 2001.[29]

People do distinguish between individual members of Congress, and Congress "as an institution." They embrace the concept of "the institution of Congress," that is, 88 percent approved of it when a question prompted them with a reference to Congress's constitutional role, historical tradition, and the physical building it occupies. Yet voters are hostile to the representatives who occupy the building—only 24 percent approved of "members of Congress." Attitudes were structured, in no small part, by concerns about the lack of representation of diverse social interests, and by perceptions about the disproportionate influence that "special interests" have in Congress.[30] Paralleling this erosion in public confidence in Congress is a loss of public faith in the idea that elections matter, as we demonstrated in Chapter 2.

CAN HOUSE ELECTIONS ENGAGE VOTERS?

It is important to consider how long citizens will remain engaged by House elections that are not competitive and not representative of the preferences that voters express at the polls. Put differently, how should we expect citizens to react if these elections continue to become even less competitive, and less representative of the partisan affiliations and social composition of the electorate? These questions become particularly important if most citizens lack strong attachments to whichever party might capture an artificial majority of seats after a given election. Will people continue to vote? Will they lose respect for Congress and the laws it passes? At what point is the legitimacy of the institution threatened? It is likely that citizens are sensitive to the effects of how (or if) they are represented. Cross-national research demonstrates that voters who support losing candidates are less satisfied with how democracy works, and are less likely to believe they have a say in government.[31] Congressional elections, as they now operate, can leave most voters in the position of having supported losing candidates. Minority constituents from districts with white representatives—who probably form a growing proportion of the electorate—are less likely to trust government, less likely to vote, and less likely to think that elections matter.

A PARTIAL DEFENSE OF U.S. HOUSE ELECTIONS

Of course, biannual contests for control of the U.S. House are not completely without suspense. In recent years, control of Congress has been so closely divided between the two major parties that if just a few competitive seats break one way or another, majority control of the House might go to the other party. In rare years when long-term changes in voting behavior begin to fundamentally advantage one party over the other, control of the House can shift for years, as happened in 1994 when growing support for Republicans in the South finally swung control of Congress to the GOP.

Even though so few incumbents are ever defeated, some scholars see congressional elections as an effective filtering process. The worst incumbents—those who do little for their constituents, or who are caught in scandals—are defeated, leaving a high quality pool of members remaining. Others note that there is substantial turnover due to the "strategic retirements" of members who know they might lose in their next election. A lack of descriptive representation, furthermore, need not be seen as a fundamental problem if the substantive interests of minorities are well represented by nonminority members. It may well be that, standing back from a particular district and getting an overall view, the political interests of African Americans may be better represented by districting that spreads African American voters around to maximize the number of liberal Democrats in Congress, rather than concentrating them in a smaller number of districts to guarantee the election of African American representatives. After initial hesitation many white voters will vote for black incumbents at the mayoral level whom they think are doing a good job. Success as substantive representation, then, may overcome some concerns about descriptive representation, provided, of course, that voters acknowledge and accept that substantive representation.[32]

A NEED FOR REFORM?

These are valid points but, taken in combination, their portrait of House elections leaves much to be desired. Elections and representatives, from these perspectives, provide rather indirect links between citizens and their government. The problem with this is that House elections are the only place in the U.S. constitutional system designed to provide citizens with close, reasonably direct engagement with the national government. Furthermore, lacking wholesale re-design of the U.S. political system, the U.S. House of Representatives is the only place where the diverse interests of society can be represented in a descriptive *and* substantive manner.

These were some of the key points the first Founders used when describing the Constitution of 1789. By design, the House was supposed to be the democratic engine driving a political system that is often insulated from public opinion through un-elected Courts, separation of powers, long terms of senators, federalism, and other institutional arrangements. The House of Representatives was designed keep citizens engaged with government, and keep government engaged with citizens. Our review of House elections and evidence from surveys of public attitudes suggest that this engagement is threatened and eroding.

Whatever its virtues, the way that we elect Congress routinely wastes many votes cast by supporters of both major and minor parties, creates barriers to descriptive representation, and produces outcomes in legislatures that do not reflect the national distribution of popular votes. For the most part this system has served the United States fairly well. However, given the current context of U.S. House elections, it may be time to reexamine how we elect Congress. In the next chapter, we assess a number of reform proposals directed at improving how Congress is elected.

NOTES

1. National Election Study measures of contact by congressional campaigns surely overestimate who is mobilized by active, competitive campaigning associated with these races. These surveys show that about three-quarters of Americans surveyed were "contacted" by an incumbent congressional candidate, and just over one-third were contacted by challengers. Yet these figures include receiving campaign mailings, hearing ads on television and radio, and reading about the candidate in the newspaper as being contacted.
2. S. Bowler and T. Donovan, "Public Opinion about Democratic Institutions: Constituencies for Change," American Political Science Association meeting, 2000, Washington D.C.
3. Incumbents do retire with strategic considerations about their electoral prospects. For example, the probability of retirement increases as the incumbents vote margin decreases, is lower if the incumbent is redistricted to face another incumbent, and is lower if the incumbent was associated with scandal. See Gary Jacobson and S. Kernel, *Strategy and Choice in Congressional Elections* (New Haven, CT: Yale University Press, 1983); Susan Banducci and Jeff Karp, "Electoral Consequences of Scandal and Reapportionment in the 1992 House Elections, *American Politics Quarterly* 22 (1994): 3–26.
4. On House elections see Paul Abramson, John Aldrich, and David Rhode, *Change and Continuity in the 1992 Elections* (Washington, D.C.: CQ Press, 1995).

5. These data are drawn from data assembled by Gary King and Andrew Gellman <http://www.harvard.edu/gking>, and reflect the difference between the first-place major party candidate and any second-place finisher. Uncontested races won by major party candidates are included. Races where there was no major party winner, or no candidate with the endorsement of a single major party (as in California under cross-filing), are omitted. If anything, these data are biased toward making earlier races look less competitive than races in recent years, given the nature of the one-party south through much of the twentieth century.

6. David Magleby, *The Other Campaign: Outside Money in Congressional Elections* (Lanham, MD: Rowman & Littlefield, 2001).

7. V. O. Key, *Southern Politics in State and Nation* (New York: Vintage, 1949); T. Holbrook and E. Van Dunk, "Electoral Competition in the American States," *American Political Science Review* 87, no. 4 (1993): 955–962.

8. In noncompetitive districts in states using closed primary elections, this may be amplified by the fact that primary election winners—who are inevitably the eventual representative—are less likely to reflect the perspective of the median voter in the district. See Gerber and Morton, 1998.

9. The trend upward is due, at least in part, to the fact that southern Democrats are now much less likely to cross over and vote with Republicans. This reflects the fact that fewer moderate Democrats can win seats in the South. Those who do win tend to come from relatively noncompetitive, safe seats, and thus have more liberal voting records.

10. See Martin P. Wattenberg, *The Rise of Candidate-Centered Politics: Presidential Elections of the 1980s* (Cambridge, MA: Harvard University Press, 1991). Paul Herrnson's work on party campaigning is a good source for the argument that the weakening of party in the electorate is giving rise to the strengthening of parties as organizations and parties in government. See Paul S. Herrnson, *Party Campaigning in the 1980s* (Cambridge, MA: Harvard University Press, 1988).

11. For similar arguments, see Robert Ritchie and Steven Hill, *Whose Vote Counts?* (New York: Beacon Press, 2001). See also David Mayhew, *Congress: The Electoral Connection* (New Haven, CT: Yale University Press, 1974); Cain Bruce, John Ferejohn, and Morris Fiorina, *The Personal Vote: Constituency Service and Electoral Independence* (Cambridge, MA: Harvard University Press, 1983); Morris Fiorina, "The Case of the Vanishing Marginals: The Bureaucracy Did It," *American Political Science Review* (1977): 177–181.

12. Jacobson and Kernell, 1983.

13. Gary Jacobson, *Money in Congressional Elections* (New Haven, CT: Yale University Press, 1980).

14. On differences in the impact of spending between incumbents and challengers, see Jacobson, 1980. A good source for a discussion of the differences in challengers' and incumbents' fund raising and vote shares is Paul Herrnson, *Congressional Elections: Campaigning at Home and in Washington* (Washington, D.C.: CQ Press, 2000).

15. For a discussion of third-party support, see T. Donovan, S. Bowler, and T. Terrio, "Support for Third Parties in California," *American Politics Quarterly* 28, no. 1 (2000): 50–57; Rosenstone et al., 1996. Minor parties do have loyal supporters but much of their vote share comes from voters who are protesting against major parties. See D. Amy, *Real Choices/New Voices: The Case for Proportional Representation Elections in the United States* (New York: Columbia University Press, 1994) for a discussion on "wasted votes."

16. This problem is known as the seats-to-votes bias. See R. Taagepera and M. Shugart, *Seats and Votes* (New Haven, CT: Yale University Press, 1989) for a discussion of this problem.

17. J. Andrew Cousins, *Electoral Reform for Prince Edward Island: A Discussion Paper*, Institute of Island Studies, 2000, University of Prince Edward Island <http://www.upei.ca/~iis/prreport.html>.

18. In both states, much of the minor party vote comes in districts where one major party fails to produce a candidate. In many states, however, Libertarians have secured permanent ballot status, and collect support even in contested races.

19. This is calculated from data in Taagepera and Shugart, 1989, 106–107. The FPTP nations include Bahamas, Belize, Botswana, Canada, Dominica, India, Malaysia, New Zealand, St. Lucia, St. Vincent, South Africa, Sri Lanka, and the UK.

20. Lijphart, *Patterns of Democracy*, 1999.

21. Mansbridge, 1999.

22. The relationship between election systems and representation of women may be indirect. Many proportional representation systems allocate seats to candidates on a "party list" based

on a party's vote share. The parties rank candidates on the list prior to an election. Many parties consciously place women high on their lists, which means that high levels of representation of women are due to the interaction between party decisions and PR election rules. See Miki Caul, "Political Parties and the Adoption of Candidate Gender Quotas: A Cross-National Analysis," *Journal of Politics* 63 (2001): 1214–1229. Even the most proportional rules, by themselves, might not produce much representation of women (see the case of Malta, which has few women legislators despite using PR).

23. There is some debate in this literature about how large a minority's share of a district must be to insure a minority candidate will win. Some place the figure at 65 percent.

24. Given the importance of the question of who gets represented, it has received considerable attention from scholars. On the representativeness of elections with regard to women, see in particular Amy, 1994; Caul, 2001; R. Darcy, Susan Welch, and Janet Clark, *Women, Elections, and Representation,* 2nd ed. (Lincoln, NE: University of Nebraska Press, 1994); Wilma Rule and J. Zimmerman, *United States Electoral Systems: Their Impact on Women and Minorities* (West Port, CT: Greenwood Publishing, 1992). On questions of race and ethnicity, see David Lublin, *The Paradox of Representation* (Princeton, NJ: Princeton University Press, 1997); Kimball Brace, B. Grofman, L. Handley, and R. Niemi, "Minority Voting Equality: The 65 Percent Rule in Theory and Practice," *Law and Policy* 10 (1988): 43–62; Bernard Grofman and Lisa Handley, "Minority Population and Black and Hispanic Congressional Success in the 1970s and 1980s," *American Politics Quarterly* 17 (1989): 436–445; Lisa Handley, B. Grofman, and Arden, 1998; Herrnson, 2000, Chapter 2.

25. D. Massey and N. Denton, "Trends in Residential Segregation of Blacks, Hispanics, and Asians: 1970–1980," *American Sociological Review* 52 (1987): 802–825.

26. See Lee Sigleman and Susan Welch, "Race, Gender, and Opinions about Black and Female Presidential Candidates," *Public Opinion Quarterly* 48 (1984): 468–475, and Handley et al., 1998, on ethnic bases of voting that may hamper minority representation; see Keith Reeves, *Voting Hopes or Fears? White Voters, Black Candidates, and Racial Politics in America* (New York: Oxford University Press, 1997) for discussion and evidence of cross-race voting; see Bernard Grofman, "*Shaw v. Reno* and the Future of the Voting Rights Act," *PS: Political Science & Politics* 28 (1995): 27–36, for a thoughtful look at recent Supreme Court rulings.

27. See Hibbing and Theiss-Morse, 1995, for an examination of how voters see American political institutions. Banducci and Karp, 1994, examine the impact of scandal on reelection.

28. Statistical Abstract of the United States, 1999, Table 485.

29. Gallup data, from <NationalJournal.com>. Polling from November 11, 2002.

30. Hibbing and Theiss-Morse found that evaluations were significantly lower among respondents who scored lowest on an index rating their perceptions of how representative Congress was (1995), pp. 118, 171.

31. Banducci, Donovan, and Karp, 1999; Anderson and Guillory, 1997; Bowler and Donovan, 2002.

32. See Jeff Mondak, "Elections as Filters: Term Limits and the Composition of the U.S. House," *Political Research Quarterly* 48 (1995): 701–727, on the lower reelection rates of poor quality representatives; see Banducci and Karp, 1994, on the tendency of poorly performing representatives to jump before they are pushed out of office. Both Pitkin and Birch discuss differences between "descriptive" and "substantive" representation and provide interesting accounts of the development of these terms through history. See also H. Pitkin, *The Concept of Representation* (Berkeley, CA: University of California Press, 1967); A. Birch, *Representation* (London: Pall Mall, 1971). Lublin, 1997, is an excellent empirical study of the representation of African-Americans while Hajnal provides a similarly interesting look at the willingness of Anglos to vote for minority candidates.

4

ARE THERE BETTER WAYS TO ELECT CONGRESS?

The discussion thus far has highlighted several problems with elections in the United States, particularly congressional elections. Some of the main problems we saw are the following: Congressional elections have limited competitiveness; they can do a poor job of translating votes into representation; and they generate little participation. Moreover, campaign costs have skyrocketed in recent years, and the permanent fundraising by incumbents associated with this is sure to erode public confidence in the institution. Finally, the winner-take-all character of these contests may inhibit both substantive and descriptive representation of American citizens. Although several of these points could be applied to both presidential and congressional elections, this chapter examines several contemporary proposals that have been offered as ways of reforming congressional elections. In the next chapter, we will address proposals that apply specifically to presidential elections. A subsequent chapter examines the issue of campaign finance separately.

Many proposals have been offered over the years to "fix" what is broken in Congress by changing the way Congress is elected. Many of these proposals require amendments to the U.S. Constitution and, as such, have had little prospect of being adopted. As examples, some have advocated eliminating bicameralism and adopting the "Nebraska Model" of a unicameral legislature.[1] James Sundquist (1986) has considered several proposals for changing American elections, and suggests a "team ticket" where ballots are structured so that voters mark a spot that represents a single vote for the presidential and congressional candidates of the same party. Sundquist has also suggested holding congressional elections two weeks after the president is elected, so that voters would know which party controlled the White House before electing a Congress. Another proposal would give the party of the president "bonus seats" in Congress to insure that the president's party had a congressional majority. Team tickets and bonus seats of this sort would probably enhance the winner-take-all nature of Congress and congressional elections.[2]

These proposals, and others of this sort, are designed to cure something that may not be the actual disease that the institution suffers from. These plans, for example, are likely to reduce the incidence or effect of divided government. These are proposals that reflect a traditional, twentieth-century American academic assumption about representation in the United States. They assume that there is a majority party that needs representation, and that elections should be reformed to ensure that they produce a cohesive party majority across all branches of government.

As we have demonstrated in previous chapters, however, the key problems with congressional elections may stem from something deeper. Election results depend little on who participates since districting plans largely predetermine the partisan distribution of seats. We suggest that the congressional elections fail to engage most citizens because they fail to offer interesting, competitive races, and because they fail at representing the diversity of America. Proposals that change elections to manufacture majorities could lead to greater mass disengagement with elections and American democracy.

How, then, should Congress be elected? We will consider here three proposals that could, in theory, increase the competitiveness and representatives of congressional elections: term limits, proportional representation, and an increase in the number of House seats.

TERM LIMITS

Many critics of the contemporary Congress advocate term limits as a way to improve representation and reinvigorate congressional elections. They note that an incumbents' ability to cultivate campaign contributions from groups lobbying Congress so outstrips challengers that there is virtually no way an incumbent can ever lose. Thus, 98 percent of incumbents are reelected in some years, with many individuals serving in the House for decades. Term limit advocates note, with disdain, that service in Congress has become a professional career. They cite arguments made about Congress at the time of its founding in favor of "amateur legislatures" and frequent rotation in office. These ideas combine into a vision of legislative members who are more concerned for the broad public good and less worried about what it takes to win their own next election. Others note that Madison and Hamilton believed the new "extended republic" would incorporate such diversity of interests into Congress that frequent rotation in office was not a major concern.[3]

Term limit proposals vary in details, but the basic idea is that incumbent members of the House would be limited to a fixed number of two-year terms. The 1994 GOP "Contract with America" proposed limiting terms of House members to twelve years. The Cato Institute, a conservative political advocacy group, recommended a total of just six years for House members.[4]

When they reach their limit, incumbents would be forced to retire and their name would not appear on the ballot. Some proposals go further and cut salary, staff, and pension benefit for legislators, in order to encourage "citizen" and oppose "professional" legislatures. The U.S. Constitution explicitly regulates congressional elections and makes no mention of term limits. This means that a constitutional amendment would be needed for term limits to apply to Congress.[5] In fact the First Congress considered over twenty constitutional amendments in 1791, including one on term limits for itself. It rejected the idea, while approving ten others (The Bill of Rights). After Republicans assumed control of Congress in 1994, they did bring term limits to a vote. In 1997, the House failed to pass several proposals for limiting terms. A proposal for twelve-year limits received the most support, but failed, 217 to 211 (it needed 69 more votes for the required two-thirds majority needed for constitutional amendments). In 1996, term limit advocates in the U.S. Senate fell just two short of the 60 votes they needed to end debate and force a floor vote on a term limits constitutional amendment.

At minimum, term limits are expected to create more open seats and thus possibly change the mix of candidates who end up winning. If congressional races are dominated by incumbents who tend to be white men, open seat races could level the playing field for women and minorities, who might otherwise not be able to unseat an incumbent.[6] Critics and advocates of limits both argue that limited terms could have even more sweeping effects on who would seek office.

Advocates suggest that if election to Congress were no longer a guaranteed "job-for-life" that members would have a different outlook on the bills they consider. As term-limited representatives, they might worry more directly about how government affects the job or business they had prior to entering Congress, since they will return fairly soon to their former life. Advocates also argue that the end of "careerism" would allow a greater variety of people to serve. A business owner, for example, might not consider running for Congress if it would take twenty years to build enough seniority to have influence in the House. Under limited terms, she could theoretically serve much less time and be on more equal footing with other members. Furthermore, by ending their perpetual concern about reelection, term limits might better focus representatives on national problems, rather than defending their own local, parochial concerns.

Critics point out that term limits would make it more difficult for people of modest means to leave their jobs and run for Congress. Why, for example, would school teachers or social workers abandon their careers of ten or fifteen years to serve no more than six or twelve years in the House? Their jobs would not necessarily be available for them when term limits force them out of office. Critics also point out that term limits would really only apply to representatives who serve for long periods. Incumbents often leave office voluntarily sooner than this. A smaller proportion of ineffective or unpopular representatives are also defeated. Empirical studies do suggest that incumbents with dubious records in offices are more likely than others to be defeated after just a few terms.[7] This means that the only incumbents to be kicked out by term limits would be, ironically, those who remain popular with their constituents over the long haul. Worse, these are the people who rise to leadership positions in the House, and thus comprise its "institutional memory."

Term limit proponents received a major shot in the arm in the first half of the 1990s by passing term limits in many states through the initiative process. In states like California and Oregon, citizens' groups are allowed to place their own proposals for constitutional amendments on their state's ballot. Term limit initiatives appeared on ballots in over eighteen states between 1990 and 1994, with nearly every proposal approved by voters in each state.[8] Election results in these states and public opinion data suggest that these proposals are quite popular with voters. Most passed with large majorities; however, a number of these state measures were struck down by state courts for violating state laws that restrict initiatives to a "single-subject." Federal courts also rejected provisions of voter-approved initiatives that would limit the terms of their state's congressional delegation, ruling that such matters required an amendment to the U.S. Constitution.[9]

WHAT WOULD HAPPEN IF WE HAD TERM LIMITS FOR CONGRESS?

Despite court decisions invalidating several state term limit measures, a number of states had legislative term limits go into effect by the late 1990s, providing a laboratory for demonstrating how such limits might affect Congress, if adopted. Since limits in most places have only recently begun to kick in, generalizations are preliminary. One of the more comprehensive studies of the effects of term limits on state legislatures concluded that the demographic composition of term limited legislatures didn't change much, apart from a possible, subtle increase in the representation of women. Otherwise, newcomers in term-limited state legislatures "displayed the same mix of occupational, educational, ethnic, and socioeconomic backgrounds as their counterparts in non–term-limited states. In California, however, representation of Latinos has increased sharply since term limits were adopted there.[10]

EVIDENCE FROM THE STATES

John Carey and his colleagues surveyed thousands of state legislators to identify how term limits might affect how legislators behave and how a legislature functions. They found that, compared to representatives in nonlimited states, those from term limit states placed a higher priority on the needs of their state than on the needs of their district. At the same time, the influence of party leadership may decline under term limits, as "rank-and-file" representatives become more assertive. The flip side of this may be that newcomers who do become leaders must rely more on others for advice, and that "incentives for cooperation" (or the leadership's ability to force consensus) may be weakened by term limits. It also seems clear that term limits do not keep politics from becoming a career for many legislators. Term limits push incumbents to run for other posts. Lower house members move on (with name recognition) to run for the state senate, and state senators drop down and serve in the lower house or seek congressional seats. Some of the most troubling findings are that citizens are less likely to know who their representative is under term limits, and so are less likely to contact their representative.

Other studies provide additional evidence that term limits might not have a dramatic effect on electoral competitiveness, nor on the nature of representation. Proponents of term limits suggest that limits will level the playing field by weakening incumbent advantages in raising campaign funds. However, the results of "open-seat" U.S. House elections suggest that new representatives very quickly develop the same fundraising advantages that long-serving members have. As soon as they are elected, interest groups and others funnel so much money their way that they can easily outspend any challenger. Thus, without changes in campaign finance laws, limits may only make the average U.S. House election more competitive once every twelve years.

PROPORTIONAL REPRESENTATION

Another reform proposal aims to increase the number of parties in Congress by changing how it is elected. Recent elections have shown that independents and candidates of "minor" or "third" parties in the United States have had some success. Ross Perot's 1992 effort was the best showing of such a candidate in eighty years. Likewise, Jesse Ventura was elected governor of Minnesota in 1998 as a Reform party candidate, and Maine and Connecticut have elected non–major party governors. These examples lead some to suggest that the future looks bright for third party movements. We expect that whatever increased support such parties have received in recent years, the United States will remain a two-party system unless its election methods are changed.[11] Nonetheless, as Table 4.1 (on page 64) illustrates, opinion polls show some support for having additional parties in Congress.

Substantial research documents a "psychological effect" associated with FPTP, winner-take-all elections. Voters rarely support a party that has no chance to win. Under FPTP elections, the only way to win is to place first. Almost by definition, small parties cannot do this. Without changing rules to reward them for the votes they receive, voters will shy away from them, even if they prefer their policies to the major parties. Hence votes and voters will flow away from small parties to the larger ones. As a consequence of this we see the system producing two large parties. In the United States, for example, no matter how much you may like a candidate such as Buchanan or Perot

TABLE 4.1   SUPPORT FOR PROPORTIONAL REPRESENTATION IN THE UNITED STATES

	NATIONAL SAMPLE, 2000 (PERCENT RESPONDING)
Continue with two-party system?	38.3
Elect candidates without party labels?	27.9
More parties to effectively challenge Ds and Rs?	33.8

Source: American National Election Study, 1,487 respondents. The question read: Which one of the following outcomes regarding political parties best represents what you would like to see happen? ONE, a continuation of the two party system of Democrats and Republicans; TWO, elections in which candidates run as individuals without party labels; or THREE, the growth of one or more parties that could effectively challenge the Democrats and Republicans?

	ARKANSAS SAMPLE, 2000	WASHINGTON SAMPLE, 2000
Leave things as they are	47.5	40
Have an additional party in Congress	40.9	56

Sources: Washington 2000 Poll, Applied Research Northwest, 404 respondents; Arkansas Poll, 2000, 770 respondents. The question read: We could elect the U.S. Congress so parties supported by, say, 20 percent of voters would hold 20 percent of the seats. This would make it more likely that an additional party could get some representation in Congress. Would you support changing things so an additional party receives some seats, or leaving things as they are with 2 large parties holding all of the seats?

or Nader, none of these candidates can win. So the "real" choice is between the two candidates from the major parties. Hence, many minor party supporters will vote for whichever of the two main party contenders they like (or vote against the one they dislike).

The range of election methods used by the world's democracies is extensive indeed. The various types can be thought of as placed along a continuum that ranges from majoritarian or *plurality* systems at one extreme, and pure, *party-list* proportional representation at the other. Majoritarian/plurality systems tend to be based on electing a single representative per legislative district, as in the United States. Proportional representation (PR) systems usually require that many representatives are elected per district, so that parties can be awarded seats in proportion to their share of the vote. Table 4.2 presents an example of this continuum, while giving examples of nations that use various election methods.[12]

Of course, this dichotomy is a great oversimplification of the distinction between majority/plurality elections (as used in the United States) and PR elections. But it does point out a key difference between how we elect our Congress and how most other democracies hold their elections. With only one member per district in the United States, only one candidate—the one who gets the majority or plurality of votes—can ever win a seat in any district. When voters become sensitive to this fact, they tend never to vote for any candidate but those of the largest two parties, so as to not waste their vote. Under various forms of PR, a vote cast for a candidate or party who might finish third or fourth may nevertheless still elect a representative from that party.

TABLE 4.2   SYSTEM OF ELECTIONS IN VARIOUS NATIONS

PLURALITY	MAJORITARIAN	SEMI-PR	MIXED-MEMBER PR	PURE-PR
United States	France	Japan	Germany	Norway
United Kingdom	Australia	(pre-1994)	Russia	Sweden
Canada			New Zealand	
India				

There are many issues involved when comparing proportional and first past the post systems; one is that FPTP tends to produce only two main political parties that can ever win anything. As we noted above, concerns over wasting a vote on minor party candidates with no chance of winning leads voters to cast a ballot for the bigger parties. PR systems tend to produce more parties that actually win seats in part because small parties *can* still win seats under a proportionality rule and so voters do not feel their votes are wasted.[13] Majority/plurality rules are said to provide more stability by eliminating the need for multiparty coalition governments. Cross-national studies of the duration of majority and coalition (multiparty) governments, however, suggest that these differences are trivial. In theory, majority/plurality elections may also help voters figure out which party to hold accountable when things go bad.

PR, in contrast, is said to better generate social consensus about what government should do by representing a wider range of interests in a legislature. This should cause a wider range of citizens to take interest in elections and lead more citizens to feel that they are actually represented by government. Comparative studies of public opinion find greater satisfaction with democracy in PR nations and also find that voter turnout is higher in nations using PR elections.[14]

METHODS OF PR ELECTIONS THAT MIGHT APPLY IN THE UNITED STATES

There are many possible ways to elect all or part of the U.S. Congress by PR. Since the Constitution insures that all states are to be represented in the Senate with two members each, it would be much easier to implement PR in House elections. The basic requirement for PR elections is having more than one member elected per district, since it is impossible to divide up a single person proportionately.

In order to implement this, Congress would be required to pass a statute (not a constitutional amendment) that reauthorizes multiple members per legislative district.[15] In 2000, Congress held hearings on a plan that would allow states to use multimember districts and PR or "semi-PR" voting methods, but no action was taken. In practice, a district would need at least three, and perhaps five members per district if seats in Congress were to be awarded in rough proportion to the distribution of votes that parties receive in the district. Studies demonstrate that with fewer than three seats at stake, the same two parties will likely win nearly all seats.

In populous states, it would be reasonably easy to divide a state into two or more distinct multimember districts. Table 4.3 illustrates hypothetical examples of how seats in Congress might be awarded if PR (as opposed to FPTP) were used to elect an imaginary state's ten-member delegation to the U.S. House. The state is divided into two geographic districts (the division could be north or south, east or west, rural or urban, etc.). Our example is set up so that District 1 happens to have a large proportion of conservative voters (who opt for Republican and Libertarians), while District 2 has a relatively large proportion of liberal voters (who support Democrats and Greens).

The example also shows that even proportional representation systems can rarely be strictly proportionate. The Democrats, in our example, earned enough votes to win 1.5 seats in District 1. Republicans, likewise, captured enough votes to win 1.5 seats in District 2. Of course it is not possible (or at least not ethical) to send one-half or three-quarters of a person to serve in Congress. Various PR systems are differentiated by the rules they use to determine how fractions of seats might be awarded to rival parties, and these rules typically favor the parties that win the most votes. Nevertheless, our example reflects that in each district a minor party could gain representation with only 20 percent of the vote.

TABLE 4.3   ELECTING A TEN-MEMBER STATE DELEGATION TO THE U.S. HOUSE OF REPRESENTATIVES

EXAMPLE 1, FOUR PARTIES

	DISTRICT 1 (5 SEATS)				DISTRICT 2 (5 SEATS)			
	VOTES	SEATS "EARNED"	SEATS (ACTUAL)	SEATS	VOTE	SEATS "EARNED"	SEATS (ACTUAL)	SEATS
Republican	40%	2.0	2	40%	30%	1.5	2	40%
Democrat	30	1.5	2	40	40	2.0	2	40
Libertarian	20	1.0	1	20	10	0.5	0	
Green	10	0.5	0		20	1.0	1	20

EXAMPLE 2, TWO PARTIES

	DISTRICT 1 (5 SEATS)				DISTRICT 2 (5 SEATS)			
Republican	56%	2.8	3	60%	38%	1.9	2	40%
Democrat	44	2.2	2	40	62	3.1	3	60

There is another important practical element of PR elections, in addition to the need for multimember districts. If there are multiple seats elected per district, some parties will need to run multiple candidates in order to gain seats in proportion to the votes they might receive. Various PR systems differ in how citizens express their votes (either for candidates directly, or for a particular party, or for both). They also differ in how votes are counted, and in how the parties control who gets to appear on ballots. Under a "closed list-PR" system, for example, voters simply mark the box of their preferred party. Votes for the party are counted to determine how many seats it wins, and the party's elite decide which party candidates get to fill the seats.

This model would probably never be acceptable to Americans, who are accustomed to voting for candidates directly. However, some versions of PR do preserve the citizen's ability to vote for candidates directly in multimember districts. PR systems in some nations are also structured to use multimember and single-member districts in tandem. This latter point is important, for it means that Congress could have members who are the exclusive representative of a local area while also having more parties in the mix elected via PR. In theory, congressional elections could be conducted with a mix of the present FPTPs and any one of the following multimember district systems we describe in brief below.

Mixed Member Proportional (MMP)   In post–WWII Germany and, more recently in New Zealand, roughly half the seats in the national legislature are elected from single-member districts, the other half by PR. This plan requires that voters mark two spots on the ballot when voting—one to elect their local representative and one to fill the PR seats. The candidate with the most votes wins the local seat. The other seats are distributed proportionately, based on the second vote. A party must win a local district or get at least 5 percent of the vote for the PR seats, in order to gain representation. Under MMP in Germany and New Zealand, the party vote (for PR seats) ultimately determines the distribution of seats in the legislature. Voters have no direct say in who represents the party in the PR seats. If a party receives 25 percent of the national vote for PR seats but its candidates win no local seats, it will receive bonus seats to insure that it controls roughly 25 percent of seats in the legislature. Mexico and Russia use a related "mixed" system, but election rules there do less to compensate parties that win few local seats.

Single Transferable Vote (STV)   This PR system is also known as preference voting, and is used in Ireland, Malta, and Australia (for their Senate). Unlike MMP, STV allows voters to fill PR seats by voting directly for individual candidates, or for the party's preranked list of candidates. Since votes can be cast directly for candidates, this method was once used in many U.S. cities, including Boulder (Colorado), Cincinnati, Sacramento, and New York.[16]

Voters simply rank candidates according to their preferences. When the total number of voters is known, the minimum number of votes needed to win a seat can be determined.[17] Voters' first preferences are counted initially—candidates with more than the minimum number are declared elected. In practice, there are often more seats than candidates who pass the minimum in the initial count. A second round of counting eliminates the candidate with the least support, and "transfers" preferences to the candidates ranked second by that candidate's supporters. This process continues until all seats are filled. Advocates of STV like it because it allows nearly all voters to see that they have some influence over who is elected—even those whose first preferred candidates lose. We will provide an example of a simpler preference voting system in the next chapter.

Cumulative Voting (CV)   Cumulative voting is another form of preference voting, where votes are cast directly for individual candidates running in a multimember district. At the end of the 1990s, several dozen U.S. cities, towns, counties, and school districts—primarily Texas and Alabama—elected their local councils with this "semi-PR" election system. Voters are allowed to cast as many votes as there are seats to fill. They can distribute their votes across a number of candidates, or they can concentrate their votes on a single candidate. If a group of voters concentrates all their votes on a single candidate, they can elect the candidate without having to win an outright plurality or majority. CV is referred to as "semi-PR" because candidates typically need a higher proportion of votes to get a seat than under MMP or STV (see Table 4.4).[18]

TABLE 4.4   APPORTIONMENT OF SEATS UNDER THREE ELECTION SYSTEMS

		NUMBER OF SEATS		
	VOTE	STV	CV	MMP
Candidate of Party A	40%	2	3	2
Candidate of Party B	35	2	2	2
Candidate of Party C	15	1	0	1
Candidate of Party D	10	0	0	0

Note: We assume a 5-seat district, and 500,000 voters. This example applies only to seats allocated from multimember districts. MMP is used in conjunction with FPTP elections, and the PR seat allocation is contingent on results in FPTP seats. If Party A's candidate won the hypothetical FPTP seat, one of their PR seats could be allocated to Party C or Party D.

WHAT WOULD HAPPEN IF WE BEGAN ELECTING CONGRESS VIA PR?

MORE PARTIES AND "FAIR" OUTCOMES

Although FPTP elections need not always produce a two-party system, PR elections in districts with three or more representatives are nearly certain to produce more than two parties that gain representation. It is less obvious just how many parties will gain effective, nontrivial levels of representation under various forms of PR. The number of parties is likely to increase as more representatives are elected per district—since this allows a smaller share of the vote to still "earn" at least one seat.

Critics note that PR might lead to too much fragmentation of the party system. Maurice Duverger goes so far as to claim that PR weakens democracy in some nations by fragmenting the party system. This can be particularly problematic in parliamentary systems, because it increases the possibility that the governing party will not have a majority. Rather than having a single majority party rule parliament, PR may produce elections where no party holds a clear majority. Coalitions of two or more parties must form the government and they may be less effective than a single-party majority. On the other hand, weak party discipline, seen at times in the U.S. Congress, is not so different from the "fragmentation" that resembles one of the most criticized cases of PR—Italy. That is, the candidate-centered U.S Congress, like the Italian Parliament, sometimes needs to build cross-party coalitions on legislation on an issue-by-issue basis.[19]

Duverger suggests that PR might be a good idea for the U.S. Congress, since our two major parties are "mere receptacles containing too haphazard a mixture of different elected members to properly represent the diverse tendencies of public opinion."[20] The composition of Congress, furthermore, has no effect on whether the president remains in office. Unlike parliamentary PR systems, the executive does not lose power in our system if she or he fails to retain a majority in the legislature; thus PR would not have the same destabilizing effects here as it might have in parliamentary systems. Others note that PR produces fewer parties when presidential and legislative elections are at the same time, and when presidential elections are decided on plurality (rather than by majority runoff).[21] As we see in the next chapter, presidential elections also work to maintain a two-party system. This point is important to remember in the next chapter when we examine proposals to reform presidential elections. Use of PR to elect Congress, combined with "alternative" or "instant runoff" election methods for the president, may be a dangerous combination if it fragments a party system more than PR for Congress might by itself.

PR systems can also be designed to limit the number of parties that can win seats. Germany and New Zealand use MMP with a rule that no party can win PR seats unless they get 5 percent of the party vote. Each nation has two large parties (on the center right and center left). In Germany, only two other parties (the Free Democrats, and, more recently, the Greens) win enough seats to ever join one of the larger parties in building a parliamentary majority. Thus, Germany is typically classified as a three- or four-party system. On the other hand, many critics of PR point to the politics of Israel, where many parties need to coalesce to form a government. Often the government is quite fragile and—critics allege—held hostage to the demands of very small extremist parties.[22]

To make the point more concrete, consider the range of candidates and parties that might gain representation in the United States, where depending on the actual plan put into place, parties associated with both Ralph Nader and Pat Buchanan could possibly gain seats. Parties associated with a range of politicians from Jesse Jackson to David Duke might also gain seats, as may parties associated with specific religions or churches. Although some would welcome the increased choice associated with more candidates, others point to the more extreme examples from countries such as Israel to argue that, if the politicking and bargaining seems excessive now with just two parties, wait until there are five or seven parties taking part.

Even if the number of parties in Congress did not increase much under PR, it is probable that PR elections would produce less distortion in translating votes into seats. Compare the second example in Table 4.2 (on page 65) to examples of vote bias from Texas and Washington displayed in Chapter 3. With two parties contesting in FPTPs, quirks of districting can cause the party with more votes to be shortchanged and win less than half the seats. Conversely, FPTPs can cause a party with a bare majority to win far more seats than the other party. With multimember PR, such distortions can be smoothed out so that each party receives seats in closer proportion to the votes they received.

MORE POLARIZATION, OR LESS?

Scholars still debate about how the presence of more parties would affect the policy choices presented to voters. A classic model suggests that in a two-party system, the sole left and right parties will converge toward the political center, since the bulk of voters are moderates. Each party can count on support from the ideological voters on their own side of the political spectrum, as those voters have no other credible candidates to support.[23]

Under PR, however, the model predicts that a party might locate in the center, with other parties staking out ideologically distinct positions that appeal to groups of voters along the ideological continuum. More parties should breed distinct choices for voters. Indeed, Alan Ware found that of eighteen nations, those with the most parties in the legislature had greater ideological differences between parties.[24] A crude form of this model would predict that America, with only two parties, should have "Tweedledee" and "Tweedledum" candidates tripping over each other to appeal to moderate voters.[25] If this is our current state of affairs, then a switch to some form of PR would probably increase the ideological distance between Democrats and Republicans, with smaller parties staking out positions in the center, or farther to the left or right of the two largest parties.

In practice, however, things don't always work out the way this model predicts. Several scholars have pointed out that in some two-party systems, the parties stake out positions that are more extreme than what their average voter might want. If parties are mostly concerned about constituents who have intense preferences about certain issues (e.g., those who contribute to their campaigns), they may adopt polarized positions that reflect those key constituents, rather than average voters. When there are just two parties, with many voters who may feel relatively indifferent about some issues, parties may have more incentive to adopt extreme positions in order to highlight— to their core constituents—how they differ from the only other credible party.[26]

If American political parties have staked out ideological positions on many issues that are more extreme than many moderate voters might want, then a switch to PR may pull the parties toward the center, or produce a new, relatively large political force in the center. There is some indirect evidence that the Democratic and Republican parties might be more polarized today than the convergence model might predict. In Ware's eighteen-nation analysis, the United States and Great Britain stood out as having relatively large ideological distances between their parties—despite the fact that there were only two main parties in each. And as we show in Chapter 2, moderates and independents feel the least represented in the United States.

This may explain why support for more parties in Congress is greater among independent voters than among strong partisans. The potential "market" for a new party may lie with these independents. When asked if we should continue electing a two-party Congress, switch to nonpartisan elections, or build additional "effective" parties to challenge the Democrats and Republicans, only 38 percent of Americans support continuing with the status quo (see page 64). Support for more parties in Congress tends to come from political independents much more than from voters who identify themselves as strong Democrats or strong Republicans. Most people, however, do not identify strongly with either party. Among these independents, barely one-quarter support the continuation of the two-party system in Congress. Independents tend to have the highest levels of dissatisfaction about the way democracy works in the United States—which, as we suggest in Chapter 2, may be due to perceptions that neither party represents their interests very well. Support for more parties, not surprisingly, is greater among those who are dissatisfied with how democracy works in the United States.

These polling data can be compared to questions from two state-wide polls that limited the response options to keeping the status quo or having more parties in Congress. Faced with this choice, there is even greater support for more parties relative to the status quo.

If the polarization model is a better picture of our present two-party system than the convergence model, then a switch to PR could, perhaps, moderate the positions that Democrats and Republicans take on many issues. With smaller, ideologically distinct parties in the mix via PR, Democrats and Republicans might be forced to move more toward the political center. Convergence theory, however, predicts that the larger American parties would be relatively centrist under FPTP, and that PR might encourage them to take more ideologically distinct positions on policies.[27]

UNSTABLE COALITION GOVERNMENTS?

One of the enduring critiques of PR is that it makes it difficult for a single party to form a majority government. With more parties in Congress, would not two or more parties need to form a coalition in order to govern? Could a president then be forced to depend on the support of one small party to get anything through Congress? Possibly. But the potential instability of coalition government might be less of a concern for the United States than other nations. For better or worse, political power in the United States is now centered firmly in the executive branch. The scope of modern presidential powers, furthermore, has increased during periods of divided and unified party government. Republican Presidents Nixon, Reagan, Bush Sr., and G. W. Bush often governed with Democrats in control of Congress. Clinton served most of his tenure with a Republican Congress. Reasonable people argue that these executives seemed little hamstrung by the fact that their party did not control the Congress.[28]

In fact, Maurice Duverger, no fan of PR in Europe, suggested that PR would "lead to a real renewal of political life" if used for the U.S. Congress, since American parties do not represent public opinion very well.[29] With a single party controlling the U.S. executive branch under our presidential system, multipartyism in one house of Congress may not change the center of gravity much in our political system.

MORE CANDIDATE CAMPAIGN ACTIVITY?

Some PR systems could possibly result in greater electoral competition. As noted in Chapter 3, the vast majority of U.S. House districts are not competitive. The same incumbents win each year, and often fail to attract any challengers. This provides little incentive for anyone to campaign actively or mobilize new voters. Under PR, multiple seats would always be at stake. If one incumbent fails to mobilize her base, another could capture a higher proportion of votes and threaten her chances of reelection. The prospect of gaining seats with a smaller share of votes, furthermore, expands the range of candidates who have the incentive to put on a vigorous campaign. Studies of candidate activity comparing similar jurisdictions that use CV and FPTP find greater candidate activity—as well as higher spending—under CV.[30]

It is also possible, however, that list-PR, a component of MMP, could depress candidate campaign activity among those who would hold the PR seats. For larger parties, candidates ranked at the top of a party's list are almost guaranteed election if their party captures anything close to its "normal" share of the vote. Many observers also suggest that local, personal-based campaigning makes little sense to candidates under list-PR, since seats are allocated based on direct votes for the party, rather than votes for individual candidates. These candidates emphasize party policy, rather than their own personal characteristics.

MORE DESCRIPTIVE REPRESENTATION

Descriptive representation entails having someone who looks like you as a representative while substantive representation means that your representative directly expresses your policy concerns. The two forms of representation need not be mutually exclusive under PR, but they may be under FPTP.[31] It is difficult to resolve questions about how well the U.S. Congress provides substantive representation under FPTP. Many think it may do a decent job at this, but the opinion data we report in Chapter 2 suggests this might not be the case. It is clear, however, that our present congressional election system does a poor job of providing descriptive representation. In 2002, only 14 percent of members were women. Only 4 percent were Latino, and less than 1 percent Asian, despite the fact that 12.5 percent and 4 percent of Americans are Latino and Asian, respectively.

Advocates of PR claim that it would increase descriptive representation of women and minorities in the United States. They point out that in many European nations, the highest proportion of women legislators are found where list-PR is used to elect all seats in the parliaments. At the top are Sweden, Norway, and Finland, where women hold about 40 percent of seats in each nation. Women hold only about 15 percent of seats that Germany and New Zealand elect from FPTP districts, but they win a much higher proportion of the list-PR seats there (45 percent in NZ). It is clear that list-PR often leads to more women in a legislature, but it is not clear that this is a general result of all PR systems.

Some suggest that any multimember district plan increases the chances that women might win. People may be less resistant to voting for women if they can cast a vote for male and female candidates at the same time—something that is possible in a multimember district. There is some uncertainty, however, about how much of the difference in representation of women under PR or FPTP is due to election rules, party behavior, or cultural factors. Moreover, PR need not automatically help women win seats. Very few women are elected under PR in Malta, for example. Women also gain more seats under list-PR because parties in many nations have made overt efforts to rank them higher on their official lists of candidates.[32] If

TABLE 4.5   REPRESENTATION OF WOMEN IN AUSTRALIAN LEGISLATURES, 1998

LEGISLATURE	LOWER HOUSE ELECTION SYSTEM	PERCENT WOMEN LOWER HOUSE	UPPER HOUSE ELECTION SYSTEM	PERCENT WOMEN UPPER HOUSE
New South Wales	99 FPTPs	16.0	PR, One 21-seat district	28.5
South Australia	47 FPTPs	29.8	PR, One 11-seat district	22.8
Tasmania	PR, Five 7-seat MMDs	28.0	19 FPTPs	10.5
Federal Parliament	148 FPTPs	22.0	PR, Six 6-seat MMDs*	31.5
Western Australia	57 FPTPs	22.8	PR, Six 5- to 7-seat MMDs	23.5
Queensland	89 FPTPs	17.9	no upper house	n/a
Victoria	88 FPTPs	18.2	22 FPTPs	20.5

Average representation of women in five PR legislatures: 26.8%
Average representation of women in eight FPTP legislatures: 17.1%

*For a half-Senate election. Other individual seats are elected for ACT and NT by FPTP, and are not included here.
Note: STV is used to elect in each PR legislature. MMD = multimember districts. FPTPs = first-past-the-post, single-member district.
Source: 1998, Women in the Senate, Senate Brief No. 3. Canberra: Parliament of Australia.

American parties behaved similarly, representation of women could increase. Australia provides an interesting test case of how different elections systems affect the representation of women. Upper and lower houses of the federal parliament and various state legislatures are elected under different election rules. Cultural factors and party attitudes about women probably vary much less within Australia than across European nations. As Table 4.5 illustrates, women tend to hold about 10 percent more seats in legislatures elected by PR. Of five places where one house is elected by PR and the other by FPTP, only one (the state of South Australia) has lower representation of women in the chamber elected by PR.

CHANGES IN CITIZEN ATTITUDES AND BEHAVIOR

A number of cross-national studies suggest that representation under PR leads citizens to be more satisfied with democracy and more likely to vote.[33] Studies that examine changes in behavior before and after a jurisdiction changed from majoritarian to PR (or semi-PR) systems find similar effects. After New Zealand changed from FPTP to MMP-PR in 1996, surveys suggest that citizens were more likely to think their vote mattered and minority citizens were more likely to vote. Our own study of the effects of adopting semi-PR elections in several U.S. cities and counties found that the switch away from majoritarian plans was associated with a rise in turnout of about 5 percent.[34]

But would PR lead to greater public satisfaction with Congress? Critics of a move toward PR for the House note that it would be unlikely to solve one of the main problems associated with Congress—public dissatisfaction with bargaining, negotiating, and partisan tactics associated with governing.[35] It is one thing for PR to make the House more representative of the American public. Making the public more content with how the legislature functions is a different matter.

Some form of two-party coalition (at minimum) would probably be necessary in order to run the affairs of a House of Representatives if no party held a majority of seats. When New Zealand's Parliament began operating under its first PR coalition government after generations of using FPTP, public contempt for government (and PR) increased.[36] However, coalition arrangements might not be too different from the status quo in the United States, where the parties in the House already must build interparty and intraparty coalitions on each legislative goal, and then build coalitions across two legislative houses and a presidency often controlled by rival parties.

INCREASING THE SIZE OF THE U.S. HOUSE

There is ample evidence then, to suggest that a switch to PR could make congressional races more competitive, while also increasing the scope of parties represented in Congress. But there is another way to broaden the scope of representation in Congress: increasing the size of the House of Representatives. Cross-national studies indicate that proportionality of election results and the number of parties in a legislature are both related positively to the number of seats in a legislature, regardless of whether PR or FPTP is used.

The reason for this is fairly simple, and somewhat mechanical. Under any election system, the smaller the place that a representative comes from, the more likely that a minority group will comprise a local majority in at least a few places. Put differently, a politically cohesive group of 50,000 voters stands a much better chance of electing their own candidate in a district of 100,000 voters than in a district of 1,000,000 voters. This is one reason that a third party (the Liberals) has been able to survive for years in Great Britain under winner-take-all FPTP. Even though they consistently finish third in national elections (behind Labour and the Conservatives), British election districts are small enough that Liberal supporters can form a plurality and win some seats. Since the election system is still FPTP, they never win seats in proportion to their national vote—but they would probably have far fewer seats if they had to compete across larger districts.

There are people who advocate increasing the size of the U.S. House for reasons unrelated to the electoral prospects of a third party. The population of America's congressional districts has grown so large in the last 100 years that few citizens stand any chance of having personal contacts with their representative. Moreover, as the population of our districts grows larger, campaign costs are sure to escalate. Each year, candidates must spend more to communicate with voters by TV and direct mail. Given what we know about incumbent advantages in fundraising, larger districts could make elections even less competitive as these advantages are amplified.

It is important to note that there is no constitutional requirement that the House have only 435 members. Congress regulates its own size by statute. The Constitution only requires that the number not exceed one representative per 30,000 people in the United States.[37] Prior to 1915, the number of House seats grew in tandem with the U.S. population. As Figure 4.1 illustrates, however, there has been no change since 1915. Cohen notes that Congress decided to stop growing in order to dilute the growing influence of immigrant voters. Whatever the reason, the effect is clear—with a fixed number of seats and a growing population, the number of people per representative has nearly tripled in the past 80 years. This puts the United States out of step with nearly all other democracies. The size of lower houses tends to increase with population, and a legislature's size tends to reflect the cube root of its nation's population. By this standard, the United States should have about 650 members in the House of Representatives, rather than 435.[38]

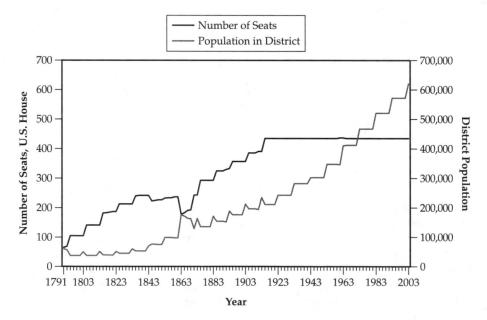

FIGURE 4.1   POPULATION OF U.S. HOUSE DISTRICTS, 1790–2000

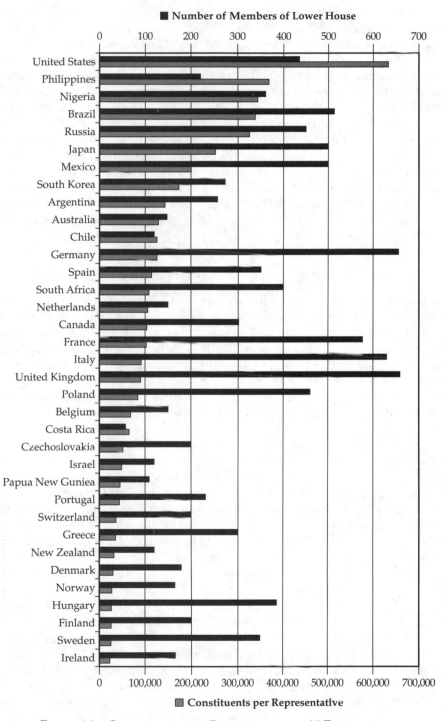

Number of Members of Lower House

Constituents per Representative

FIGURE 4.2   CONSTITUENTS PER REPRESENTATIVE IN 35 DEMOCRACIES

Figure 4.2 (on page 77) demonstrates that each member of the U.S. House now represents over 600,000 constituents, compared to about 90,000 per representative in Britain and less than 30,000 per representative in Norway, Finland, Sweden, and Ireland. Only India (a nation of over 1 billion people) has more constituents per representative than the United States. Representatives in sprawling, populous nations such as Nigeria, the Philippines, Brazil, and Russia all have fewer constituents than a member of the U.S. House. The figure shows the reason why: These nations with large populations, as well as many less populous democracies, have bigger legislatures. In fact, all of Europe's biggest democracies, though less populated than the United States, have more members in their national legislature. The British Parliament has 659; France's National Assembly has 577; Germany's Bundestag has 656, and Italy's lower house has 630. Relative to many of the world's most economically advanced democracies, the United States has a fairly small legislature.

WHAT WOULD HAPPEN IF CONGRESS HAD MORE MEMBERS?

At present, there seems to be limited impetus for increasing the size of the House. Despite the addition of four states and the tripling of the U.S. population since the size of the House was frozen at 435, Congress has rarely examined the issue. On February 23, 2001, Representative Alcee Hastings (D-Fla.) introduced H.R. 506, a resolution to create a commission to study the size of the House of Representatives and the method by which representatives are chosen. Hastings claimed that the United States has become the second most "under-representative" democracy in the world (after India).

Even if the commission was established and issued a report, it is unlikely that incumbent members of Congress will see it in their interest to admit more members to their ranks. It seems reasonable to assume that if the number of members of the House increased, the average representative might have less chance of being a major player inside Congress. More representatives may mean more "back-benchers," unless Congress somehow increased the number of leadership posts to be handed around to members. At the same time, smaller districts with closer ties between the representative and constituents might make it easier for constituents to keep track of the behavior of members.

It is difficult to find empirical studies that might help us draw conclusions about the effects of less populated congressional districts. Smaller congressional districts would make it easier to draw district lines that provide representation for spatially concentrated minorities, without having to resort to the "bizarre" shaped districts that the U.S. Supreme Courts has frowned upon. Smaller districts might also produce many of the same effects as a switch to multimember district PR: more parties, greater descriptive representation, more proportionate translation of votes to seats, and, perhaps, less campaign cost per candidate. A major study of participation in U.S. cities and suburbs found that larger places were a deterrent to participation.[39]

This does not mean, however, that House elections would become more competitive by definition if House districts were smaller. Although campaign costs might be reduced, incumbents would still seek reelection in FPTP seats, where all they need is a plurality to retain their seat. Incumbents may still use personal-style campaigning, name recognition, and pork-barrel politics to maintain their advantage over challengers. A bigger U.S. House, with less populous districts and lower campaign costs, may produce many challengers in new districts, but, given the nature of FPTP, it is likely that many incumbents would eventually run unopposed. Still, the benefits may improve upon the current state of affairs.

CONCLUSIONS

Electoral reforms of the kind we have discussed here are always fraught with the uncertainties that changes may bring. Some effects of institutional change can be harder to predict than we might like to think. Reformers of all stripes often state that the particular change they favor has many upsides and very few downsides (all known) with much more confidence than is warranted. But in the case of New Zealand some of the consequences of the shift from FPTP to MMP have surprised some observers despite the fact that the change itself was thoroughly discussed beforehand. There are, then, uncertain effects attached to all institutional shifts. For example, if PR caused Congress to become more fragmented than it is under the current system there might be calls for a stronger presidency along the French model. On the other hand, it is easy to make too much of these kinds of thought experiments. And if reformers err by too readily dismissing downsides, opponents of reform err by overstressing uncertainty and unexpected consequences. After all, if we push the logic of fearing surprises too far we would hardly ever get out of bed in the morning since you never quite know what could happen that day. Opponents of reform obviously stress words like *risk* or *uncertainty* or *gamble* because the words make the effects of reform sound much more dangerous than they actually are.

Some of the changes proposed above seem to have relatively little scope for unintended consequences. Increasing the size of the House and adopting term limits might seem to have little room for surprises; not least because we have experienced those reforms at the state level. Adopting PR for Congress, however, may well have more scope. But the question remains whether uncertain and unspecified changes outweigh the known downsides of the current system.

NOTES

1. Abraham McGlaughlin, "Which Governs Better: One House or Two? *Christian Science Monitor* 9, no. 210 (September 24, 1999).
2. James Sundquist, *Constitutional Reform and Effective Government* (Washington, D.C.: Brookings, 1986).
3. See, as examples of advocacy of term limits, George Will, *Restoration: Congress, Term Limits, and the Recovery of Deliberative Democracy* (New York: Free Press, 1992); John Fund, "Term Limitation: An Idea Whose Time Has Come," in *Limiting Legislative Terms*, ed. G. Benjamin and M. Malbin (Washington, D.C.: CQ Press, 1992). Petracca (1992) discusses the concerns of reelection in relation to term limits. In contrast, Anthony King argues that even without term limits, modern politics shows the triumph of running [for office] over governing. See Anthony King, *Running Scared: Why America's Politicians Campaign Too Much and Govern Too Little* (New York: Martin Kessler Books, 1997). For interpretation of Madison and Hamilton, see Benjamin and Malbin, 1992.
4. Doug Bandow, "Real Term Limits: Now More than Ever," *Policy Analysis*, no. 221 (March 28, 1995).
5. The Constitution was amended in 1951 to limit the president's tenure to two terms.
6. Gary Moncrief, Joel Thompson, Michael Haddon, and Robert Hoyer, "For Whom the Bell Tolls? Term Limits and State Legislatures," *Legislative Studies Quarterly* 17 (1992): 37–47. A decade after the term limits movement, the effects of limits on representation of women may have been smaller than expected. See Robert A. Bernstein and Anita Chadha, "The Effects of Term Limits on Representation: Why So Few Women?" in *The Test of Time: Coping with Legislative Term Limits*, ed. R. Framer, J. Rausch, and J. Green (Lanham, MD: Lexington Books, 2002).
7. Mondak, 1995; Steven R. L Millman, *Effects of Term Limits on the Quality of Members of the U.S. House: Testing the Mondak Model*, MA thesis, Department of Political Science, 1997, Western Washington University.
8. These ballot initiatives only qualify after securing a certain number of signatures from registered voters. We discuss this in Chapter 6. In Washington, voters rejected that state's first term limit initiative in 1991, but passed a second, less restrictive version in 1992.
9. On voter support for term limits, see J. Karp, "Explaining Support for Legislative Term Limits," *Public Opinion Quarterly* 59 (1995): 373–391; T. Donovan and J. Snipp, "Support for Legislative Term Limits in California," *Journal of Politics* 56 (1994): 492–501.
10. The "clock" that limits incumbents in many states did not run out until the late 1990s, or even after 2000. Some courts, like Oregon's, waited until limits were to take effect fully before rejecting them in 2002. The following section relies heavily on John M. Carey, Richard G. Niemi, and Lynda W. Powell, *Term Limits in the State Legislatures* (Ann Arbor, MI: University of Michigan Press, 2000).
11. See the examples of the chances for third-party success in Paul Herrnson and John C. Green, *Multiparty Politics in America: Prospects and Performance*, 2nd ed. (Lanham, MD: Rowan & Littlefield, 2002). For a general overview of third parties in the U.S., see Rosenstone et al., 1996.
12. For those interested in electoral systems there are several excellent treatments. See Enid Lakeman, *How Democracies Vote* (London: Faber, 1974); D. Rae, *Political Consequences of Electoral Laws* (New Haven, CT: Yale University Press, 1971); David Farrell, *Electoral Systems: A Comparative Introduction* (London: Palgrave, 2001).
13. Again, this is an oversimplification. Canada has multiple parties, but uses plurality rules. Regionalism gives Canada more parties. Likewise, Australia has at least three or four relevant national parties, but uses majoritarian rules to elect its lower house. A form of majoritarian voting used in Australia, the Alternative Vote, helps some smaller parties survive, as do PR elections used to elect the Australian Senate (see Bowler and Grofman).
14. Anderson and Gilloury (1997) study the impact of electoral institutions on reactions to loss. Also see Amy, 1994, and Andre Blais and R. K. Carty, "The Psychological Impact of Electoral Laws: Measuring Duverger's Elusive Factor," *British Journal of Political Science* 21 (1991): 79–93.
15. This was allowed by law until Congress passed a statute in the late 1960s that required each House district to elect only a single member.

16. Leon Weaver, "The Rise, Decline, and Resurrection of Proportional Representation in Local Governments in the United States," in *Electoral Laws and Their Political Consequences*, ed. B. Grofman and A. Lijphart (New York: Agathon Press, 1986); Kathleen Barber, *Proportional Representation and Election Reform in Ohio* (Columbus, OH: Ohio State University Press, 1995). See also S. Bowler and B. Grofman, eds., *Elections in Australia, Ireland, and Malta under the Single Transferable Vote* (Ann Arbor, MI: University of Michigan Press, 2000).
17. The total number of voters is v, and the number of seats to be elected is s. The "quota" for a seat is s+1/v
18. Lani Guinier, long concerned with issues of minority representation, has also long been an advocate of CV as a means of addressing minority underrepresentation. For a detailed study of America's experience with CV elections, see S. Bowler, T. Donovan, and D. Brockington, *Electoral Reform and Minority Representation: Local Experimentation with Alternative Elections* (Columbus, OH: Ohio State University Press, 2003).
19. On fragmentation of governing abilities under PR, see M. Duverger, "Which Is the Best Electoral System?" in *Choosing an Electoral System*, ed. B Grofman and A. Lijphart (Westport, CT: Praeger, 1984); Mark Rush, 1998.
20. Duverger, 1984, p. 36.
21. M. Shugart and J. Carey, *Presidents and Assemblies: Constitutional Design and Electoral Dynamics* (New York: Cambridge University Press, 1992); Mark P. Jones, *Electoral Laws and the Survival of Presidential Democracies* (Notre Dame, IN: University of Notre Dame Press, 1995).
22. Studies of the survival of coalition governments often point to the greater fragility of administrations, the larger the number of parties in government. See, for example, M. Laver and N. Schofield, *Multiparty Government* (New York: Oxford University Press, 1996). Other examples about this aspect of PR point to the problems in German politics in the inter-war period, or the problems in France just after WWII as examples of dysfunctional political systems.
23. A. Downs, *An Economic Theory of Democracy* (New York: Harper, 1957).
24. Alan Ware, *Political Parties and Party Systems* (New York: Oxford University Press, 1996). Ware based this on surveys of party experts reported by M. Laver and W. B. Hunt, *Policy and Party Competition* (London: Routledge, 1992).
25. Or, as the more cynical put it, "Tweedledum and Tweedledumber."
26. This is called the "directional" theory of voting, in contrast to the "spatial distance" model defined by Downs, 1957. For examples of it used, see S. MacDonald, O. Listhaug, and G. Rabinowitz, "Issues and Party Support in Multiparty Systems," *American Political Science Review* 85 (1991): 1107–1131; S. Merrill and B. Grofman, *A Unified Theory of Voting* (New York: Cambridge University Press, 1999).
27. The example of New Zealand is especially instructive. Regarded as an archetypical majoritarian system underpinned by a first-past-the-post electoral system, the country moved to list PR in 1993. This experiment in electoral system design on a grand scale has produced a number of studies on effects of electoral system change.
28. On arguments that presidents have sufficient (or even excessive) power over Congress, see A. Schlesinger, Jr., *The Imperial Presidency* (New York: Houghton Mifflin, 1973); Michael Lind, "The Out-of-Control Presidency," *New Republic* 14 (August 1995): 18–23; Nat Hentoff, "The President Who Makes War against the Constitution," *Village Voice* 43, no. 6 (February 10, 1998): 48–49.
29. Duverger, 1984.
30. Bowler, Donovan, and Brockington, 2003.
31. Lublin, 1999; Mansbridge, 1999; Herrnson, 2000, Chapter 2.
32. On the representation of women and electoral systems, see Amy, 1994; Caul, 2001; Darcy, Welch, and Clark, 1994.
33. Anderson and Gillory, 1999
34. For New Zealand, see Banducci, Donovan, and Karp, 1999. For the United States, see S. Bowler, D. Brockington, and T. Donovan, "Election Systems and Voter Turnout: Experiments in the United States," *Journal of Politics* 63 (2001): 902–915.
35. Rush, 1998.
36. On New Zealand, see J. Karp and S. Bowler, "Coalition Government and Satisfaction with Democracy: An Analysis of New Zealand's Reaction to Proportional Representation," *European Journal of Political Research* 40 (2001): 57–79.
37. This would be about 9,100 representatives, given today's population.

38. For a historical study of the size of the House and of House districts, see Andrew Cohen, "Increasing the Size of Congress Could Limit Campaign Spending," CNN.com Law Forum, accessed at: <http://www.cnn.com/2000/LAW/06/columns/fl.cohen.campaign.06.30/> on November 22, 2002; C. Kromkowski and Kromkowski, "Why 435?" *Polity* 24 (1991): 129–145. On the cube law, see R. Taagepera, "The Size of National Assemblies," *Social Science Research* 1 (1972): 385–401.
39. J. Eric Oliver, *Democracy in Suburbia* (Princeton, NJ: Princeton University Press, 2001).

5

ELECTING THE PRESIDENT

One of the more common words used to describe the 2000 presidential election was *debacle*. Albert Gore received over 500,000 more votes than George W. Bush nationwide, but the election ultimately depended on whether five Supreme Court justices would allow the State of Florida to count disputed ballots cast. The reasons for this are complex, but center on the fact that our presidents are elected by the electoral college with votes allocated by a "winner-take-all" basis in nearly every state. American presidents have never been elected by direct vote of the people. Whoever receives a majority (not a plurality) of electoral college votes becomes president, regardless of the popular vote.

Every state, and the District of Columbia, has a number of electors equal to its number of representatives in Congress. The Constitution allows each state the discretion to determine which candidate, or candidates, will receive the state's electoral college votes. In the past, state legislatures themselves made such decisions. Beginning in the 1830s, many states changed their laws and began allocating electors based on popular votes cast in the state. Today, all but one state has decided to award all of its electors to the candidate who wins a popular vote plurality in the state. Two states, Maine and Nebraska, allocate their electors by congressional district—the candidate who wins a district receives one electoral college vote.

After the polls closed on November 8, 2000, it became clear that the election was going to be one of the closest in history—and the outcome in Florida was the closest of any state. Regardless of the popular vote total, neither Gore nor Bush had a majority of electoral college votes without winning Florida. Whoever won Florida would be president. On election night, the first TV exit-poll projections gave the state to Gore, but these estimates were soon retracted. Later in the evening, the networks predicted Bush would win. Once the votes were counted, Bush appeared to have won the state by a mere 1,100 votes. Another partial recount reduced the margin to about 500 votes—or a difference of less than .0001 percent. It became clear that voter errors, voter confusion, and mechanical failures of counting machines might have cost Gore far more than 1,000 votes, and the Gore campaign pressed for further counts.

What followed was an awkward, weeks-long process of county-by-county recounts, lawsuits, and recriminations that led to the Supreme Court's 5–4 decision of December 12. The conservative Court majority that had for years deferred to the judgment of the states on matters of state law, ruled that Florida's own courts were unable to determine how to apply Florida election law, and that all recounts should cease.[1] This decision made Bush president. Subsequent examination of uncounted ballots by a consortium of journalists and academics found that, by using Florida's standards for determining the intent of voters whose ballots were not counted by the machines, Gore would have won Florida with a narrow margin.[2]

THE LOGIC OF THE ELECTORAL COLLEGE

Although 2000 is an extreme example of what can go wrong with America's presidential election system, it should not be seen as an isolated case. The 2000 election was indeed rare. It was only the fourth time in the history of the republic that the popular vote winner did not end up president (the other occasions being 1824, 1876, and 1888). However, it also reflects something less rare. Presidents are often unable to make claims about having received a popular vote majority. Since the Civil War, eleven of thirty-four presidential elections (32 percent) have produced winners who did not receive a majority. Furthermore, in contests with three or more candidates, winners may not always be able to claim that they were the public's most preferred.

HOW TO LOSE THE PRESIDENCY BY WINNING THE MOST VOTES

Imagine two states, one with 4,500,000 voters and nine electoral college (EC) votes, and one with 4,800,000 voters, and ten electoral college votes. If Gore won with 55 percent of the vote in the first state (2.475 million votes), he receives all nine EC votes. If Bush won the second state with a 45 percent plurality in the other (2.16 million votes), he receives all ten of its EC votes. Gore wins more votes, but less electors. In reality, the odd results in 2000 reflected outcomes like this; Gore piled up lots of votes in California and New York while Bush won Florida and other mid-sized states by narrower margins. Things are exacerbated by the fact that EC votes are based on a state's population, not the number of voters that come to the polls. In two states with identical populations, 50 percent support might be reached with 2 million votes in one state, and 1.5 million in the other.

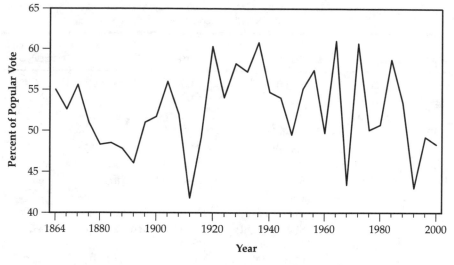

FIGURE 5.1   TRENDS IN VOTE SUPPORT FOR U.S. PRESIDENTS

Source: Federal Election Commission

As Figure 5.1 illustrates, most of these submajority elections are not rare. Table 5.1 (on page 86) lists data from twelve presidential elections since 1900 (out of twenty-five total). In each of these, minor candidates combined to poll at least 5 percent, and/or polled enough support to prevent the winner from receiving at least 50 percent of the popular vote. Some of these examples show that it is quite possible for third candidates to have received substantial popular support without affecting the winner's claim to a majority mandate—as occurred when Robert LaFollete won over 16 percent of the vote in 1924. Despite the presence of modestly successful third candidates in 1904, 1916, 1980, and 1996, the winning candidate could still lay claim to a majority or near majority. At first glance, this suggests that the electoral college functions fairly well. Presidents are often elected with substantial popular support when more than just two candidates mount serious campaigns for the White House.

In some years, however, third candidates capture well over 10 percent of the vote—such as in 1912, 1924, 1968, 1992. At the same time, it is possible for minor candidates with much lower levels of support to collect enough votes to deny the president a majority, as occurred in 1916, 1948, 1960, and 2000.[3] In close elections, minor candidates capture enough support to present difficult-to-answer "what if" questions. What would happen if people who voted for the minor candidates had thrown their support to one of the major candidates? Would it make any difference if electoral college votes were awarded differently than winner-take-all, by state? What if the third-place or fourth-place candidates were not on the ballot? What would the voters who

TABLE 5.1   "MINOR" CANDIDACIES AND PRESIDENTIAL
VOTE SHARE IN THE TWENTIETH CENTURY

YEAR	CANDIDATE	PARTY	VOTE	WINNER	WINNER'S SUPPORT
1904	E. Debs	Socialist	3.00%	T. Roosevelt (R)	56.4%
1904	S. Swallow	Prohibition	1.90		
1912	T. Roosevelt	Progressive	27.40	Wilson (D)	41.8
1912	E. Debs	Socialist	6.00		
1916	A. Benson	Socialist	2.80	Wilson (D)	49.2
1916	J. F. Hanley	Prohibition	1.20		
1920	E. Debs	Socialist	3.40	Harding (R)	60.3
1920	P. Christensen	Farm Labor	1.00		
1924	R. Lafollete	Progressive	16.60	Coolidge (R)	54.0
1948	S. Thurmond	State's Rights	2.40	Truman (D)	49.5
1948	H. Wallace	Progressive	2.40		
1960	E. Hass	Socialist Labor	0.07	Kennedy (D)	49.7
1968	G. Wallace	American Ind.	13.50	Nixon (R)	43.4
1980	J. Anderson	independent	6.60	Reagan (R)	50.7
1980	E. Clarke	Libertarian	1.10		
1992	R. Perot	independent	18.90	Clinton (D)	43.0
1996	R. Perot	Reform	8.40	Clinton (D)	49.2
1996	R. Nader	Green	1.50		
2000	R. Nader	Green	2.80	Bush (R)	48.0
2000	P. Buchanan	Reform	0.60		

Note: The list includes all presidential elections from 1904 to 2000 in which minor candidates polled more than 5 percent and/or the winner polled less than 50 percent.

preferred the minor candidates have done? Who would they support? The answers to these questions become troublesome when minor candidates capture more than just a trivial fragment of the vote in a close election. Who would have won the presidency in 1948, or 1968, or 1992, or 2000, if the choices available to voters, or the election system, were different?

WHAT DO WE EXPECT FROM PRESIDENTIAL ELECTIONS?

Given the federal nature of America's political system, the president is the only figure who comes close to representing a national constituency. However, presidential elections are fifty separate state-by-state, winner-take-all contests. Candidates who appeal to a minority perspective can never win a single electoral college vote unless their support is heavily concentrated within a particular state. This reflects the fact that at the time the Constitution was drafted, the first Founders viewed states as the relevant minority worthy of protecting when they designed the presidential election system we use today.

In presidential elections today, relevant political minorities are no longer states or regional interests—minorities can be ideological, economic, ethnic, racial, or other social groups. Since a minority group, or small coalition of minorities, can rarely win the popular vote in any given state, their only recourse is to attempt to gain influence within one of the large parties that can. With region-specific or state-specific political minorities largely absent today,[4] the electoral college now helps maintain a two-party system. Defenders of it note that it maintains a *national* two-party system—due to the centralizing force of having each party list a single presidential candidate on the ballot in all states and then allocating each state's electors on a winner-take-all basis.[5] The nation's ultimate electoral prize is effectively off-limits to all but the two largest parties. Third party efforts should thus prove unattractive to candidates who stand no chance of winning—and to voters, who don't want to waste their vote on a doomed candidate.

The benefits of this, we are told, are many. Presidents are assured of getting popular majorities, or at least large pluralities, that lend them the legitimacy they need to govern. The system should also encourage national unity by forcing minority groups to seek their peace within one of the major parties, rather than by fragmenting the political order with their own presidential candidates.[6] And whatever the uncertainty that multicandidate presidential contests of recent decades might have produced, analysis of public opinion data demonstrate that had George Wallace (1968), John Anderson (1980), or Ross Perot (1992) run "head-to-head" against the Democratic or Republican candidates they challenged, each would have lost.[7] We suspect that the same could be said about Perot in 1996 and Ralph Nader in 2000. Probably neither would have won in a two-candidate race.

Defenders of the electoral college illustrate some of what many citizens probably expect from their presidential election system. A single candidate who represents the nation should win, rather than one who represents a coalition of various states. The winner should have some claim to a large plurality of the popular vote, if not a clear majority. As a corollary to this, the winner of a multicandidate race should be one whom most voters prefer relative to all others. Put differently, the winner should win due to popular support rather than due to the presence of a third candidate on the ballot who might divide a majority of voters who are opposed to the candidate who actually wins. Presidential elections should produce an unambiguous winner whom most voters preferred. At present, they do not do this.

WHAT IS GAINED BY HAVING MORE THAN TWO CANDIDATES?

Some of the defects of the electoral college might be remedied if there were some way to limit election choices to just two candidates. As a practical and constitutional matter, however, this is not possible. Even though America's two-party systems have been quite static, they have changed at times when third or forth parties fragment the outcomes of presidential elections and re-define what (and who) the major parties represent (e.g., 1860, 1892, 1912, 1968). Limiting presidential elections to two choices would restrict the ability for elections to realign our party system when change is needed. There is also ev-idence that minor parties mobilize new voters when they mount presidential campaigns. In 1992, Perot's presence on the ballot increased turnout nearly 3 percent. Likewise, many of Nader's voters in 2000 may not have come to the polls had he not been on the ballot. In 2000, Nader and other minor candi-dates may have added 2.5 percent to turnout. In 1968, Wallace may have boost-ed turnout by 2.3 percent.[8]

These mobilization effects may seem small, but they can have large con-sequences. Some attribute the GOP takeover of Congress in 1994 to the sus-tained political activity of Perot supporters who gravitated toward the GOP after being brought into the political arena by Perot's 1992 presidential cam-paign.[9] Similarly, Nader's candidacy in 2000, and the perception that it cost Gore the White House, may affect how future Democratic candidates reach out to voters Nader brought into the electoral mix. In large and small ways, then, these "failed" candidacies may help make the major parties more represen-tative of society over the long haul. But the benefits of multicandidate elections clash with the workings of the electoral college.

WHY THE ELECTORAL COLLEGE FAILS

The electoral college may be failing to meet many people's expectations for presidential elections, particularly since 1968. As we noted before, no president has been elected with a popular majority since 1988. In three elections after that, one was elected with a modest plurality (Clinton in 1992), and one plu-rality winner actually lost (Gore in 2000). Analysis of opinion data from 1992 suggest that many Perot voters probably would have lined up behind the eventual winner, Clinton, if Perot had not been on the ballot. The election may have been much closer without Perot. Had Wallace not been on the 1968 bal-lot, Humphrey might have defeated Nixon.[10]

It is possible that had enough supporters of Wallace in 1968, or Perot in 1992, or Nader in 2000 switched their support to the second-place finisher, these elections would have produced different presidents each year.[11] This re-flects another shortcoming of the electoral college—it need not produce a de-finitive, "most-preferred" winner. If a substantial proportion of the minor candidates' supporters in 1968, 1992, or 2000 preferred their third-placed can-didate the most, but liked the second-place finisher more than the actual win-ner, then presidential elections are producing inefficient, if not perverse, results. Winners may not only lack popular majorities; it is possible that a winner can be the *least* preferred major-party candidate of a substantial ma-jority of voters.

This problem is something different, and perhaps more problematic, than the occasional nuisance of a candidate winning the electoral college while losing the popular vote. As we shall demonstrate below, Bush probably could not have won under election systems designed to account for how voters rank their preferences across more than two candidates. After the election, journalists and academics can pour over opinion data to make judgments regarding "what if" questions about whether minor party voters preferred the first place candidate more than the second place candidate. Ultimately, however, this is something the election system should answer.

The electoral college fails on other grounds. Winner-take-all allocation of electors means that a major party candidate can take for granted states that are safely in her party's column. Conversely, the other candidate has no incentive to campaign in a state that is a bastion of support for the other party. Entire areas of the country that have safe pluralities for one party—California, New York, Texas—can be left out of the presidential campaign. Presidential elections are thus highly targeted affairs. Candidates campaign where the polls show a state remains close, and drop in on "safe" states when they need to raise money. Hundreds of millions of dollars in TV ads are beamed into a few "battleground" states, while others see nothing. This limits the ability for a campaign to mobilize voters, and may depress turnout.

REFORMING THE ELECTORAL COLLEGE

How, then, can presidential elections produce a winner with a claim to majority support when voters are presented with more than just two candidates? Reform proposals can be lumped into two categories—those that preserve the logic of the electoral college, and those that do not. The first category of proposal retains the idea that presidents are elected by the states, not by voters directly. Each state retains a number of electors equal to its representation in Congress. This means that small states, even those with just three electors, are overrepresented in presidential elections, while populous states remain underrepresented.

Electoral college reform proposals differ regarding what should be done with the actual flesh-and-blood electors. At present, each party files a list of possible electors in every state before the November election. After the election, each of the winning candidate's electors then casts one of their state's votes for president on a date in December. In practice, they nearly always vote for the candidate who won their state (since that is the candidate they pledged to support), but they are not legally required to do so. Since electors are picked from among the party's loyalists, "faithless" electors have not been a large problem. Only eight have failed to vote for their party's presidential nominee since 1948.[12] Since faithless electors are a minor issue, we focus on two proposals designed to change how states allocate electoral college votes. The Constitution leaves the method of allocating electors to the states. This means that either of these plans could be adopted on a state-by-state basis, if states decide to change their election laws.

WINNER-TAKE-ALL BY CONGRESSIONAL DISTRICT

As we noted in Chapter 4, any election system produces more proportionate outcomes when there are more districts. The electoral college today can be thought of as forty-nine separate winner-take-all districts (forty-eight states and the District of Columbia). Win a state and you get all the electors. Two states, Maine and Nebraska, allocate their electors to whomever wins in each congressional district. If this method were used in all states, presidential elections would become 436 winner-take-all contests within congressional districts. Since each state also has two "at large" electors due to their U.S. Senate representation, the candidate with the most votes in each state would likely get these electors as a bonus.

However such a plan is designed, it would reduce the electoral college's ability to turn a close *two-candidate* election into an electoral college landslide. Table 5.2 uses actual election results to illustrate how candidates would have done under two alternative methods of allocating presidential electors. It illustrates that Carter won just over 50 percent of the popular vote in the 1976 election but the winner-take-the-state method gave him 55 percent of electoral votes that year. However, if electors were contested congressional district by district, the electoral vote would have been a tie. In each of the elections listed here, the actual winning candidates would have won fewer electors if electors were awarded by congressional district.

If the goal of an election is to produce an unambiguous winner, there are problems with this proposal. Even though it is still winner-take-all, it can make the results of a close two-candidate race more ambiguous. In 2000 the popular vote plurality winner (Gore) would have lost by even more electoral votes under such a plan. In 1976 the popular vote majority winner would have been denied an electoral vote majority, leaving a joint session of Congress to select the president. Moreover, this plan still leaves supporters of third candidates having little role if their support is spread evenly across the United States.

PROPORTIONAL ALLOCATION OF ELECTORS, BY STATE

Another plan would fully eliminate the winner-take-all nature of allocating electors. States would become multimember districts, with electors awarded in proportion to a candidate's vote in the state. Given the nature of PR, larger states with more electors would be able to have more proportionality in allocation than states with few electors. In states with just three or four electors a candidate would likely need at least 25 or 30 percent to secure an EC vote,

TABLE 5.2 OUTCOMES WITH DIFFERENT METHODS OF AWARDING ELECTORAL VOTES

	POPULAR VOTE	ACTUAL EC TOTAL	EC PLURALITY, BY CD	EC PR, BY STATE
2000				
Gore	48.4%	266 (49%)	251	257
Bush (W)	47.9	**270** (51%)	**287**	258
Nader	2.7			20
others	1.0			3
1996				
Clinton	49.2	**379** (70%)	**345**	262
Dole	40.7	159 (30%)	193	220
Perot	8.4			49
others	1.7			7
1992				
Clinton	43.0	**370** (69%)	**324**	232
Bush	37.5	168 (31%)	214	203
Perot	18.9			102
1980				
Reagan	50.7	**489** (91%)	**396**	**273**
Carter	41.0	49 (9%)	142	221
Anderson	6.6			35
others	1.9			9
1976				
Carter	50.1	**297** (55%)	269	**270**
Ford	48.0	240 (45%)	269	258
others	1.8			10
1968				
Nixon	43.2	**301** (56%)	**289**	231
Humphrey	42.7	191 (35%)	192	225
Wallace	13.5	46 (8%)	57	79
others	0.6			2
1960				
Kennedy	49.8	**303** (56%)	**278**	266
Nixon	49.5	219 (41%)	245	266
unaffiliated	0.7	15 (3%)	14	5

Note: Bold numbers represent outcomes in which candidate wins an electoral college majority.

Sources: 1996 and 2000, author's calculations; 1960–1992, 1996, Stephen Wayne, *Road to the White House* (New York: St. Martin's), p. 311.

unless fractions of electoral votes could be awarded. And as we discussed in Chapter 4, PR plans can also include some minimum threshold for candidates to win anything.

Table 5.2 describes how some presidential election results might have looked if states had awarded electors on a proportional basis, without a minimum qualifying threshold. Proportionality is also enhanced here by allowing fractions of electors to be awarded. Under these conditions, nearly all winners would have received fewer electors. Kennedy (1960), Nixon (1964), Clinton (1992), Clinton (1996), and either major party candidate in 2000 would have been denied an EC majority, which would have required Congress to pick the president. This plan allows candidates who lack regional support to gain electors, but in doing this it substantially reduces the EC's ability to manufacture a decisive victory out of a popular vote plurality or slight majority. This also reduces the EC's propensity to exaggerate a winning candidate's electoral mandate. In its present form, the EC translated Reagan's 50.7 percent popular vote majority in 1980 into a decisive (if deceptive) 91 percent EC landslide. Had electors been awarded by PR, Reagan would have been reduced to a narrow four-vote EC majority. Even this may understate how PR allocation of electors would change outcomes. Voters respond to incentives created by different election rules. If PR had been used in 1980 to award electors, for example, independent candidate John Anderson probably would have received more votes, since his supporters would be less inclined to see their votes as wasted.[13]

The hypothetical results in Table 5.2 are meant to illustrate how the institution of the electoral college, acting as a force independent of voter preferences, often determines who will be president and distorts the nature of the mandate they received in an election. Alternative methods of allocating electors would have put six of these elections into the hands of Congress. Having such an outcome occur six times in forty years may be worth avoiding, and the EC deserves credit for doing this. But as noted above, using the EC to manufacture majorities comes at a cost. In 2000, it did a particularly bad job of reflecting the preferences of voters, and in 1968 and 1992 it produced winners with ambiguous claims to being the person whom most voters preferred relative to all other candidates. Under either of these reform proposals, outcomes would be no less ambiguous. Each increases the odds that no one wins an EC majority. This means that each state's delegation in Congress would cast a single vote to select the president. California, New York, Delaware, and Rhode Island would each have the same weight. Since most contemporary third party candidates have no supporters in Congress, decisions would be controlled by the major parties.

If our goal is to increase Congress's role in selecting the president, then these EC reform plans would possibly be on target. However, if our goal is to insure that the president is the candidate preferred by most voters, these reforms fail. Due to staggered Senate terms and the power of incumbency, one major party could easily control a state's congressional delegation while the other party's candidate won more votes in the state's presidential contest. There is no assurance that the tally of partisan control of each congressional delegation would look anything like the distribution of votes cast for the party's presidential candidates. In fact, had PR been used to allocate electors in the 2000 presidential election, Gore would probably still have lost if the outcome was determined by Congress. Republicans controlled more state delegations than did Democrats and they may have supported Bush despite Gore winning more popular votes.

DIRECT ELECTION OF THE PRESIDENT

The second category of reforms is based on the idea that the EC is anachronistic. Presidents in most democracies, even federal systems like Russia, are elected by direct popular vote. There are different variants of direct election, depending upon the electoral system. Under a runoff system, for example, the winner has to receive 50 percent of the popular vote in one of two rounds. A direct election method could provide a cure to the problem with the 2000 U.S. presidential elections. With Gore ahead by 500,000 votes nationally, a few hundred votes in Florida would have been less relevant.

RUNOFF ELECTIONS

Some nations guarantee that presidents have a popular-vote majority mandate by use of nationwide runoff elections, in which one round of voting is used to winnow the candidate field down to the top two candidates. A second election is held between the remaining candidates on another day. If runoff elections were to be used as part of a nationwide vote to directly elect the U.S. president, this reform would require a constitutional amendment. It is conceivable, however, that individual states could use runoff elections to decide who would get their state's electoral college votes without such an amendment.

Both the French and Russian presidents, probably the two most powerful executive positions in any democratic nation, are directly elected by a runoff system. A runoff system is also used to elect mayors in many U.S. cities, including Los Angeles, San Francisco, and Seattle. The first round is typically held according to "first past the post" rules. If, in that first round, a candidate gains over 50 percent of the vote then she or he is elected. This was the case for Russian President Vladimir Putin in 2000 when he received just under 53 percent of the first-round vote. Conversely, if no candidate gains a majority in the first round, a runoff election is held a few weeks later. This was the case, for example, for Putin's predecessor—Boris Yeltsin—in 1996, and also for the French presidential elections of 1995 and 2002.

TABLE 5.3   RUSSIAN PRESIDENTIAL ELECTION 1996

CANDIDATE	FIRST ROUND	SECOND ROUND*
Yeltsin	35.3%	53.8%
Zyuganov	32.0	40.3
Lebed	14.5	—
Yavlinski	7.3	—
Zhirinovski	5.7	—
Others	5.2	—

*Column does not add to 100 since Russian voters had an "against all," i.e., "a none of the above."

Typically, the period between the two rounds is one of intense horse-trading. Eliminated candidates are still free to urge their supporters to vote for a candidate left in the race, and those still in the race compete for such endorsements. So, for example, in the 1996 Russian presidential race (see Table 5.3), Boris Yeltsin successfully engaged in serious negotiations for the endorsement of Alexander Lebed. Similarly, in the 1981 French presidential election, the Socialist candidate Mitterrand ran second in the first round, but won the second round with support of Communist voters. Mitterrand then rewarded the Communist party with four of forty ministerial (cabinet) posts.[14]

Runoff elections may help ensure the winning candidate receives over 50 percent of the vote.[15] But runoff elections often—but not always—see a decline in turnout in the second round. Perhaps most important of all, however, is that runoff elections produce an odd set of second round choices—particularly if one segment of the electorate is represented by several candidates in the first round.

The French presidential election of 2002 provides a dramatic example of this last point. So many candidates (sixteen) ran in the first round that the vote of the major parties became fractured, especially on the left. The runoff, then, featured a race between a center-right party under Jacques Chirac and an explicitly fascist candidate, Jean Marie Le Pen. In the second round, then, left-wing voters had a choice between a right-wing candidate they did not like and an extremely right-wing candidate they despised. Chirac won the presidency with 82 percent of the second round vote, even though fewer than 20 percent of voters had supported him in the first round—his main appeal to the majority of the electorate being that he was not Le Pen.

ALTERNATIVE VOTE/PREFERENCE VOTING

Some nations have elections designed to protect against a problem that is common in the United States—our candidates are often elected from a crowded field with only modest pluralities. Preference voting allows voters to rank

TABLE 5.4   FRENCH PRESIDENTIAL ELECTION RESULTS

CANDIDATE (PARTY)	FIRST ROUND	SECOND ROUND*
1995		
Jacques Chirac (RPR)	20.7%	52.6%
Lionel Jospin (PS)	23.3	47.4
Edouard Balladur (RPR)	18.5	
Jean-Marie Le Pen (FN)	15.1	
Robert Hue (PCF)	8.7	
Arlette Yvonne Laguiller (LO)	5.3	
Philippe de Villiers (MPF)	4.8	
Dominique Voynet (Verts)	3.3	
2002		
Jacques Chirac (RPR)	19.8%	82.1%
Jean-Marie Le Pen (FN)	16.9	17.8
Lionel Jospin (PS)	16.1	
Francois Bayrou (UDF)	6.8	
Arlette Yvonne Laguiller (LO)	5.7	
Jean-Pierre Chevenment (MC)	5.3	
Noel Mamere (Verts)	5.2	
Oliver Besancenot (LCR)	4.3	
Jean Saint-Josse (CPNT)	4.2	
Alain Madelin (DL)	3.9	
Robert Hue (PCF)	3.4	
Bruno Megret (MNR)	2.3	
Christina Taubira (RLP)	2.3	
Corine Legpage (MCAP)	1.9	
Christine Boutin (FRS)	1.2	
Daniel Gluckstein (PT)	0.5	

*Percentage of votes cast where voters marked a preference. About 4 percent of those voting in the second round cast spoiled (blank) ballots as a protest.

Note: RPR = Rally for the Republic (conservative); PS = Socialist Party (center-left); FN = National Front (right-populist); PCF = French Communist Party (left-communist); LO = Workers Struggle (left); Verts (Greens); UDF = Union for French Democracy; MC = Citizen's Movement; LCR = Revolutionary Communist League (left-communist); CPNT = Hunting, Fishing, Nature and Traditions; DL = Liberal Democracy; MNR = National Republican Movement; RLP = Radical Left Party (left); FRS = Social Republican Forum; PT = Worker's Party.

Sources: 1995, Fischer Weltalmanach <http://www.electionworld.org/election/france.htm>; 2002, Parliamentary Summary, Vacher Dod Publishing. <http://www.politicallinks.co.uk/politics2/Bulletin/Archives/European%20Elections/FrancePres.asp>.

candidates in order of their most-to-least preferred choices. Under the Alternative Vote (AV, as it is known in Australia), if no candidate has a majority when everyone's first choices are counted, subsequent rounds of counting are conducted until one candidate has a majority.

AV, known in the United States as "Preference Voting" and as "Instant Runoff Voting" was recently adopted for San Francisco city elections. It was devised in 1870 by a professor at MIT named A. R. Ware. This system is used in Australia to elect that nation's House of Representatives from single-member districts. It can be used whenever a single candidate is to be elected, and the act of marking AV ballots is pretty simple. The voters rank their first-most-preferred candidate by marking "1" next to her name, their second-most-preferred candidate is marked "2," and so on. The winning candidate is the one who gains over 50 percent of the vote. Sometimes this is obvious. If over 50 percent of the voters put a "1" next to the name of a particular candidate, then that candidate wins.[16] Sometimes, however, no candidate receives 50 percent of the vote, as in the example below:

TOTAL NUMBER OF FIRST PREFERENCES GIVEN TO EACH CANDIDATE

CANDIDATE A	CANDIDATE B	CANDIDATE C
45	40	15

Here is where the voters' second and third preferences come into play. Candidate C is listed as the first choice of just fifteen voters. In one sense, then, C should *not* be a winner since so few people like him. So let us look at those people who ranked C first and find out whom they placed as second choice, and use those second choices to help decide a winner.

As an analogy, imagine the following: You are in a restaurant and the waiter asks what you would like for dessert. The choices are apple pie, berry pie, and chocolate cake. You say "chocolate cake" only to have the waiter come back a few minutes later to tell you that the chocolate cake is all gone, leaving only apple and berry pie, so what would you like, given you can't have chocolate cake. The same holds for C's supporters: C can't win, so if the voters can't have C who would they pick? We could hold a runoff election, but having people's second choices already listed on the ballot means there is no need (hence the name "Instant Runoff").

Under this AV/preference voting method, the candidate who has the fewest first choices is eliminated and the ballots of those people who voted for him are examined to see whom they placed second. Those votes are added to the totals of the candidates still in the race. That is, those fifteen voters who put C first would have put A or B second. Let us say, for the sake of simplicity, that all of C's fifteen voters put A second. As the weakest candidate, C is eliminated and those fifteen second choices are added to A's vote total in a second round of counting:

	CANDIDATE A	CANDIDATE B	CANDIDATE C
First round	41	43	15
Second round	56 (41+15)	43	eliminated
	winner		

This example illustrates one of the main properties of AV—by counting and transferring preferences marked on ballots, this election system can, in effect, manufacture a majority winner out of a coalition of voters who support similar candidates. Voters from the same side of the political spectrum may be divided about their preferred candidate (as with the left in the first round of the 2002 French presidential election). In our example, many may prefer A but some like C, and they all may like A and C more than B. By ranking each other's candidates second, AV allows supporters of C and A to build a coalition.

A preferential system like this is used to directly elect the president of the Republic of Ireland.[17] Table 5.5 shows results from the Irish presidential election of 1997. Voters could rank as many as five candidates. After the counting of voter's first choices, Mary McAleese had the lead with 45.24 percent. If a crowded field had produced third, fourth, or lower place candidates with combined support greater than the second place candidate, the lower ranking finishers would be removed sequentially. That is, the last placed candidate would be eliminated first, with his supporters' second preferences then distributed amongst the remaining candidates. The next remaining candidate would then be eliminated, and his preferences transferred. This process would continue until one candidate had a majority. In the 1997 Irish example, the combined total of all the candidates below second place was less than that of the candidate in second place, so they were eliminated as a group, and their supporters second-choice votes were transferred to the two remaining candidates.[18] After the transfers, McAleese won decisively with 58 percent support.

The chief executive—mayor—for the city of London is directly elected by a similar preferential system. In London, voters mark their first and second choices only. If no candidate receives over 50 percent of the vote then everyone but the top two candidates are excluded. This is different from the Irish method, which would eliminate candidates sequentially if lower-placing candidates had enough combined support to affect who the top two candidates would be. This is possible in Ireland because voters are asked to put numbers next to several candidate's names reflecting whom they liked most and least. By contrast, London voters were presented with a ballot listing candidate names, next to which were two columns: one for a first preference and the other for a second preference. Voters marked an 'X' in each column.[19]

TABLE 5.5   ALTERNATIVE VOTE RESULTS: IRISH PRESIDENTIAL ELECTION, 1997

CANDIDATE	COUNT 1	COUNT 2	FINAL TOTAL
Mary McAleese	574,424 (45.24%)	+131,836	706,259 (58.67%)
Mary Banotti	372,002 (29.30%)	+125,514	497,516 (41.33%)
Dana Rosemary Scallon	175,458 (13.82%)	—	—
Adi Roche	88,423 (6.96%)	—	—
Derek Nally	59,529 (4.69%)	—	—
Exhausted			66,060

The two candidates with the most first-preference votes make it past the first round of counting. All remaining candidates are eliminated, and their supporters' second-preference votes are distributed among remaining candidates. Table 5.6 shows the results of the first direct mayoral election in London in 2000. Although Livingston had just 39 percent of voter's first preferences, he won with a decisive 58 percent after preferences were transferred from supporters of lower-placing candidates.

The possibility that a candidate might not gain many first-choice votes but nonetheless be someone whom many voters like as their second choice, does not seem to have occurred to those who designed London's system. Yet, from the 2000 London election results it seems that Kramer—the Liberal Democrat candidate eliminated in the first count—had more total votes (first- and second-choice votes combined) than one of two candidates who remained in the count, due to Norris (Conservative) having more first-preference votes.

TABLE 5.6   PREFERENCE VOTING RESULTS: MAYOR'S RACE, LONDON, 2000

NAME	PARTY	FIRST PREFERENCE	SECOND PREFERENCE*	FINAL**
Ken Livingstone	Independent	667,877 (39.0%)	178,809 (12.6%)	776,427
Steve Norris	Conservative	464,434 (27.1%)	188,041 (13.2%)	564,137
Frank Dobson	Labour	223,884 (13.1%)	228,095 (16.0%)	—
Susan Kramer	Liberal Democrat	203,452 (11.9%)	404,815 (28.5%)	—
Ram Gidoomal	Christian Peoples Alliance	42,060 (2.4%)	56,489 (4.0%)	—
Darren Johnson	Green	38,121 (2.2%)	192,764 (13.6%)	—
Michael Newland	British National Party	33,569 (2.0%)	45,337 (3.2%)	—
Damian Hockney	UK Independence Party	16,324 (1.0%)	43,672 (3.1%)	—
Geoffrey Ben-Nathan	Pro-Motorist Small Shop	9,956 (0.6%)	23,021 (1.6%)	—
Ashwin Kumar Tanna	Independent	9,015 (0.5%)	41,766 (2.9%)	—
Geoffrey Clements	Natural Law Party	5,470 (0.3%)	18,185 (1.3%)	—

*2nd preference votes are only used if no candidate receives more than 50 percent of 1st preference votes.
**If no candidate receives more than 50 percent of 1st preference votes, the top two receive 2nd preference from remaining candidates.

The Irish system is a marked improvement on the London version, since voters can rank more than just two preferences, and since candidates are eliminated sequentially. Had it been used in London, we could have seen if the voters who supported lower-ranking candidates might have preferred Kramer to Norris, or Kramer to Dobson (Labor), or Dobson to either of these.

Defenders of these preferential systems point out that far fewer votes are wasted than under simple plurality rules like those used in the United States. Minor candidates cannot win, but their supporters find that a vote for them still has some value. Voters get the satisfaction of supporting their favorite candidate without the risk of letting their least-preferred candidate win. In the example above, pretend that C's voters think he is the ideal candidate. At the same time, they loath Candidate B, and think that A is not as bad as B, but not as great as C. Under American-style plurality elections, a vote for their dream candidate would mean that B wins. Under AV, they could vote for C, *and* help A win. Smaller parties are said to benefit because this system allows them to show the major parties how much they depend on the smaller party's support. In this case, A would govern, owing an obvious debt of gratitude to C's supporters.

There are two broad lines of criticism of preference voting. First, do voters understand it? The simple answer is yes. Just as people can figure out how to order food if some menu choices are not available, so can voters figure out how to order candidates. After all, if consumers can deal with the fact that Baskin Robbins can offer thirty-one flavors to choose from, then voters can presumably manage ranking three or four candidates. Current practice in Australian national elections not only demands that voters turn out and vote but that they also rank order *all* the candidates. If voters are having trouble with the system when even the least interested are compelled to vote, we should see lots of spoiled ballots. Yet, even here, with 95 percent turnout in 1998, only 4 percent of ballots were spoiled. Voters are perfectly capable of managing the demands of this electoral system.[20]

Another criticism is that AV appears to help minor parties less than might be expected because candidates from small parties are typically excluded from the count quite early on. Small parties, by definition, have relatively few people who rank them first, and so their voters' second-place preferences simply go to candidates of the largest parties. Australian and Irish elections essentially remain two-party contests. And, in general, being a "second choice" can still be problematic. A candidate could be the second choice of every single voter but, because no one placed her or him first, be eliminated at the first round. AV, then, tends to help maintain the position of the major parties although it does force them to work harder to appeal to a broader cross-section of voters.

WHAT IF PREFERENCE VOTING WERE USED IN THE UNITED STATES?

Preference voting could be used to elect the president directly, or to award a state's slate of electors to a single candidate most preferred by the state's voters. In Florida's 2000 election, for example, it is quite likely that many of those people who voted for Nader would have placed Gore second. Under AV, Nader would have been eliminated and his supporters' second-place preferences then counted, possibly making Gore the winner of the state's 25 electors.[21] In other states Gore won, Buchanan or Libertarian supporters could have tipped those electors toward Bush with their second-choice votes.

Given the quirks of the electoral college, using AV on a state-by-state basis would not guarantee that the popular vote winner would be the electoral college winner. It would have to be used in conjunction with direct, popular-vote election of the president to make certain that winners are the majority preferred candidate. Direct elections would require an amendment to the Constitution and, as we discuss in Chapter 8, any system used to directly elect the president on a national basis would probably require dramatic changes in the mechanics of how elections are conducted.

Table 5.7 provides an admittedly simplistic portrait of what the 2000 U.S. election might have looked like had AV been used to directly elect the president. Table 5.8 provides a similar illustration based on the 1992 election. In order to simulate what might have happened if voters could have rank-ordered the candidates in these two elections, we make a number of assumptions, some realistic, others less so. First, since we have no way of knowing what people would have done if AV were used, we assume that their first choices are reflected by the votes that were actually cast under our current simple plurality election rules. That is, the "first count" used in Tables 5.7 and 5.8 reflects the actual votes these candidates received. We also assume that the same number of voters would have come to the polls. Using these assumptions, we can plug in various scenarios and see what might have happened if certain proportions of, say, Nader voters ranked Gore second under AV.

It is important to point out how these assumptions are somewhat unrealistic. If AV were actually used, people who considered supporting a minor candidate but ultimately voted for a major-party candidate may have been more likely to stick with the minor candidate when marking their first choice. Put differently, the actual first count under AV may better reflect sincere preferences, rather than the votes candidates actually received by simple plurality rules. Second, a different election system might have altered which voters were mobilized. AV might have drawn more minor party supporters to the polls.

That being said, these simulations illustrate how direct election of the president by AV can produce a winner who has popular vote majority, even

TABLE 5.7   SIMULATED ALTERNATIVE VOTE OUTCOMES
FOR 2000 PRESIDENTIAL ELECTION

EXAMPLE 1:

	1ST COUNT	2ND COUNT	3RD COUNT	4TH COUNT	5TH COUNT
D/Gore	48.384%	48.491%	48.600%	48.734%	**50.795%**
R/Bush	47.869	47.975	48.224	48.531	49.218
G/Nader	2.735	2.741	2.745	2.749	
Rf/Buchanan	0.426	0.427	0.431		
L/Browne	0.365	0.366			
others	0.221				

Note: For the second count, the 2nd choices of all "other" candidates are randomly distributed in proportion to the original vote share of the five top candidates. In the 3rd count, 68 percent of Browne supporters' 2nd choices are directed to Bush, 30 percent to Gore, and 1 percent to Nader and Buchanan, respectively. In the 4th count, 69 percent of Buchanan supporters' 2nd choices go to Bush, 30 percent to Gore, and 1 percent to Nader. In the 5th count, 75 percent of Nader supporters' 2nd choice votes go to Gore, 25 percent to Bush.

EXAMPLE 2:

	1ST COUNT	2ND COUNT	3RD COUNT	4TH COUNT	5TH COUNT
D/Gore	48.384%	48.491%	48.503%	48.525%	**50.051%**
R/Bush	47.869	47.975	48.304	48.705	49.948
G/Nader	2.735	2.741	2.753	2.775	
Rf/Buchanan	0.426	0.427	0.439		
L/Browne	0.365	0.366			
other	0.221				

Note: For the second count, the 2nd choices of all "other" candidates are randomly distributed in proportion to the original vote share of the five top candidates. In the 3rd count, 90 percent of Browne supporters' 2nd choices are directed to Bush, and 3.3 percent to Gore, Nader, and Buchanan, respectively. In the 4th count, 90 percent of Buchanan supporters' 2nd choices go to Bush, 5 percent each to Gore and Nader. In the 5th count, 55 percent of Nader supporters' 2nd choice votes go to Gore, 45 percent to Bush.

TABLE 5.8   SIMULATED ALTERNATIVE VOTE OUTCOME
FOR 1992 PRESIDENTIAL ELECTION

	1ST COUNT	2ND COUNT	3RD COUNT	4TH COUNT
D/Clinton	43.006%	43.162%	43.204%	49.850%
R/Bush	37.447	37.583	37.765	**50.107**
I/Perot	18.905	18.974	18.988	
L/Marrau	0.279	0.280		
other	0.362			

Note: For the second count, the 2nd choices of all "other" candidates are randomly distributed in proportion to the original vote share of the four top candidates. For the 3rd count, 90 percent of Marrau supporters 2nd choices go to Bush; 5 percent to Perot and Clinton, respectively. For the 4th count, 65 percent of Perot supporters' 2nd choices go to Bush, 35 percent to Clinton.

when several candidates fragment the voting. Table 5.7 (on page 101) presents outcomes based on different scenarios. In the first example, we assume that 75 percent of Nader voters would have ranked Gore second, and that Gore would have received just under 70 percent of the second choices from Buchanan and Browne (Libertarian) supporters. Under these conditions, Gore would win 50.8 to 49.2 percent, or a margin of about 1.6 million votes. The second Table 5.7 example might be considered a "best case" scenario for Bush. Here, we assume that Bush would have captured 45 percent of Nader supporters' second choices and 90 percent from Browne and Buchanan. Even with these generous assumptions about how Green and Libertarian voters might have ranked Bush, he still would have lost, albeit by a very narrow margin.

In reality, we cannot tell how the minor candidates' supporters would have rank-ordered the candidates. Opinion surveys don't usually detect enough supporters of minor candidates for us to know who they would prefer if they ranked a second choice. The 2000 NES, however, did capture a number of Nader supporters proportionate to their share of the actual voting population. When asked for whom they would vote for if they could cast a second-choice vote, 45 percent said no one. Only 30 percent said Gore, and 15 percent said Bush. If AV were used, the Nader ballots without second-place rankings would be considered "exhausted" and no longer counted in subsequent rounds. Still, the NES data suggest Gore would have had a 2:1 advantage over Bush in second choices transferred from Nader voters during the last round of counting. In other words, Gore would still probably have won under AV.

Table 5.8 (on page 101) reports the simulation of the 1992 presidential election, when Ross Perot received 18 percent support as the third-place candidate. It is unlikely that the incumbent, George Bush (the elder) could have won under AV. Our example illustrates the level of support Bush would have needed from supporters of other candidates if he were to have beat Clinton. The main point here is that 65 percent of Perot's voters would have had to place Bush second for him to catch Clinton. The 1992 NES postelection survey found that 80 percent of Perot voters considered voting for Bush or Clinton. Just about half said they considered Clinton, the others said Bush. If this serves as a benchmark for their potential second choices under AV, Bush could not have won. Of course, we can never know. Our election system is not designed to account for the preferences of most voters.

DISCUSSION

In the twentieth century, the American presidency became the single most powerful political institution in the United States. This was probably not envisioned by the original authors of the Constitution. Their vision had the legislature supreme, with the president being an administrator rather than the focus of control over much of public policy. Under such arrangements, the peculiar compromises used to design our presidential election system—indirect election by states, malapportionment of state influence in the electoral college, a winner-take-all logic, might not be seen as too troubling.

Today, however, the American political system has invested tremendous power in the institution of the presidency. The growth of presidential power and presidential dominance over Congress—over matters of trade, national security, intelligence, use of the war power, regulation of the environment, and management of the economy, grew since World War II, and reached new heights after September 11, 2001, with President George W. Bush. Presidents also remain able to institutionalize their political vision for generations by appointing life-tenured members to the federal courts. Given such stakes, presidents should be elected on the basis of popular support rather than the arbitrary effects of antiquated election rules.

Our political system is no longer the loose federal arrangement that the first Founders had in mind when they designed the electoral college. The Civil War, two World Wars, the Depression, the civil rights and suffragette movements all helped to put an end to that vision of state-centered federalism. But our presidential election system remains the same, for no compelling reason. States remain represented *as states* in Congress, via the U.S. Senate. There is little reason in the modern era to continue representing them as states in the election of the president.

It is critical that with such power invested in a single public office, election rules should maximize the likelihood that the president be the candidate who was most preferred by voters. Our election system does this at times, but it is not well-suited for doing so with certainty. We risk, then, a future where election rules produce presidents with tremendous power, but dubious claims to legitimacy. Such leaders may have only a tenuous hold on power without something like a sustained national security crisis to maintain their popular support.

NOTES

1. Howard Gilman, *The Votes That Counted: How the Supreme Court Decided the 2000 Presidential Election* (Chicago, IL: University of Chicago Press, 2001).
2. The National Opinion Research Council recount project, sponsored by the *New York Times*, *Washington Post*, *Wall Street Journal*, and other papers, was to release its report in September 2001. The terrorist attacks on September 11 delayed release of the report for weeks. The study reported likely results under several scenarios. Gore would have won if all counties had adhered to Florida election law when accepting absentee ballots, and under four other possible scenarios, including one that accounted for ballots where voters punched a choice for a candidate and then also wrote the candidate's name on the ballot (these are defined as spoiled ballots under Florida law). Bush would have won if illegal absentee ballots remained in the count, and under other scenarios. Bush would have won if the U.S. Supreme Court had not blocked the narrower recount rules prescribed by the Florida Supreme Court in December of 2000.

3. Several candidates, each getting less than 0.07 percent of the vote, combined to deny Kennedy or Nixon the possibility of a majority.

4. Slave owners, "yeomanry," "manufactures," and "merchants" either no longer exist, or they are no longer as spatially concentrated in a given set of states as they were in the eighteenth century. The electoral college (EC) was designed to protect such spatially concentrated, state-specific minorities (who may comprise a majority within a state). Given social and economic diversification across the nation—or the nationalization of economic practices and social relations, this mode of protecting minority interests may no longer be as relevant as it was back then.

   At the same time, if the institution of the EC rewards state-specific minorities more than others, logic would suggest it provides incentives for some such minorities to persist. That is, the EC created a payoff for racially segregationist politics well into the twentieth century, long after slave society ended formally.

5. Compare this to Canada, where many parties do not compete nationwide. Distinct two-party systems thus exist in the western and eastern parts of the country as well as in Quebec. Only one party—the Liberals—has nationwide reach.

6. Nelson Polsby and Aaron Wildavsky, *Presidential Elections: Strategies and Structures of American Politics* (Chatham, NJ: Chatham House, 2000); John Bibby, *Politics, Parties, and Elections in America* (Belmont, CA: Wadsworth Publishing, 1995).

7. Dean Lacy and Barry Burden, "The Vote Stealing and Turnout Effects of Third Party Candidates in U.S. Presidential Elections: 1968–1996," paper presented at the American Political Science Association Meeting, 1999, Atlanta, GA.

8. Dean Lacy and Barry Burden, "The Vote Stealing and Turnout Effects of Ross Perot in the 1992 Presidential Election," *American Journal of Political Science* 43 (1999): 233–255; Barry Burden, "Did Ralph Nader Elect George W. Bush? Analysis of Minor Parties in the 2000 Election," paper presented at the American Political Science Association Meeting, 2001, San Francisco, CA. Burden finds that had small numbers of Buchanan votes switched to Bush in a few states in 2000, Bush would have won a clear electoral college majority without Florida.

9. Stone and Rappoport, 2001a, 2001b.

10. See Michael Alvarez and Jonathan Nagler, "Economics, Issues, and the Perot Candidacy: Voter Choice in the 1992 Election," *American Journal of Political Science* 39, no. 3 (1995). They estimate that the 1992 election would actually have been much closer with Perot out of the race, giving Clinton a smaller margin of victory over Bush. See also Burden, 2001; Lacy and Burden, 1999.

11. Lacy and Burden, 1999, p. 4; Burden, 2001.

12. By the way, the electoral college has no "campus"—electors meet in their respective state capitols to cast their state's votes. For more details see Stephen J Wayne, *Is This Any Way to Run a Democratic Election? Debating American Electoral Politics* (New York: Houghton Mifflin, 2001). He notes six faithless electors, plus one elector who placed the 1988 Democratic vice presidential nominee above the presidential candidate. In addition, one Gore elector abstained to protest the 2000 election result.

13. Lacy and Burden's analysis suggests Anderson took more potential votes from Reagan than from Carter.

14. James W. Davis, *Leadership Selection in Six Western Democracies* (Westport, CT: Greenwood, 1998).

15. Sometimes, however, that may not be true. So many people spoiled their ballots in the second round of the French presidential election that President Jacques Chirac beat Lionel Jospin with less than 50 percent of those who voted in the second round. Since the second-round voters were asked to mark an X next to one of two candidates this is not likely a result of voters being able to manage the system. In the second round there were 6 percent invalid votes (1.9 million) and Chirac won with 53 percent of the *remaining* ballots. In the first round of nine candidates, invalid voting ran at just 2.8 percent.

16. For a good overview of electoral systems, see David Farrell, *Electoral Systems: A Comparative Introduction* (New York: Palgrave, 2001).

17. Technically, Ireland uses the Single Transferable Vote system where the district magnitude is 1, and so the quota is 50 percent +1. STV is a form of preferential voting very similar to AV except that it is most commonly used in multimember districts. It is used to elect the Australian Senate and the lower houses of Ireland and Malta. See Bowler and Grofman, 2000, for a review.

18. That is, no matter how the votes of the three lowest candidates transferred, they would all be eliminated.
19. A photo of the ballot may be found at <http://www.electoral-reform.org.uk/sep/publications/leaflets/london.htm>.
20. See Bowler, Donovan, and Brockington, 2003, for a review of studies on voter understanding of preferential voting.
21. AV would not have made the Florida contest any less close. However, if all minor candidate supporters that finished behind Nader ranked Bush second, their support would still have Bush short of a majority under AV.

6

THE NOMINATION PROCESS, OR WHO GETS ON THE BALLOT?

The reforms discussed in Chapter 5 address the question of how the president should be elected. This begs a second, equally important question: How do we decide who appears on the presidential election ballot? For the most part, presidential candidates represent political parties when they seek office, although a few minor candidates run without a party, as independents. For major party candidates, the first stage of the presidential election involves winning a party's nomination. Some minor candidates first tried and failed to win a major party's nomination (e.g., John Anderson in 1980). Others have simply skipped this stage and tried to start their own party (George Wallace in 1968, Ross Perot in 1996), or run as an independent (Perot in 1992).

THE POWER OF NOMINATION RULES

Given the current state of our election rules, only major party nominees can be elected president. The importance of nomination should not be understated. As one famous political scientist said: "The nature of the nominating process determines the nature of the party: He who can make the nominations is the owner of the party." Control over nomination is also colorfully known as the "secret garden" of politics.[1]

Rules governing party nomination of presidential candidates effectively determine how the field of candidates will be reduced to just two, who will be presented to voters, and who has any chance of winning. The same is true for most other elected positions that carry a party label. The stakes associated with nomination rules are thus huge. If voters are given just two viable choices in the general election, who gets to determine what those two choices will be?

In the United States, state laws regulate who can list candidates on the state's presidential election ballot in November. The two major party's candidates automatically qualify to be listed on all state ballots. However, state laws vary quite a bit in the degree of difficulty that third party and independent candidates face when trying to qualify for a general election ballot listing. Most minor candidates for president fail to get ballot access in all but a few states, and even the most successful often fail to qualify in all 50. In 2000, Buchanan was listed on 49 ballots, while Nader qualified in just 44 states. Buchanan had the advantage of winning the Reform nomination— based on Perot's showing as a Reform Party candidate in 1996, the party was prequalified in several states for 2000.

The point is that winning a major party's nomination is the only certain route for being listed on the November presidential election ballot in all American states. How then should these two nominees be selected? Is the selection a private matter to be controlled exclusively by the party, and by official members of the party? Is it a public matter that all voters should be allowed to participate in if they wish? Do public or private nomination processes produce different candidates? As we see below, the United States is unlike most other democracies regarding the level of direct public control over the selection of a party's official nominee.[2]

PRESIDENTIAL NOMINATIONS BEFORE 1972

Beginning in the early 1900s, several American states began requiring that major parties pick their nominees for state partisan offices in public, primary elections held months before the November general election. In most states, if a voter checks a party affiliation when registering to vote, she may vote in that party's primary election and pick the party's nominees for state offices elected in November. Since the president is elected nationally, however, each state sends delegates to a national party meeting (a nominating convention), where the party's presidential candidate is selected.

For much of our history, the delegates sent to these conventions were picked by state and local party leaders and by elected officials in each state. Delegates were often loyal to leaders of their state's party, not to any particular presidential candidate. Candidates seeking the presidency had to cultivate favor with these party elites in order to win the nomination. This gave party officials, rather than voters, direct control over who would run for president under the party's banner. It was often a mystery who would win a party's nomination prior to the convention, as candidates bargained and built coalitions among the party elite in their attempts to win support of a majority of delegates.[3]

THE "POST-REFORM" NOMINATION PROCESS

By 1972, however, new state laws and new rules of the Democratic and Republican national party committees changed how delegates to the nominating convention would be selected. After 1972, most were picked directly by voters in primary elections or, in some states, at public meetings known as caucuses. Starting with the Iowa caucuses in mid-January 2004 and the New Hampshire primary a week or so later, each presidential candidate seeking a party's nomination spends months contesting primaries and caucuses in state after state. The final primaries are held in early June. As many as a dozen candidates may begin the campaign for a party's nomination at the beginning of the process. While these candidates still must seek the support of their party's leaders and elected officials, they now must also pitch their campaigns directly to voters. A states' slate of delegates to the national convention is awarded based on the popular support candidates receive in the state's primary or caucus.

In some states, parties award all the state's delegates to the first place candidate in the primary—regardless of how crowded the field is or how small the winner's plurality might be. Other states use proportional allocation of delegates, usually with some minimum threshold required to win any delegates. Since 1972, conventions themselves have played no role in deciding the nominees. Despite crowded candidate fields, lengthy primary seasons, and proportional allocation of delegates in some contests, a front-runner usually emerges fairly early. By the time the last primary is held—two months before the conventions—one candidate has always had a majority of delegates. Thus, we nearly always know each party's nominee far before the primary season is over.[4] Conventions, rather than being a place where party officials bargain about who their candidate shall be, have become highly choreographed, government-subsidized coming-out parties for a party's nominee.

INITIAL FEARS ABOUT THE POST-REFORM NOMINATION PROCESS

Many political scientists, journalists, and others were not optimistic about the new, public nomination system as it was being adopted in 1972. They argued that the old system worked well and produced candidates who clearly represented the mainstream voters of each party. After all, party elites knew better than anyone that the number one priority for selecting a candidate was picking a winner. If a candidate was "too ideological," too far beyond the mainstream, or too disliked by voters in the political center, the candidate would probably lose. State and local party elites may all have different goals and expectations associated with backing a candidate, but they could probably agree that they would all gain nothing by backing a loser.

Only candidates who had a serious chance of winning could offer them the promise of something in return for their support. The reformed nomination system, it was feared, would take control of nominations away from party elites and put it in the hands of "amateurs" who might be motivated less by winning in November, and more by ideology or narrowly defined principles.

PARTY OFFICIALS LOSE CONTROL?

Early observers predicted that primaries would weaken the strength of party elites and organizations, as they no longer controlled who would be nominated. Some worried that the open and fluid primary process, coupled with awarding of delegates in some states by PR, could leave too many candidates standing at convention time and so not produce a clear choice. The concern was that candidates from the ideological extremes of a party could rally their die-hard supporters, dominate primary elections (which have notoriously low turnout), and steal their party's nomination from the electable candidates whom old party elites would have rallied behind. It was expected that post-reform nominees might often have little mainstream support, and thus be crushed in the general election.[5]

These critics argued that nomination reforms that were designed to make the nomination process more democratic, by taking control away from party bosses, would end up making the general election presidential choices less likely to represent the majority of voters. By opening a party's nomination to all comers, early observers also worried that nominees would end up being more likely to reflect the influence of narrow interest groups, or extremists. In fact, voter nomination of candidates via primaries has allowed people like David Duke to win the Republican nomination for governor in Louisiana, and for supporters of Lyndon Larouche to win Democratic nominations for lower level races in other states. These unelectable, fringe candidates won their nominations in low-turnout primaries, over the objections of officials in the respective parties.

INCREASED FRAGMENTATION OF PARTIES?

Postreform primaries and caucuses, furthermore, were much more public than the old boss-dominated system, meaning that conflict within the party would be on display for all to see. Primary elections could also lead to divisive intraparty conflicts and factionalism that would linger beyond the convention and weaken the eventual nominee.[6]

There is some evidence that losing candidates and their supporters have been disgruntled with their party's eventual choice. It seems that every four years, party convention organizers are faced with finding a tactful way to keep a losing candidate—particularly bitter losers like Buchanan—from gaining too much of the prime-time spotlight. Consider Ronald Reagan's insurgent, antiestablishment movement in 1976, and John Anderson's campaign in the Republican party in 1980; as well as Pat Buchanan (1992 & 1996) and John McCain (2000) within the GOP. Or Ted Kennedy (1980), Gary Hart (1984), Jesse Jackson (1988), and Jerry Brown (1992) within the Democrats ranks.

Some of these failed primary candidates did not back their party's eventual nominee enthusiastically. Two of them (Anderson and Buchanan) eventually bolted their party and mounted a third-party challenge against it. More recently, Republicans made great efforts to bring John McCain back into the party fold after 2000 primaries. McCain lost the nomination to Bush after a series of bitter primary fights where the candidates highlighted disagreements over policy and style. More visible to many voters, perhaps, were personal attacks that left McCain unwilling to meet with Bush for weeks after he withdrew from the primaries.

WITH HINDSIGHT, INITIAL FEARS PROVED WRONG

In reality, the postreform primary nomination method cannot be faulted for failing to produce clear winners. Experience since 1972 shows that the public primary and caucus election method nearly always does a good job of ensuring that each major party's presidential nominees have won a solid majority of the votes cast in their party's primaries. Since 1972, the system has always been able to produce candidates who are unambiguous winners of the party's nomination. Every major party nominee since 1972 won a majority of delegates prior to the convention.[7] Every party convention since 1972 has thus been able to confirm the nominee with a majority of delegates on the first ballot. Voters who may have backed a loser in the primary, moreover, eventually rallied behind their party's nominee. Public opinion polls show that the winner from the primary season eventually becomes the first choice of party voters. Contemporary research also demonstrates that fears about the effects of divisive primaries were "overstated substantially."[8]

As we see later, however, the current process may prevent all but the best-financed candidates from having a chance to win a party's nomination. Nominees win clear majorities of delegates and votes and solidify support among their party's voters, because their challengers for the nomination are so easily dispatched. Front-runners have been able to eliminate challengers months before the primary season begins. Voters in a few early states participate in contested nomination elections, but after that, most primaries and caucuses are nearly always irrelevant.[9] It's no wonder, then, that someone always wins a majority of delegates and votes. In most primaries, there is often just one viable candidate left on the ballot.

CONTEMPORARY PROBLEMS WITH PRESIDENTIAL PRIMARIES

THE WEALTH PRIMARY

After nearly thirty years of experience with using direct voter primaries and public caucuses to select party nominees, we can better evaluate problems with this nomination system. In hindsight, it seems that critics of the 1972 reforms failed to realize that elite control of the nomination process would be largely unaffected by the switch to primary elections. The nature of control has shifted, however, from state and local party elites to major campaign donors. In eleven of twelve Democratic and Republican nomination contests since 1980, the candidate who raised the most money *in the year prior* to the first primary election ended up winning the party's nomination.[10] The only exception is 1980, when John Connelly raised slightly more early money than the eventual GOP nominee, Ronald Reagan. Reagan, however, had actually been spending and raising money since his 1976 presidential campaign, and thus can be seen as outspending Connelly prior to the first primary of 1980.

Candidates seeking a party's nomination now spend years before an election building networks of major donors.[11] The process is not unlike the old system of soliciting the graces of the old party elites. The difference is that today candidates must seek early support from major economic elites, interest groups, and wealthy individuals. Party elites can influence who the nominee will be if they can steer such donations to a particular candidate. In several nomination contests, groups that reflect the traditional donor base of a party lined up behind a single candidate before the primary season. And it's important to note that traditional party elites still have a large presence at the conventions: About one-third of Democrat and one-fifth of Republican delegate slots are reserved for the traditional party elites. Every Democratic member of Congress, members of the DNC, and all Democratic governors are preselected to attend their convention. By observing early contribution records, and by gauging the sentiments and behavior of contributors, party elites, and preselected "superdelegates," the media can identify each party's front-running candidates well in advance of any primary votes being cast.[12] We take up the question of campaign finance reform in Chapter 8. For the moment we simply note money as one the factors that have made nomination contest outcomes quite predictable.

PARTY CONTROL IS ALIVE AND WELL

Since the primary battle takes months and requires that candidates establish and maintain field operations in dozens of states in advance of each party's primaries, early money is critical. Once voting begins in January, there is little time to raise new money nor time to establish well-financed campaign organizations in each state. Fundraising during the primary season is made even more difficult due to the Federal Election Campaign Act of 1974, which requires that candidates accept donations of no more than $1,000 if they are to receive federal matching funds. Under the old rules, a candidate could emerge relatively late in the process and mount a serious campaign by raising millions from a few contributors.[13] Today, if a front-runner begins the primary season with a fundraising advantage, it is nearly impossible for a challenger to catch up, regardless of how well she does in the early primaries.

Support from party officials, elected officials, and groups aligned with these actors reinforces front-runner fundraising advantages. In addition to providing the party-preferred candidate a bank of early delegates, state-level officials can also provide campaign manpower to their preferred candidate. In 2000, for example, even though Al Gore's campaign funds were not dramatically larger than Bill Bradley's at the start of the primary season, Gore was seen as the overwhelming favorite because so many Democratic "superdelegates" (party officials who attend the convention and vote for the nominee) were known to support him. Furthermore, it was also clear—even before the primaries began—that Gore would benefit much more than Bradley from the support of various voter mobilization resources affiliated with state parties and organized labor.

FRONT-LOADING AND THE POWER OF EARLY MONEY

The move toward greater use of primaries and public caucuses has coincided with other changes that dampened the potential effects of popular control over nominations. For reasons beyond the scope of this book, states have been scheduling their presidential primaries earlier in the year. This means that most of the delegates are selected early in the primary season, making early money even more important. In 1976, fewer than half of the Democrats' delegates were awarded only after the eleventh week of the primary season. This allowed candidates to enter the nomination contest later, and gave voters in states with late primaries some influence in the process. By 1996, however, so many primaries were "front-loaded" that most of the delegates were allocated just after the fourth week. In 2000, late primaries (actually held in early March) in states like New York and California were nearly irrelevant, even though neither party had an incumbent president seeking renomination. In addition, many of the large states still award delegates on a winner-take-all basis in Republican primaries, which greatly favors front-runners. Thus, once the first few primaries are conducted, the race is essentially over. Many challengers drop out shortly after the New Hampshire primary, even if they win primaries in some early states.[14]

There is a good deal of irony in the switch toward supposedly greater popular control over party nominations in the United States. The new system is different from the "party-centered" one it replaced in that the eventual nominee is determined much earlier now. The new process has created a "candidate-centered" nomination process, but not one in which the contest leads to competitive contests for the nomination. There are no more contested conventions, where rival factions of the party might be represented by various candidates and forced to bargain and compromise about the party's future. Yet the reforms left a system that favors party insider-candidates as much as before. Now, however, there is usually only a single insider candidate in the field from the start, even in years when there is no incumbent president seeking renomination.

Despite all the worry about the effects of reforms and all the hoopla associated with primaries and caucuses, there is usually less mystery today about who a party's nominee will be than under the old convention system of nominations. The public, moreover, appears to be unhappy with the major party nominees that are produced from this process. A June 1992 Pew Center poll found that 61 percent of Americans were "not satisfied" with the presidential candidates for 1992. Only 6 percent were "very satisfied." In July of 1999, several months before the field of presidential candidates for 2000 would be narrowed, just 11 percent were reported being very satisfied with the candidates.

INSTITUTIONS TRUMP MOMENTUM:
THE 2000 NOMINATION CONTESTS

The 2000 presidential nomination contest illustrates these issues well. Since President Clinton was finishing his second term, both parties would need a new candidate to nominate. One might expect that each party would have had wide-open contests for their nominations.

THE DEMOCRATS

Well before the first primary, however, clear frontrunners emerged in each party. As vice president under Clinton, Al Gore was able to cultivate the loyalty of many party insiders, superdelegates, and donors, as well as key support from organized labor. Gore raised $27,800,000 by December 31, 1999, compared to $27,100,000 for his only challenger, Bill Bradley (D-N.J.). Gore went on to raise more money than Bradley in every month of the 2000 primary season but February.

Despite relative balance in their preprimary fundraising, Gore's nomination was never in much doubt, particularly after Bradley lost the New Hampshire primary on February 1st. Gore received 49 percent to Bradley's 46 percent—with Bradley winning about as many votes as George Bush did on the GOP side but losing by collecting just 6,500 fewer votes than Gore. Democratic national rules made sure that no Democratic primaries would be held between New Hampshire and the first week of March. This meant that

Bradley had one month to build support after his narrow loss in New Hampshire. Falling 6,500 votes short of a killer "Bradley Beats Gore" headline, he had difficulty building media and fundraising momentum before March 7th, when sixteen Democratic caucuses and primaries were held. On that day, Democrats would allocate just under one-half of all non–super-delegate convention delegates. Bradley lost in every state that day, withdrew immediately, and left Gore unchallenged.

THE REPUBLICANS

On the Republican side, there were several candidates seeking the 2000 GOP nomination—Texas Governor George W. Bush, former Transportation Secretary Elizabeth Dole, New Hampshire Senator Bob Smith, Ohio Congressman John Kasich, millionaire Steve Forbes, Arizona Senator John McCain, Utah Senator Orin Hatch, former Tennessee Governor Lamar Alexander, Gary Bauer, Alan Keyes, and former Vice President Dan Quayle—jockeying for publicity and contributions through 1998 and 1999.

By the end of June 1999, Bush had collected over $36 million—far more than any other candidate. Citing fund-raising problems, several candidates quit the race in quick succession.[15] Thus, before any voting began, the fundraising primary reduced the Republican field from eleven to seven, with many of the remaining candidates, having never held office, probably unelectable (Forbes, Keyes, and Bauer).

By January 2000, Bush had raised nearly $60,000,000—and had twenty times more money in the bank than any of his remaining challengers. Forbes's personal fortune may have been formidable, but his campaign fund was still dwarfed by Bush's. In the January 24th Iowa caucuses, the first contest that voters participated in, Forbes received 30 percent and placed second after he spent millions of dollars and months of his time there. Bush won the Iowa caucus with 41 percent—which took a total of just 35,000 votes.

Other candidates also began to fall away so that, after just one week of voting in a few very sparsely populated states, the crowded Republican field was down to just Bush, McCain, and Keyes.[16] As Figure 6.1 illustrates, hardly any Americans were paying attention to the contest prior to Iowa or New Hampshire. But by the time that even one-fourth of Americans were beginning to think and talk about the presidential election, New Hampshire and Iowa were history, as were most of the candidates seeking nomination.

Many casual observers hearing news of the February 1st, 2000, New Hampshire primary would have believed that John McCain had a decent chance of winning the Republican nomination, or at least making a contest of it. McCain won New Hampshire with 48 percent, and beat Bush by nearly 20 percent. The effect of this victory meant a tremendous surge in press coverage and fundraising potential for McCain. As Figure 6.2 (on page 116) illustrates, he gained 15

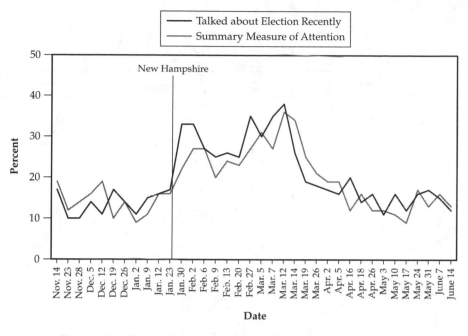

FIGURE 6.1   PUBLIC INTEREST IN THE 2000 PRESIDENTIAL ELECTION

Source: CNN Polling Data.

percent in terms of national name recognition immediately after New Hampshire, and he surged past Bush (and Gore) in national polls measuring favorable attitudes about candidates (see Figure 6.3 on page 117). Although he lost the next major primary (South Carolina), he defeated Bush on February 23 in Michigan, the first large state to hold a primary.

Prior to January, many people responding to polls had not heard of McCain and had heard little negative about Bush. Figure 6.2 suggests that McCain was closing the familiarity gap by January. Uncertainty about McCain, as a non–front-runner, was being reduced considerably as the primary season unfolded. Figure 6.3 illustrates the momentum that New Hampshire might provide a non–front-running candidate like McCain. After New Hampshire, he began to be rated more favorably than Gore or Bush. For a brief period in February 2000, pundits began suggesting that McCain, rather than Bush, might be the Republican Party's best bet for the November election. Polls showed that McCain was particularly popular among a large block of independent voters. In the end, however, he had little chance, and the nomination contest was not at all close, as Bush's greater ability to raise money and his popularity with core Republican voters took their toll.

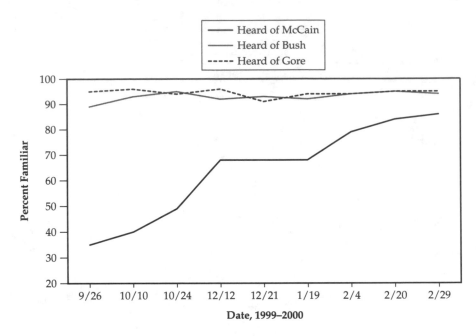

FIGURE 6.2   PUBLIC FAMILIARITY WITH PRESIDENTIAL CANDIDATES, 2000

Source: CNN Polling Data.

THE DEATH OF POST–IOWA/NEW HAMPSHIRE MOMENTUM

Other candidates seeking a party's nomination have had a similar post–New Hampshire boost. In 1976, Jimmy Carter's early success in the Iowa caucuses (collecting just 14,000 caucus votes—enough to finish second to a slate of uncommitted delegates) and a win in New Hampshire (with just 28 percent support) helped him emerge from a crowded field with enough momentum to lock up the Democratic nomination before June. Similarly, in 1984 voters' levels of information about Gary Hart (D) went from almost nothing before New Hampshire to reach levels similar to those associated with the Democratic frontrunner (Walter Mondale) immediately after New Hampshire. However, just as Hart was doomed to lose the 1984 Democratic nomination, so was McCain doomed to lose the GOP nomination in 2000. Neither Hart nor McCain was a player at his party's nominating conventions.

Outsider and underdog candidates still bank on the hope of replicating Carter's 1976 nomination campaign. Many spend months campaigning in Iowa and New Hampshire, and little time anywhere else. In 1988, for example, Senator Paul Simon (D-Ill.), Congressman Richard Gephart (D-Mo.),

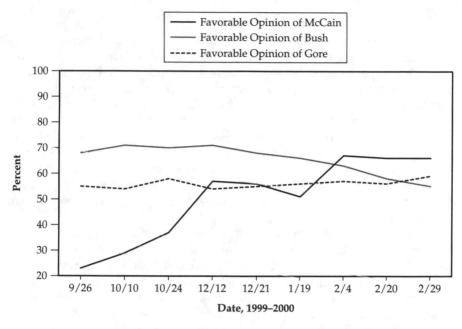

FIGURE 6.3   PUBLIC ATTITUDES ABOUT PRESIDENTIAL CANDIDATES, 2000
Source: CNN Polling Data.

Governor Michael Dukakis (D-Mass.), and Governor Bruce Babbit (D-Ariz.), Robert Dole (R-Kans.), Congressman Jack Kemp (R-N.Y.), former general Al Haig (R), and Pierre du Pont (R-Del.) each spent at least 100 days campaigning in Iowa and New Hampshire in the seven months prior to February. Another four candidates spent at least sixty days in the two early states. In addition to time, candidates tend to spend the maximum amounts of money allowable by law in these states, but not on primaries in larger states. If you don't live in Iowa or New Hampshire, chances are the candidates will not be spending much time or money in your state.[17]

Despite this, wrestling a party's nomination away from the early front-runner with a "bounce" from an early win in Iowa or New Hampshire is nearly impossible now. Since 1976, underdog winners from Iowa or New Hampshire have seen their support in national opinion polls go up after their win, including Carter in 1976 (up 12 percent), Hart in 1984 (up 27 percent), Senator Paul Tsongas (up 26 percent), Patrick Buchanan in 1996 (up 20 percent), and McCain in 2000 (up 15 percent).[18] Only Carter, however, has won a nomination. In every year since 1980, the front-running candidate who led in the last poll conducted *before* Iowa still ended up winning the nomination.[19]

THE DECK IS STACKED AGAINST CHALLENGERS

Why did the McCain effort end up like so many other challenges to party-preferred front-runners? The compact primary schedule makes it much harder for challengers to gain momentum in votes and contributions. Jimmy Carter had time to translate his momentum into contributions and votes. McCain had much less time. In 1976, one-half of voter-allocated Republican delegates were awarded by the eleventh week of the primary season. In 1984, one-half were awarded by the tenth week. In 2000, half were awarded after the first six weeks. The "shelf-life" of momentum may be only two or three weeks, after which challengers have a hard time making up any remaining gap in familiarity compared to the front-runner.[20] In addition, most Republican primaries held after New Hampshire are winner-take-all, meaning that a strong second-place finish gets nothing.

Table 6.1 illustrates how these election rules advantage early front-runner candidates and make challenges to such candidates quite difficult. In 2000, it took 1,034 delegates to win the Republican presidential nomination. Eighty-five percent of all delegates, about 1,750, would be allocated based on public voting in primaries and caucuses. In the first set of primaries contested between January 24 and February 29, McCain and Bush ran about even, with Bush winning 1,724,129 votes (or 47.7 percent) to McCain's 1,689,085 votes (or 46.7 percent). Bush won 179 of the 315 delegates awarded in these primaries and caucuses (57 percent), compared to 114 delegates (or 36 percent) for McCain. Bush held the edge because he won more in "winner-take-all" contests, including Virginia (56 delegates), and South Carolina (37 delegates) and assorted caucuses in U.S. territories. McCain's victories in two states, Michigan and New Hampshire, were aided by "open" primary rules that allowed voters not formally registered as Republicans to participate in the Republican primary. Despite his delegate lead, Bush might have appeared slightly vulnerable in late February.

On March 7th alone, however, seven states held contests to award 549 delegates. All but two of these states (Ohio and New York) awarded their delegation winner-take-all to the plurality winner. The two largest states (California and New York) restricted participation to registered Republicans only. This meant that a candidate emerging from New Hampshire as a challenger to an early front-runner had just about one month to build campaign organizations to contest seven primaries, stretched coast-to-coast, held on the same day. A close second-place finish in most of these states would result in no delegates. Table 6.1 demonstrates what McCain faced. He won 42 percent of the votes cast on March 7th compared to 53 percent for Bush. This was enough to give Bush 77 percent of the delegates that day. Had there been more viable candidates left between New Hampshire and March 7th, votes would have been more dispersed and McCain would probably have won even fewer delegates.

TABLE 6.1 DELEGATE ALLOCATION IN THE 2000 REPUBLICAN PRESIDENTIAL PRIMARY

DATE	STATE	DELEGATES	BUSH VOTES	BUSH DELEGATES	McCAIN VOTES	McCAIN DELEGATES
24 Jan	Iowa	25	41.0	10	4.7	1
1 Feb	New Hampshire	17	30.3	5	48.5	10
8 Feb	Delaware	12	50.7	12	25.3	0
	Alaska	23	36.0	9	36.0	9
19 Feb	South Carolina	37	53.4	34	42.0	3
22 Feb	Michigan	58	41.5	6	49.1	52
22 Feb	Arizona	30	35.7	0	60.0	30
26 Feb	territories	26		26		0
29 Feb	Virginia	56	52.7	56	44.0	0
29 Feb	North Dakota	19	75.7	14	18.9	4
29 Feb	Washington	12	57.8	7	38.9	5
		315		179		114
7 Mar	New York	93	50.8	67	42.9	26
7 Mar	Connecticut	25	46.3	0	48.7	25
7 Mar	Georgia	54	66.9	54	27.8	0
7 Mar	Maryland	31	56.2	31	36.2	0
7 Mar	Maine	14	51.0	14	44.0	0
7 Mar	Massachusetts	37	32.0	0	64.7	37
7 Mar	Missouri	35	57.9	35	35.3	0
7 Mar	Ohio	69	58.0	63	36.9	6
7 Mar	Rhode Island	17	36.5	0	60.2	17
7 Mar	Vermont	12	35.3	0	60.3	12
7 Mar	California	162	52.2	162	42.9	0
		549		426		123
Total Delegates		**864**		**605**		**237**

Bush ended March 7 holding claim to 605 delegates from primaries and caucuses held up to that date, plus many more delegates from among the party elite who are given automatic slots at the convention. Since he needed 1,034 delegates to be nominated, McCain was effectively finished, even though there were three months of primaries remaining to be conducted in twenty-nine states. Without any competitive or meaningful contests remaining, media coverage of presidential primaries dries up. In 1996, for example, 79 percent of network news reporting on the Republican nomination, from January 1995 to June 1996, was dedicated to Iowa and New Hampshire.[21] As Figure 6.1 (on page 115) illustrates, Americans' attention to the presidential contest faded quickly after March 7.

Few Americans believe that they have any say in this awkward nomination process. A poll conducted in June 2000 by the Shorenstein Center for the Press, Politics, and Public Policy found that 75 percent believed that "big money" and "party elites" controlled the nomination of presidential candidates. Only 15 percent believed that voters had influence in the process. Feelings of lack of influence were even greater among independents. Another Shorenstein Center study by Thomas Patterson found that Americans preferred almost any alternative primary system over the current version. A similar poll from the Pew Center, described in Table 6.2, shows that most Americans believe voters have too little influence in the process, and that party leaders and political donors have too much. If turnout in presidential elections is any indication, many Americans may also be unimpressed by the presidential candidates that the current system produces.

WHAT DO WE EXPECT FROM PRESIDENTIAL PRIMARIES?

What then, needs fixing? That depends on what we expect from party nominations. If we wished to design a system that allowed for nominal public participation in a party's selection of its nominee, while also maximizing the chances that a candidate of the party elite will win the nomination, the present system may be optimal. Over the last twenty years, it has a good record of doing this. Since 1972, the only two candidates who might not have been the preferred choice of their party's organizational and elected elites going into the primaries—Carter in 1976, and, perhaps, Reagan in 1980—both managed to win the presidency. Reagan also managed to win the loyalty of most of the GOP elite who might have opposed him earlier.

On the other hand, if we want a system by which voters in every state play a role in selecting the nominees, and a system in which voters are engaged with the process, then the presidential nomination process needs to be

TABLE 6.2 ATTITUDES ABOUT WHO HAS INFLUENCE
IN SELECTING PRESIDENTIAL NOMINEES

	TOO MUCH	ABOUT RIGHT	TOO LITTLE	DON'T KNOW
Large Political Donors	74	16	6	4
The News Media	64	30	5	2
Party Leaders	46	38	12	4
The Average Voter	8	28	62	2

Note: Question wording: How much influence do you think _____ have on which candidates become presidential nominees: too much, too little, or about the right amount?

Source: Pew Center Poll, September 1999.

reformed. If the goal is to produce two nominees who best reflect the preferences of the average (or median) voter nationally, then outcomes would be improved by opening participation in primary elections to a larger group of voters. If the goal is to produce nominees who best reflect what the party's most loyal voters want, then participation should be restricted.

OPENING PRIMARY ELECTIONS

Debates about reforming of the presidential primary system center around a number of issues. Some suggest that a process controlled exclusively by the parties is not representative of most voters, who are politically moderate. Each party's nominee may reflect the bedrock partisans in their respective party, but the system is biased against producing candidates who might challenge a party's position on a broad range of issues. Democratic candidates nominated by Democrats, from this perspective, will be committed to Democratic programs, and Republicans to Republican programs. This creates a possibility that voters are not presented with presidential candidates who support a mix of both Democratic and Republican programs, nor with candidates who actively promote policies that both parties might resist (e.g., campaign finance reform).

This raises questions about who should be able to vote in a party's primary. If participation is limited to loyal, registered partisans, nominees may be less likely to reflect the policy preferences of the average voter. When primary elections allow independents or voters of any party to vote as well, then the median voter participating in picking the nominee can shift toward the political center. A study of the effects of primary nomination rules used for congressional elections provides evidence of this moderation effect. Members of Congress elected from states that use open primaries are more likely to have voting records that match their constituents preferences than representatives from states where primaries are open to partisans only.[22]

CLOSING PRIMARY ELECTIONS

Despite the fact that the post-1972 nomination system has mostly worked thus far to help party insiders win, the possibility exists, in theory, that an outsider candidate could essentially "steal" the nomination from a party. That is, if elite money fails to concentrate in the hands of a single candidate early on, and a crowded field survived the first primaries with no clear front-runner emerging, anything could happen. A candidate with little money, and limited support among the party hierarchy, could win just as many delegates as any other candidate, and force a "brokered" convention under such conditions. Democrats worried about this possibility in 1988, when the presumed front-runner, Gary Hart, withdrew from the race over allegations of adultery. The prospect of an outsider like Jesse Jackson affecting the nomination might be greater for Democrats, since they require much more proportional allocation of delegates in each state. This could make it more difficult for a party elite preferred candidate to win a majority of delegates prior to the convention.

Stronger party elite control of nominations could be produced by stricter use of winner-take-all delegate allocations, and by requiring that only registered party voters participate in a party's primaries. The U.S. Supreme Court has ruled that state and national party officials have substantial discretion in deciding who gets to participate in their primaries and caucuses (see *CA Demo. v. Jones*). Democratic National Committee (DNC) rules encourage states to limit participation in Democratic nomination contests to registered or declared Democrats. Republican national rules allow their state parties slightly more discretion.

The effects restricting participation to party loyalists can be illustrated with an example from Washington state's 2000 presidential primary. In Washington, any voter could participate in the Republican primary. Voters were asked, however, to first declare if they were affiliated with the Republican party or if they considered themselves independent or Democrat. New Hampshire uses a similar process and all ballots cast for Republican candidates are used to allocate delegates. Thus McCain, or similar candidates, can succeed there by making appeals to independent and cross-over voters.

In Washington, however, party officials count only those ballots cast by declared Republicans when allocating Republican delegates. As Table 6.3 illustrates, McCain was clearly preferred by independent voters, while Bush was clearly preferred by those who declared themselves to be loyal Republicans. McCain received 48 percent of all votes cast for Republican candidates, and Bush received 48.3 percent. If all ballots cast for GOP candidates were used to allocated delegates, and delegates were awarded proportionate to the candidates' vote shares, McCain and Bush would have won equal delegate shares.[23] If, however, only declared Republican's votes are counted and delegates are awarded winner-take-all, Bush wins all the state's delegates. The point is, rules matter.[24]

FIXING THE PRIMARY SCHEDULE

If we expect primary elections to engage more of the public, then closed primaries would probably be a move in the wrong direction. Open primaries, by definition, allow for a broader base of participation. However, party officials claim that such primaries will dilute the party's message by allowing any candidate to run under their label.

If we expect primaries and caucuses to provide meaningful voter participation in the selection of candidates—not just for citizens in a few small states—it should be made more competitive. This means that more than one

TABLE 6.3   CANDIDATE PREFERENCES, REPUBLICAN VERSUS INDEPENDENT
PRIMARY VOTERS: WASHINGTON STATE, 2000 PRESIDENTIAL PRIMARY

BALLOTS CAST FOR REPUBLICAN CANDIDATES BY ALL VOTERS

Bauer	2,870	0.3
Bush	402,287	48.3
Forbes	5,136	0.6
Hatch	2,263	0.3
Keyes	21,122	2.5
McCain	399,980	47.9

Total votes cast for Republican candidates = 833,658

BALLOTS CAST FOR REPUBLICAN CANDIDATES BY INDEPENDENT/UNAFFILIATED VOTERS

Bauer	1,401	0.4
Bush	118,234	34.5
Forbes	3,387	1.0
Hatch	1,240	0.3
Keyes	9,369	2.7
McCain	208,879	61.0

Total votes cast by independent voters = 342,510

BALLOTS CAST FOR REPUBLICAN CANDIDATES BY DECLARED REPUBLICAN VOTERS

Bauer	1,469	0.3
Bush	284,053	57.8
Forbes	1,749	0.3
Hatch	1,023	0.2
Keyes	11,753	2.4
McCain	191,101	38.9

Total votes cast by declared Republicans = 491,148

Source: Washington Secretary of State.

viable candidate is remaining when most citizens still have their chance to vote. Ideally, this could be done so that citizens also have some time to learn about the candidates before they vote, and before all but the last candidate drops out of the race. At present, the nomination system looks like a football season with just one or two preseason games and then a Super Bowl featuring two mismatched teams. There are no "regular season" games that let voters learn about the candidates before the season is over.

There are a number of proposals for fixing problems with the primary schedule, including going back to the calendar that existed in 1976, when most delegates were not awarded until after nearly three months of voting in the primary system. Other proposals include the following.

Regional Primaries   In 1999, the National Association of Secretaries of State advocated a system wherein states in the same region have their primary on the same day. There would be four regions (east, south, midwest, and west). In 2004, the eleven eastern states would have their primary in early March. The South would have theirs in early April, the Midwest in early May, and the West in early June. The order of primaries would rotate every four years, with the South going first in 2008, the Midwest in 2012, and the West in 2016. Iowa and New Hampshire would retain their privileged positions and go first and second each time. A Shorenstein Center poll found 47 percent of Americans like the regional primary idea, with 39 percent favoring the current system, given this alternative (15 percent were undecided).

Apart from rotating the region that holds the first big primary, this plan is not too different from the system used in 2000. Front-loading is reduced somewhat, which could make it easier for some candidates to challenge front-runners.

The Delaware Plan   Delaware's state Republican Chair proposed a plan for 2004 that would have four separate days of primary voting, with the thirteen smallest states, including Delaware and North Dakota, going first. Over the next three or four months, primaries would be held on the same day in other states. The second primary would include the smallest remaining states, the third the next smallest remaining, and the last would include largest states. On the last day of voting, 50 percent of delegates would be awarded. Advocates say this would allow "grass-roots" candidates to have a chance to do low-cost "retail politics," build momentum in small states, and still allow voters in big states to have real influence. This plan was approved by the Republican National Committee (RNC) rules committee, and by a committee at the 2000 Republican National Convention, but ultimately it was not approved in 2000. RNC Chair Haley Barbour opposed changing the primary calendar in a way that would have the Republican nominee decided after the Democrat's.

The Shorenstein poll found 41 percent approved of this as an alternative, compared to 40 percent supporting the current system. This plan eliminates front-loading and could probably help keep more candidates in the race for a longer period.

National Primary   Others suggest having a national primary in May or June, an idea that has been attributed to Woodrow Wilson. Voters in all states would go to their caucuses or primaries on the same day. The intent of this reform is to shorten the nomination process dramatically. If the date is set late enough, it could also help to sustain voter interest in the candidates until the major party's conventions. As Thomas Patterson notes, for this system to work there would have to be some kind of early "activation" events. Without publicized debates or "beauty contest" primaries in some place like

New Hampshire before the vote, citizens would be voting in a low information environment. Patterson notes that party officials are not at all interested in such a plan, but Shorenstein Center polls found that 56 percent of Americans favored this, and only 32 percent favored the current system when this was an option.

The best-financed candidates would continue to have advantages under all three of these plans. Those advantages might be muted somewhat under the first two, as non-front-running candidates would have more time to translate success in early primaries into fundraising. A national primary would eliminate any opportunities for this. However, a single day of voting would probably insure a fairly crowded field of candidates. This could make it more difficult for a front-runner to consolidate support and win an outright majority of delegates.

Party Conventions   This plan would go back to the days before 1972, and have direct party control over delegate selection. Although this would reduce direct public influence over the choice of nominees, it could be a more competitive system in some ways. In the preprimary days, candidates were often still building their coalitions of supporters during the convention. This means that factions within the parties could have some ability to affect the bargaining that produces the eventual nominee. The system would also require much less voter involvement. The Shorenstein poll found that voters also preferred this system to the current one. Given public discontent with a "closed" political process in general, it is hard to imagine that this plan would retain much support if used.

PARTY CONTROL OF NOMINATIONS OUTSIDE THE UNITED STATES

The introduction of primaries was a direct attack on the power of "King Caucus"—as nomination inside the party was known in earlier days of the republic. In most established democracies, public participation in the selection of party nominees is far more limited than is the case with primary elections. In fact primary elections, where voters are allowed to choose candidates, are unheard of in most other nations.

Outside the United States, the way that candidates are actually selected varies both between countries and political parties but, generally speaking, outside the United States, the nomination procedure is firmly in the hands of the party. The selection of party leaders is especially important since these are the people who, should their party win the election, become head of the executive. In practice this also means that many candidates for a nation's top executive office are ones who are already serving as elected officials of some kind, often in the national legislature.

NOMINATION BY PARTY IN THE LEGISLATURE

Most commonly, candidates for prime minister are members of the national legislature, although in some countries candidates may be leaders of a state or province. In Germany, successful leadership of a party at the state level is often a path to becoming leader of the national party. In January 2001, for example, Edward Stoiber, leader of the main right-wing party in the state of Bavaria, was chosen to lead the German CDU/CSU in the elections of that year.

In some parties, members of the party caucus in the legislature are the only ones who make the choice of party leader. This restricts the choice of party leader to a very small number of people. For example, it was a few hundred members of the Conservative party caucus in Parliament that chose one of Britain's most famous politicians in recent times, Mrs. Thatcher. And it was this same group who failed to reelect her as party leader and chose her successor.[24] In the United States, this would be like the majority party in Congress picking who the president would be.

PARTY MEMBERS SELECT NOMINEE

Another way in which leaders are chosen might involve giving a voice to the party organization outside the legislature. Some parties, for example, conduct a mail ballot of their membership. Since 1997 the British Conservative party has moved away from a process that only consults members of the legislative caucus toward one that involves individual members. The party caucus now chooses two candidates and then individual members are allowed to choose between them. This happened for the first time in 2001.

It should be noted that, although these kinds of elections sound similar to American-style primaries, there is an important difference. Voting is restricted to party members and party membership typically means much more than simply voting for a party or registering to vote for it. Outside the United States, party membership is more like joining and paying dues in order to be a member of a private club. Individuals must pay a monthly fee to become a member of a party. In return, these members may get a say in picking the party's candidates. Very few citizens who might support the party at the polls actually become dues-paying members. Typically, just about 10 percent of the population actually join a party as an official member—a little more in some countries, a little less in others. These are the only people eligible to vote on party matters.

It cannot be stressed strongly enough that simply declaring affiliation at the polling place or at the time one registers to vote, as in the United States, is not enough to qualify to vote on a party's nominee elsewhere in the world. Thus, in nations outside the United States where a party gives members a say in picking nominees, far fewer people are involved with selecting nominees than in the United States. A rough equivalent to having dues-paying party members decide the nominee would be if American parties allowed only those who worked on campaigns to vote in primaries.

PARTY ORGANIZATIONS SELECT NOMINEES

There are other versions of leadership selection that allow some participation by various parts of the party organization. Parties outside the United States exist more as permanent social and political organizations than they do inside the United States. While this picture has changed over the past generation or so, parties often retain strong links to social organizations. Many left-wing and left-of-center parties, for example, have strong ties to organized labor. For the British Labour party these ties are given expression in selecting party leaders. Labour's choice of leader candidate is produced by a complicated electoral college procedure involving various components of the party. Thirty percent of votes in the college go to the party caucus in the legislature, 30 percent to rank and file member organizations (the people who pay the monthly dues to become members) and 40 percent to labor unions.

Other political parties may nominate the leader at a convention, as in Germany, Sweden, and Norway. In such cases local and regional parties send delegates to the convention who then vote. Under a convention model, while some members may have a say, not all members get a vote. In 1998 for example, Gerhard Schroeder was nominated chancellor candidate by the 515 members of the party convention of the SPD in Leipzig. Some other parties rely on members of what are, roughly, the equivalent of the Democratic or Republican National Committees—as is the case for some parties in Italy and France.

Thus there are three broad ways in which party leaders outside the United States are chosen: by party caucus in the legislature; by vote of individual members (remembering that membership here has a very restricted sense); and by appeal to party organizations. This last has two different varieties: a convention model and one based on allowing national committees to have a say. Some party procedures combine elements of these ways but all procedures have the effect of keeping control of nominations within the party.

Table 6.4 (on page 128) presents a quick overview of the number of parties in various nations that use these three methods of leadership selection. As can be seen, this table underscores the variety of methods employed. To the extent that there have been changes over the past few years, it has been to allow dues-paying party members a slightly bigger say in candidate selection in some instances. Even with this trend it is all very far away from the American system of primary elections. Although these alternative methods of selection may seem impossibly elitist to Americans, many overseas

TABLE 6.4 PARTY LEADERSHIP SELECTION:
NUMBER OF PARTIES USING LEADER SELECTION SYSTEM BY COUNTRY

	PARLIAMENTARY PARTY	NATIONAL COMMITTEE	PARTY CONGRESS	PARTY MEMBERS
Australia	2			1
Austria		1	4	
Belgium		1	1	5
Canada			2	2
Denmark	6		3	
Finland			6	
France		2	2	5
Germany		1	3	
Ireland	3			1
Italy		3	1	
Netherlands	5		1	1
New Zealand	1			
Norway			5	
Sweden			6	
UK			1	2

Source: Susan Scarrow, Paul Webb, and David Farrell, "From Social Integration to Electoral Contestation: The Changing Distribution of Power within Political Parties," in *Parties without Partisans*, ed. Russell Dalton and Martin Wattenberg (Oxford: Oxford University Press, 2000), p. 143.

observers see American-style primaries granting a shocking degree of say to ordinary voters. After all, many voters typically have only a minimal commitment to a party or its ideas. Every few years such a voter may mark a ballot in a given party's favor. Even for those who repeatedly vote for the same party this is very far from having a real stake in that party's ideals. For parties outside the United States, the party belongs to those who are active within them.

Voters overseas, then, are free to choose between parties, but not to tell parties how to conduct their business. Outside the United States, ordinary voters are thus rather like consumers while party members are much more like shareholders. When it comes time to consider how a particular firm should be run, it is the owners—the shareholders—who are the only ones who have a say. Consumers (voters) are perfectly free to grumble or even choose a different party. If consumer-voters really want a say over how things are done, they should join the party. Just because you rented the video of "Toy Story" does not entitle you to tell Disney how to run its theme parks, but being a Disney shareholder does. For non-Americans, primaries essentially amount to giving people who rented the video a say over who should be on the board.

CONCLUSIONS

Given winner-take-all rules used in the United States, general elections present voters with just two credible choices in most situations—the Democrat or Republican candidate. This means that many voters who do not like these candidates are forced to sit out the election, or to choose what might seem to them as the lesser of two evils.

Without new general election voting rules that provide independents, or smaller parties, greater ability to cast effective votes (such as AV, see Chapter 5), the only way to make *general election* outcomes better reflect most voters' preferences is improve the way that we select the two major party's nominees. Rules that strengthen party elite (or elite campaign donor) influence over nominations—such as front-loading, the use of superdelegates, closed primaries—can produce choices between two candidates well representative of their party's core supporters but farther from the median voter than what might be produced in more open, competitive nomination contests.

It is not often that political scientists argue in favor of weaker party control over nominations. Ideally, we would prefer that candidates of a particular party provide clear and consistent messages that all of their party agrees upon. This makes a candidate's party label a more easily used cue for voters. Open nominations can make this less certain to occur. But we see a dangerous trade-off here. Closed nominations *used in combination with* plurality, winner-take-all rules, and America's free-wheeling campaign spending environment, increase the risk that candidates will be elected to the single most powerful elected position without solid claim to reflecting the preferences of most voters.

NOTES

1. The quotation is from E. E. Schattschneider, 1942, while the term *secret garden* is used in one of the very few comparative studies of nomination politics by M. Gallagher and M. Marsh, *Candidate Selection in Comparative Perspective: The Secret Garden of Politics* (Thousand Oaks, CA: Sage Publishing, 1987).
2. Davis, 1995; See also Herrnson and Green, 2002, for a full set of challenges the smaller parties face.
3. Ceaser, 1979; see also Lonna Atkeson, 2000.
4. William G. Mayer, ed., *In Pursuit of the White House: How We Choose Our Presidential Nominees* (Chatham, NJ: Chatham House, 1995).
5. David Broder, *The Party's Over: The Failure of Politics in America* (New York: Harper Collins, 1972); Nelson Polsby, *The Consequences of Party Reform* (New York: Oxford University Press, 1983). Tom Campbell, and other prominent moderate Republicans in California politics could say "I told you so." He has consistently warned his party of these dangers and he almost succeeded in changing the primary rules to help avoid this problem but was blocked by the courts. For a full account of the attempt to introduce the "open primary," see Bruce Cain and Elisabeth Gerber, *Voting at the Political Fault Line* (Berkeley, CA: University of California Press, 2001).
6. See Sullivan, 1977; Bernstein, 1977.

7. The 1976 GOP nomination was quite close. Ford won 18 of 28 primaries and had a majority of delegates at the convention. Reagan may have won more primary votes, due to his big win in California. See Richard M. Pious, *The Presidency* (Reading, MA: Addison-Wesley, 1995).

8. Lonna Atkeson, "From the Primaries to the General Election: Does a Divisive Nomination Race Affect a Candidate's Fortunes in the Fall?" in *In Pursuit of the White House, 2000*, in ed. William G. Mayer (Chatham, NJ: Chatham House, 1999); Lonna Atkeson, "Divisive Primaries and General Election Outcomes," *American Journal of Political Science* 42 (1998): 256–271; Pious, 1995.

9. The sequencing of primaries is yet another example of how rules shape outcomes. States jostle to move their primaries. California moved its primary earlier in the process in order to gain more influence at the crucial stage where bandwagons get rolling; several Southern states did the same thing in bundling together primaries in Super Tuesday in a more successful attempt to make their states more important in the nomination process.

10. William G. Mayer, "Forecasting Presidential Nominations."

11. M. Hagen and E. Lascher, in Mayer (ed.), 1999.

12. Emmett H. Buell, Jr., "The Invisible Primary," in *In Pursuit of the White House, 1996*, ed. William G. Mayer (New York: Chatham House, 1995).

13. Anthony Corrado, "The Changing Environment of Presidential Campaign Finance," in *In Pursuit of the White House, 1996*, ed. William G. Mayer (Chatham, NJ: Chatham House, 1995). After 2003, the limit increased to $2,000.

14. M. Hagen and W. Mayer, in *In Pursuit of the White House, 2000*, ed. William G. Mayer (New York: Chatham House, 1999).

15. Kasich quit in July of 1999, then Alexander withdrew in August after a poor showing at a straw poll in Iowa that had nothing to do with winning delegates, but everything to do with looking credible to campaign donors. Quayle withdrew in September saying he could never compete against Bush's money. Dole withdrew in October, citing similar concerns. Bush decided against matching funds, which allowed him to ignore the $1,000 contribution limit.

16. Hatch withdrew two days after getting just 1 percent in Iowa. Forbes placed a distant third to McCain in New Hampshire on February 1st, and was thus written off in the second week of voting. Bauer collected less than 1 percent in New Hampshire, and withdrew three days later. Forbes withdrew one day after finishing third in the February 8 Delaware primary. Bush won Delaware with a total of just 15,000 votes.

17. Charles D. Hadley and Harold W. Stanley, "The Southern Super Tuesday: Southern Democrats Seeking Relief from Rising Republicanism," in *In Pursuit of the White House, 1996*, ed. William G. Mayer (Chatham, NJ: Chatham House, 1995).

18. Pre-2000 opinion data from Buell 1999, in Mayer (ed.), 1999.

19. William G. Mayer, "Forecasting Presidential Nominations," in *In Pursuit of the White House, 1996*, ed. William G. Mayer (Chatham, NJ: Chatham House, 1995); Emmett H. Buell, Jr. "The Invisible Primary," in *In Pursuit of the White House, 1996*, ed. William G. Mayer (Chatham, NJ: Chatham House, 1995).

20. Buell, 2000.

21. Gerber and Morton, 1998.

22. Most states reward the plurality winner, no matter how close the contest, with bonus delegates in excess of their proportion of the vote.

23. Washington's Republicans decided to count only Republican voters but also to award delegates proportionately.

24. Since Britain is a parliamentary system and the Conservatives were the governing party, this changeover in party leader also meant a changeover in prime minister.

7

DIRECT DEMOCRACY

One practical issue faced by a democracy is how to accommodate the idea of popular sovereignty. For most countries, including the United States, representative democracy is the basic device for doing this. European societies are typically most explicit in declaring the elected representatives as the embodiment of sovereignty. In Britain, for example, the main constitutional doctrine is that Parliament is sovereign, not the people themselves. The citizens' role in governing, then, is to elect a representative who makes laws. In practice, the same may be said to apply in the United States, at least at the national level.

In the United States, however, the Constitution begins with an explicit statement about "We the People." The Bill of Rights guarantees a "right for citizens to petition the Government for a redress of grievances" and states that "the people" retain rights in addition to those enumerated in the Constitution. The Declaration of Independence stands as another example that the American political tradition places sovereignty in the hands of "the people." But does this mean that citizens can, or should, vote on laws directly? Is it possible to give expression to the popular voice through direct democracy?[1] For the most part, the answer to this question in the United States has been "no." Despite this language of popular sovereignty, the United States stands as one of the few well-established democracies never to have held a national vote on a major question of public policy. Advocates claim that direct democracy could better engage citizens with their national government, make policy more responsive to the public, and lead to a "civic maturation" of American society.

WHAT IS DIRECT DEMOCRACY?

THE REFERENDUM

There are two basic forms of direct democracy—the referendum and the initiative. The referendum process, noted in the French constitution, is the most common form in Europe. Under this process the government places a question before the voters, who then vote yes or no on the matter. Examples include referendums in Canada about the status of Quebec, and several European nations that have held referendums on joining the European Union (EU), or on renegotiating membership in the EU. Ireland has also put separate ballot questions about the legality of divorce and abortion before citizens. Typically, the questions considered in these referendums have been very important and often very divisive. As such, national referendums are not conducted very often. France, for example, has had just nine since 1958. National referendums have been used with some frequency in Australia, and have also been used in nearly all of the European democracies.

The major point about referendums is that it is the government (the executive) that usually decides whether to hold a referendum. Not only that, the government decides on what topics to hold a referendum, what kind of question to ask, and, sometimes, what kind of majority is needed in order to make a referendum result one that has to be acted upon (if at all). Despite their control of the agenda, governments can sometimes be surprised by the results. President Mitterrand of France, for example, expected a much larger show of support for his 1992 referendum on joining the EU, and Danish voters have several times upset attempts to move to greater European Union. By and large, however, governments rarely lose referendums. If those in office think they will lose a referendum they can often decide not to hold one. However, in Europe, direct voting via referendum has almost become a prerequisite for constitutional political change.[2]

THE INITIATIVE

The initiative process allows voters (or some organized group) to define the issue or question to be voted on. Initiatives are qualified for the ballot after a certain number of signatures are collected. Twenty-four of the American states have some kind of initiative, as does Switzerland. Italy has had a form of national initiative since 1970, and New Zealand adopted advisory initiatives in 1996. After unification, some German states adopted initiatives. In the late nineteenth century, U.S. populist and progressive reformers expressly copied the earlier Swiss example, although the referendum was used in the United States at least as early as 1778, when Massachusetts referred its constitution to voters for approval. It failed.[3] The initiative was first allowed in South Dakota in 1898 and first used in Oregon in 1904. By the early 1920s most (nineteen) of the states that currently use the process had the initiative in place.

GROWING POPULARITY OF DIRECT DEMOCRACY

The lack of direct democracy at the national level in the United States stands in contrast to expanded use of direct democracy in many other advanced democracies, and in the American states. Even Britain, from which America

---

How Initiatives Work

There are five basic steps in the initiative process:

1. The proposal is drafted.
2. The proposal is forwarded to the attorney general for titling and summary along with a $200 deposit. This deposit is refundable upon qualification for the ballot.
3. Third, petitions are circulated among voters. In California, proponents have 150 days to gather signatures. Petitions must be signed by a number of registered voters equal to at least 5 percent of the votes cast for all candidates for governor at the last election. At least 8 percent are required for constitutional amendments.
4. The secretary of state's office verifies that the correct number of signatures have been gathered.
5. The proposal is voted on. If the initiative receives more yes votes than no votes, it becomes law.[4]

---

inherited its tradition of constrained popular democracy, has used regional referendums to decide issues of political devolution. Governments in other British-influenced democracies, including America's northern neighbor, Canada, and Australia referred major constitutional questions to a national vote in the past decade.[5] Direct democracy remains highly popular in nations that use it to decide on national questions.[6] Majorities of survey respondents in fourteen European nations also support the Swiss model of direct democracy.[7]

The absence of any national process of direct democracy in the United States also conflicts with U.S. popular opinion. Various polls show majorities of Americans support the use of direct democracy at the national level. As the American public's perceptions of Congress have soured,[8] public regard for the initiative process remains firm. Unlike most other advanced democracies, however, the American public's desire for expanded democratic practices have not been satisfied with any use of direct democracy at the national level.

As initiative use has exploded in many states, citizens have remained supportive of the initiative process.[9] Surveys reveal that familiarity with direct democracy does not breed contempt for its expanded use. A poll (spring, 2000) of voters in Washington state found 78 percent thought that initiatives were a "good thing." Sixty-nine percent of California respondents offered the same evaluation in 1996, as did 62 percent of Arkansas voters in 2000. Sixty-three percent of Washington voters also supported expanding initiative use to the national level.[10] Another recent poll found 68 percent of Americans supported having initiatives at the state level, with 57 percent supporting a national initiative.[11]

This array of public opinion data—usually showing strong support for general principles of direct democracy—should not detract from the fact that widespread approval of the initiative process coexists with worries, among voters and elected officials in west coast states, about the health of the initiative process as it is now used. In these states where initiatives are widely used, voters and legislators agree that the process needs reform—however they do not agree about how the process should be improved.

Critics point out that too many initiatives appear on ballots in some states, on a wide array of topics that voters might not understand. More worrying, well-funded groups proposing or opposing a ballot measure can spend as much money as they want—spending on many ballot initiative campaigns runs into tens of millions of dollars. Many measures that pass are then invalidated in court. Those sympathetic to the initiative process note initiatives are still used to advance major reforms.

Voters and elected officials in western states agree that initiatives often make bad laws, and that campaigns are misleading. They agree that some public official or public office should take a more active role, *before the election*, to review the constitutionality of measures prior to a public vote. Beyond that, voters and representatives disagree. Legislators desire greater ability to affect or amend initiative decisions after voters approve them—voters, not surprisingly, are opposed to this. In 1997 a majority of California voters expressed support for requiring super-majorities to pass initiatives, and a near majority supported having legislators cast votes on measures before the public.[12]

WHY CITIZENS LIKE DIRECT DEMOCRACY

The initial supporters of direct democracy in America were the Populists and Progressives of the late nineteenth and early twentieth centuries. There are important differences between the two strands of thought; Populist support for the initiative was anchored in a more anti-elite and antigovernment strand of thought than that of the Progressives.[13]

Populism was characterized by (1) a concern for individual self-interest and the common person's aspiration for political equality and social and economic opportunity, (2) an assumption that the common people are trustworthy and competent, and (3) a mistrust of a concentration of power in the hands of elites. Progressives were more interested in the mechanics of good government and put their faith in the educated professional class. They distrusted party bosses, and their support of the initiative can be interpreted not as an attack on representative government but as an attempt to fix it by trying to diminish the influence that special interests and party machines had over legislatures.

By and large, the current proponents of direct democracy hold similar kinds of views. Arguments in favor of expanding the initiative process to other states and to the national level are grounded in the idea that the initiative gives meaning to the notion of popular sovereignty in a way that no other institution can. Other political institutions typically involve some intermediary—such as legislatures—between citizens and the exercise of policy-making power. A large amount of the cynicism about politics that we discussed earlier in this book can be seen as frustration with the lack of responsiveness of these intermediaries.

Results from a 1997 California Poll presented in Table 7.1 and Table 7.2 (on page 136) illustrate these sentiments. These opinions suggest that citizens see themselves as peers with legislators when it comes to making decisions on laws, and that despite confusing and expensive initiative campaigns designed to sway public opinion, they believe voters can be trusted more than legislators. Citizens clearly like the idea of having a more effective voice in politics, as we have seen in previous chapters. In California, a place with great experience in using initiatives, they see direct democracy as a way to give people an effective voice. Table 7.1 lists responses to an open-ended question asking Californians what was the "best thing" about direct democracy there. Forty-four percent replied that it gives people a voice.

If we compare responses in Table 7.2 with the attitudes about politics presented in Chapter 2, then the argument in favor of expanding use of the initiative process becomes quite straightforward. Citizens have a declining regard for politics and government that is tied to declining regard for politicians—that is, at some level many no longer feel that government is *their* government. Initiatives place greater responsibility for what governments do in the hands of the voters.

TABLE 7.1   REASONS CALIFORNIANS SUPPORT DIRECT DEMOCRACY

	N	PERCENT
Gives people a voice	445	44
Allows direct participation	113	11
Allows for policy change	107	11
Forces issues onto the agenda	71	7
Makes voters aware of issues	41	4
Gets attention of politicians	19	2

Cells are numbers of volunteered responses to the open-ended question, "In your opinion, what is the best thing about proposition elections in California?" Respondents could make multiple responses.(e.g., respond "allows for policy change" and "gives people a voice").

Source: Field Research Institute, 1997, California Poll number 97-03, 1,007 respondents.

TABLE 7.2   VOTER EVALUATIONS OF REPRESENTATIVE VERSUS DIRECT DEMOCRACY

	ELECTED REPRESENTATIVES PERCENT	VOTING PUBLIC PERCENT	OTHER*
Who do you feel generally enacts more coherent and well-thought-out government policies?	38	44	18
Which do you feel is better suited to decide upon highly technical or legal policy matters?	49	37	16
Which do you feel gives more thorough review to each particular aspect of a proposed law?	46	39	15
Which do you feel is better suited to decide upon large scale government programs and projects?	30	55	15
Which do you feel is more influenced by special interest groups?	57	29	16
Which do you feel can be trusted more often to do what is right on important government issues?	19	64	17

*other = responded "both," "neither," or "don't know."
Source: Field Research Institute, 1996, California Poll number 9606, 1,023 respondents.

AGGREGATING PREFERENCES: DIRECT VERSUS REPRESENTATIVE DEMOCRACY

The initiative process also marks one of the few times it is possible to find a majority opinion on a particular topic or issue. Without, for example, direct election of the president, there is no mechanism in the United States to discover the opinion of the majority of voters. Voter opinions are generally expressed through representative institutions, institutions that, as we have seen in previous chapters, may well not reflect what the majority wants.

One theme of this book is that different electoral arrangements can produce different outcomes, and some might work better to reflect majority preferences for candidates or public policy. Figure 7.1 gives a simple example of a thirty-person society with two groups of people—we call them As and Bs. There are 16 Bs, and 14 As. Pretend that the As prefer a completely different set of public policies than the Bs, and that both groups vote as a block. In Figure 7.1, we divided these people into six legislative districts to illustrate how representative governments can distort popular preferences. As can be seen, the As win four of the six seats (two-thirds) yet are a minority opinion overall (fourteen out of thirty). Under these arrangements, the As can govern

District 1	District 2	District 3
A A A B B	A A A B B	B B B B A
Majority A	Majority A	Majority B

District 4	District 5	District 6
A A A B B	B B B B A	A A A B B
Majority A	Majority B	Majority A

FIGURE 7.1   A MAJORITY OF LEGISLATIVE DISTRICTS NEED NOT MEAN MAJORITY RULE

Note: Two groups of voters A and B are distributed into six districts. There are 14 "As" and 16 "Bs." The As have majority status in four of six districts.

and pass laws via the legislature. Without an initiative process, the Bs are left out. Of course we could have shifted district lines and produced different results, but one point should be clear: Voting majorities in a legislature need not reflect voting majorities in a state or nation.

Direct democracy may complement representative democracy by allowing popular majorities another vehicle for affecting policy. By giving voters a direct say in policy making, it may help address feelings of discontent with current processes and institutions and thus engage citizens with democracy.

In a moment we will look at four major forms of direct democracy that could be adopted at the national level in the United States. There are a number of practical questions associated with each of these, but before examining these we should first look at some of the main objections to direct democracy *per se*. Many critics of direct democracy do not simply object to the expansion of the initiative to other states or the national level, they often want to see current use of the initiative process halted and rolled back altogether.

CRITICISMS OF DIRECT DEMOCRACY

ORIGINAL INTENT

The intent of the first framers was for a *republican* form of government. By that, scholars typically mean that representatives govern, rather than direct popular majorities. This idea is expressed strongly in David Broder's objections to initiative use in the United States.[14] It is always difficult to know what the original intent of the Framers was; what we have are their words. The stress on checks and balances as well as staggered terms and federalism all suggest, independent of their writings, that the Framers really were deeply suspicious of majority rule. But these things can also be seen as reflecting their fear of the new national government, as much as popular sovereignty *per se*. In fact, Madison wrote in *The Federalist* No. 43 that republics derive their power "directly and indirectly from the great body of the people." He said states were free to "innovate" their forms of government and would remain "republican" as long as they were not "aristocratic or monarchical."[15] In 1903, the U.S. Supreme Court largely concurred, and allowed states to adopt the initiative process.[16]

Nor should we interpret the silence of the constitution on the question of the initiative process as necessarily implying disapproval. The Framers' education and their own experience of previous governments could imply that they knew that elements of direct democracy were consistent with a republican or representative democracy. Their silence could thus be seen as tacit approval.[17]

LAWS ARE POORLY WRITTEN

The drafting of initiatives is different from the legislative process. Proponents need not consult with all the groups affected by their legislation when they draft it. The drafting process also generates concerns over how thoroughly special interests dominate, since proposals can be drafted to suit their concerns at the expense of the general good. However, as we see below, well-financed, narrow interests have great difficulty convincing voters to approve their proposals.

Having amateurs or narrow interests draft laws rather than legislators, some argue, means that bad laws will result. There is, probably, something to this argument. Most successful initiatives are challenged in court, and many are invalidated in part or in whole. As Elisabeth Gerber notes, however, the same can be said of many pieces of legislation introduced by the executive and the legislature.[18] Moreover, legal challenges would seem to offer a self-correcting device. Proponents of an initiative will, presumably, be wary of the proposal being overturned and so try harder to write better laws. The same self-correction process should also be true by virtue of the election campaign: Badly drafted laws give ammunition to opponents.

TOO MUCH MONEY AND "SPECIAL-INTEREST" INFLUENCE

Money is as valuable a commodity for initiative elections as it is for any election. Simply collecting signatures to qualify can, for big states, cost upwards of $1 million. Campaigns themselves can cost tens of millions of dollars. In November 1998, with twelve measures on the California ballot, more than $192 million was spent on campaign activity for initiative proposals alone. The most expensive measure was Proposition 5 (Tribal Casinos) with $92 million spent collectively to qualify, support, and oppose the initiative.

TABLE 7.3   SPENDING FOR AND AGAINST INITIATIVES, BY TYPE OF CONTRIBUTOR

CONTRIBUTOR TYPE	TOTAL AMOUNT	PERCENT SPENT ON "YES"	PERCENT SPENT ON "NO"
Economic	$98,680,452	22	78
Citizen	$33,483,959	88	12

Source: Elisabeth Gerber, *Interest Group Influence in the California Initiative Process* (Public Policy Institute of California, 1998).

With this kind of money at play, the argument that special interest groups can dominate the process is, on the face of it, quite plausible. It seems clear that money will get a proposal onto the ballot. But the empirical evidence offers a more cautious conclusion than the one critics might suggest. Table 7.3 reports figures relating to spending on a series of California propositions from 1976 to 1996, according to whether the relevant players were narrow-interest groups ("economic" groups) or more broadly based citizen groups. As can be seen from Table 7.3, economic groups did greatly outspend citizen groups—spending nearly three times as much. The bulk of economic group spending, however, is to defeat proposals. This kind of pattern supports the argument that narrow economic groups do not use the initiative process to try and impose their own policies. After all, it is probably much cheaper for them to lobby the legislature. Rather, special interests are on the defensive and are not always successful.[19]

Table 7.4 shows that when it comes time to vote, special interests do not hold sway. As can be seen, when a citizens' group supports an initiative and economic interests oppose it, the proposals pass 64 percent of the time—despite the spending advantages that economic groups typically have. In contrast, when economic groups propose a measure (e.g., insurance reforms, tort reforms) and citizens' groups oppose it, the pass rate is only 29 percent. Others have used a different method of analysis and arrived at similar conclusions. The argument that special interests dominate, while popular and frequently voiced, is thus is not borne out by the data.

TABLE 7.4   PERCENTAGE OF INITIATIVES PASSING, BY GROUP SUPPORT AND OPPOSITION

	CITIZEN SUPPORT	ECONOMIC SUPPORT
Citizen opposition	43	29
Economic opposition	64	20

Source: Elisabeth Gerber, *Interest Group Influence in the California Initiative Process* (Public Policy Institute of California, 1998).

VOTERS ARE INCOMPETENT

Another objection is that voters are not competent to decide complex matters of public policy. True enough, levels of public information on ballot measures often tend to be low. Moreover, voters cannot rely on the usual "cues" that apply to candidates, such as party or incumbency, when they vote on ballot measures. Lacking information, many fear that voters will be easily duped by big initiative spending campaigns.

In the United States, voters may compensate for lack of information by just voting "no" when in doubt. Thus, the pass rate for initiatives is around 40 percent overall. One consistent finding seen in several studies is that campaign spending against propositions can help to increase the *no* vote. That is, negative spending has an impact but there is less evidence that spending in favor increases the *yes* vote. Voters are not, then, duped into passing anything that appears on the ballot. In fact, research shows that voters can make use of cues—from ads and from endorsements—to help orient their vote in line with their own self-interest. Endorsements by members of the political elite are especially useful since they enable voters to anchor their vote in party loyalties. If a famed right-wing politician strongly supports a proposal (and is listed in the ballot pamphlet or on TV as such) then voters of both left and right know how to orient themselves. Voters have many sources of easily available information that allow them to find such cues. Other research shows when overall spending is high then voters find it easier to orient their vote. Rather than acting to manipulate voters, higher spending campaigns inform them. This is a point we must remember when we address the issue of campaign finance reform in Chapter 8.[20]

MINORITY RIGHTS

If direct democracy means untrammeled majority rule, then one of Madison's main fears comes to the fore. Direct democracy allows majorities to be tyrannical over minorities. This opens the possibility of oppression of racial and ethnic minorities by the majority. In fact, the 1990s saw several waves of antiminority initiatives—against immigrants, non-English speakers, gays and lesbians, and affirmative action policies. Some scholars worry that minority gains via the legislative process will be undone by tyrannical and discriminatory majorities via the initiative process.[21]

Empirical evidence from the United States and Switzerland suggests that some concerns about the antiminority effects of initiatives are overstated. Donovan and Bowler analyze ballot measures relating to the civil rights of gays and lesbians to find that only 18 percent of state-wide initiatives aimed at restricting gay rights are passed. While this figure may be troubling for gays, this is a pass rate lower than for ballot propositions as a whole. Courts invalidated nearly all anti–civil rights initiatives affecting any group that did pass. A similar pattern holds for Switzerland. That is, there are relatively few measures restricting minority rights that pass, with passage rates for antiminority measures at 20 percent at the national level and 23 percent at the local level. There is a much higher pass rate of antiminority measures (62 percent) at the cantonal (state) level and there is some evidence even in the Donovan and Bowler study that direct democracy elections conducted in less populated areas may well have more of an antiminority edge. Their work suggests that minorities would have less to fear from a national initiative, since the electorate would be more heterogeneous, and, as such, less able to tyrannize any particular minority.[22]

A study of voting on California propositions by Hajnal and his colleagues asks a deceptively simple question: How often do minority voters end up on the winning or losing side of an issue? After all, if minorities win as often as everyone else, the initiative can hardly be seen as repressive of minorities. As Table 7.5 shows for a sample of initiatives in California between 1990 and

TABLE 7.5 PROBABILITY OF BEING ON THE WINNING SIDE OF DIRECT DEMOCRACY BY DEMOGRAPHIC GROUP

VOTER GROUP	PROBABILITY OF WINNING
White	63
Black	60
Asian American	60
Latino	58*
Income—low	61
Income—high	63
Education—no high school	60
Education—B.A.	63
Age—under 30	62
Age—over 65	61
Gender—woman	63
Gender—man	62
Region—Southern California	63
Region—Bay area	63
Ideology—conservative	62
Ideology—liberal	62
Partisanship—Republican	62
Partisanship—Democrat	62

*significantly different from mean voter p < .01.

Source: Z. Hajnal and E. Gerber, "Tyranny of the White Majority? Race, Ethnicity, and Outcomes in Direct Democracy in California," presented at the Midwest Political Science Association, April 2000. Probabilities and their significance levels were calculated from models estimated by Hanjal and Gerber, holding all other variables at their mean levels using a simulation procedure developed by G. King, M. Tomz, and J. Wittenberg, "Making the Most of Statistical Analysis," *American Journal of Political Science* 44 (1998): 341–355.

1998, with the exception of Latino voters this is not true for minorities as a whole. The Latino exception is a serious one to note but, even here, a majority of Latino voters are on the winning side of an issue a majority of the time.[23]

In principle it is possible for majorities to repress minorities through the initiative process. But it also remains possible for majorities to do this via legislatures. Minority populations do need entrenched legal rights and safeguards not subject to amendment by the initiative or legislature. Contemporary research on the use of direct democracy in the American states illustrates that the major critiques of direct democracy are, at best, overstated.

LESSONS FROM THE AMERICAN STATES

The growing use of initiatives in the American states gives us the opportunity to study the effects of initiatives. Since about half the states use initiatives, and half do not, scholars have been able to assess how initiatives might affect politics and policy where they are used. By extension, this might tell us something about what would happen if some form of direct democracy were used at the national level.

EFFECTS ON POLICY

A number of scholars propose that the initiative process causes public policy to better reflect the preferences of voters. The reasoning here is somewhat different from what we presented in Figure 7.1. Rather, the mere existence of initiatives can change how legislators behave. If legislators know that someone might pass a popular measure by initiative, they have greater incentives to do it themselves. Even if they don't, initiative votes can send "signals" to legislators about what the public wants done.[24] In states without initiatives, legislators face different pressures and have fewer clear signals about what the public wants. Thus, a number of studies find that certain public policies in initiative states—spending on programs, abortion regulations, death penalty laws, and some civil rights policies—more closely match public opinion in those states than in noninitiative states.[25]

It is also clear that initiatives lead to the adoption of electoral reform and "governance" policies that legislators might not prefer. By giving groups outside the legislature a tool to craft policies, initiatives can advance policies that run counter to the self-interests of elected officials. States with the initiative process thus are more likely to have adopted policies that constrain how legislators govern: term limits, supermajority requirements for new taxes, tax and expenditure limitations, and campaign finance reforms.[26] One problem with this, however, is that legislators may have greater difficulty writing coherent budgets in initiative states.[27]

EFFECTS ON POLITICS

A body of democratic theory proposes that people learn how to be citizens by making decisions in groups and by participating in politics. Greater democratic participation has an *educative* role and can breed civic maturation. If this is so, initiatives—by forcing people to deliberate about public issues—might lead to a more engaged, informed, and interested citizenry. Direct voting on policy matters increases discussion about public policy and, at least at a minimal level, forces voters to think about the issues put on the ballot.

A number of recent studies show that there might be some merit to the idea that direct democracy makes citizens more engaged with politics. Comparisons of behavior and attitudes between states that use initiatives frequently and those that do not demonstrate that initiatives are associated with increased voter turnout, particularly in off-year elections. The presence of highly visible initiatives on a state ballot may also be associated with higher levels of general knowledge about politics. Our own research has found that citizens in states with frequent initiative use feel more competent when participating in politics, are more likely to think that they "have a say," and are more likely to think that officials care about what they think.[28] In other words, the use of initiatives may combat some of the cynicism about politics we describe in Chapter 2. Similar results regarding the relationship between efficacy and direct democracy have been found in Switzerland.[29]

MAJOR FORMS OF DIRECT DEMOCRACY

If direct democracy were to be adopted in the United States at the national level, what might it look like? There are four basic models to discuss: the nationwide referendum, a national advisory initiative, a nationwide indirect initiative, and the nationwide binding initiative. Apart from advisory votes, all of these proposals would probably require a constitutional amendment to enact.

NATIONAL LEGISLATIVE REFERENDUM

As we noted earlier, governments in European nations, Australia, and Canada have, over the past few years, offered their citizens a chance to vote directly on a number of highly salient and important issues. In 2000, for example, Australia went to the polls to decide whether to remove the queen as head of state and replace her with a president. Australia's choice of a national anthem was also a national referendum issue. By and large, however, referendums have often been used to allow voter ratification of major constitutional changes proposed by a government, as was the case with Canada's failed 1992 referendum on new constitutional arrangements designed to accommodate Quebec.

The advantage to such a process is that it allows voters a say on key issues and provides popular legitimacy to elite proposals. This is important when designing new political institutions and when adopting some major policy changes. Referendums on institutional changes directly address the concerns of citizens that were described in Chapter 2. Consider, for example, the popular legitimacy of joining the European Union in a nation that decided the question by a public vote, compared to another nation where legislators simply imposed their decision to join on a skeptical public.

The downside of the referendum process is that it is one driven largely by political elites and not by voters or groups from outside of government. The timing of the election, the phrasing of the question, and, in some instances, the interpretation of the result are typically left to the government of the day. However, the referendum process could help break partisan deadlocks that some see as plaguing the American political system. If a simple majority in one chamber of Congress were able to place a question before the public in a *binding* vote, legislators could have a tool to force a floor vote on contested popular bills that might otherwise die. Legislative referendums could also give Congress another way to challenge a presidential veto (by going to the people). Referendums might also allow legislators some cover from difficult votes, by allowing voters themselves to decide matters. Legislative referendums modeled after the European practice could also provide a faster method for amending the U.S. Constitution.

ADVISORY INITIATIVES

Another model is the advisory initiative as used in New Zealand. Registered voters can sign a petition requesting the government hold a vote on a particular issue. For a vote to take place, petitioners must collect signatures equal to some threshold—in New Zealand, the threshold is 10 percent of all registered voters. The equivalent of this in the United States would be about 12,500,000 people as of 2002. A citizen-initiated referendum is not binding on New Zealand's government or on Parliament, and the government can ignore the result if they wish.

One idea behind advisory initiatives is that it allows enough legislative discretion for minority groups to be protected from an oppressive and well-organized majority. Demands for initiatives in New Zealand stemmed from seemingly widespread opposition to attempts to decriminalize homosexuality and ban discrimination on the grounds of sexual orientation.[30] If initiatives are merely advisory, citizens can use them to send signals to government, but governments may ignore badly drafted or oppressive laws and develop their own response. Advisory votes let citizens express their opinion on issues that they feel are not being adequately addressed by legislators. Moreover, under this system groups outside government get to set the agenda.

One major downside to advisory initiatives is that governments can simply and completely ignore the views of voters. Since 1994, three referenda have come about as the result of citizen's petitions in New Zealand: on fire service staffing levels (1995); on the number of representatives in Parliament (1999); and on changes to the criminal justice system (1999). In each case the public has overwhelmingly supported the proposal of the petitioners. However, governments have (so far) almost completely ignored the results. If governments do ignore the views of voters it would seem to open up the possibility of making trust in government drop even further. At minimum, however, an advisory vote that produces a definitive outcome can make it difficult for rival parties to each claim to follow the public's wishes while they pursue opposite policies.

INDIRECT INITIATIVE

Some forms of direct democracy allow citizen groups a direct say in writing laws, yet still incorporate the legislature in the process. In one version—the indirect initiative—voters sign a petition favoring a piece of legislation that is presented to the legislature before any popular vote. If the legislature fails to approve the measure, or amends it in a way not acceptable to those who proposed the measure, then it is placed on the ballot. Some American states allow their legislature to put an alternative proposal on the ballot along with the original initiative. Versions of this process are found in nine U.S. states and some European nations, most notably Switzerland, Austria, Spain, and Italy. In some places, if the legislature accepts the initiative proposal, it need not go to popular vote.

Swiss national initiatives are indirect in the sense that the government may accept the proposal, reject it (and trigger a public vote), or reject it and offer voters the initiative and a rival proposal. Swiss initiatives may be formulated only on constitutional questions and can't be changed by Parliament and the government. For such an initiative to be organized, the signatures of 100,000 voters (approximately 2 percent of eligible voters) must be collected within eighteen months. Of the 104 Swiss national initiatives that qualified between 1891 and 1991, roughly 10 percent were approved by voters (6 were accepted by parliament). As with the U.S. states, then, voters are clearly unwilling to approve everything they see on the ballot.

The Swiss government always takes a stand on these proposals—usually in opposition. Governments have recommended accepting only three of the ninety-eight proposals voted on in the 100 years from 1891 to 1991.[31] Sometimes the government responds to initiatives with a counterproposal (generally less far-reaching) in the hope that the people will vote for its proposal over the initiative. The possibility of a double "yes" vote exists: Voters may approve both the initiative and the counterproposal. A procedure determines which of the two proposals become law if both secure a majority. The Swiss have used national initiatives to make decisions about compulsory military service, the existence of an army, environmental issues, and immigration policy.

The indirect initiative may be regarded as an adjunct to constitutional government because it adds an additional check or safeguard on the exercise of legislative power. In effect it involves giving the electorate a veto over the works of politicians. Citizens use initiatives to propose new laws and to undo laws that a legislature might pass. Like all vetoes, it may be used to frustrate good laws as well as foil bad ones, but that drawback applies equally to every policy-making process whether it be legislative (direct or representative) or judicial.

A more formal direct democracy veto procedure is the *abrogative referendum* found in Italy and Switzerland. Voters circulate a petition to require that some existing law be put to a popular vote. Thus voters can initiate a process to repeal legislation. Italian voters used this process in 1993 when a referendum canceled their existing electoral law. In this way, Italian voters managed to place electoral reform on the political agenda—by repealing the old law, they forced parliament to write new ones. The threat of additional referendums forced parliament to draft laws that responded to public disgust with the election system. Switzerland, too, has such a system in place, although it is harder to use in some respects than the initiative process. Voters have ninety days to gather signatures to challenge a law. Roughly 7 percent of bills in the Federal Assembly have been challenged this way, the challenge being successful 60 percent of the time.[32]

Again, like the advisory initiative, indirect initiatives allow the possibility for the legislature to tidy up badly drafted laws proposed by citizens, and to either stop or at least delay repressive ones. The disadvantages of these indirect initiative processes are that if legislators can amend or modify a proposal, then they have the ability to cut the teeth out of any proposal. Moreover, it is not always clear what happens after a law is passed by voters or abrogated by them. Under some circumstances the legislature can, after a suitable delay, simply reintroduce a piece of legislation (under the abrogative system) or amend it away (under the indirect system).

A NATIONAL INITIATIVE

A direct citizens' initiative process of the kind found in American states is not used at the national level anywhere in the world. The closest example is that of Switzerland, which has, technically, an indirect process. A direct national initiative would allow public votes on citizen-drafted laws, leaving the legislature with no role in shaping the proposal. If constitutional initiative amendments are allowed, legislators and courts could have virtually no role in the process. Initiatives that deal with statutes only, on the other hand, could be reviewed by courts and amended by legislators just like any other law. In 1977, Congress held hearings on a Joint Senate Resolution that would have provided for a national statutory initiative process.[33]

Introducing a binding, direct national initiative for the United States, even if only for statutory laws, may present some difficult practical problems. Scaling up the process from the state to a national level may be a stumbling block. It is not necessarily clear that having initiatives in such a large electorate is feasible. If the California model were scaled up to the national level, it would take approximately 6 million signatures to qualify an initiative for a vote. Spending on campaigns could run into hundreds of millions of dollars. There is also the question of turnout. In many U.S. elections, turnout is below 50 percent. Although initiatives might stimulate turnout, what level is required to give "majority" approval of direct legislation a measure of legitimacy? This is an important question when elected representatives are completely shut out of the legislative process. Italy requires at least 50 percent turnout for a direct vote to be valid. These factors may well present too many practical objections.

Other practical questions concern the kind of *federal* majority that would be required to approve something—an issue if any of these forms of direct democracy should be adopted by the United States. Switzerland requires a double majority—a majority of voters and a majority of cantons (states) must approve an initiative. Australia requires the same thing for legislative referendums. This kind of provision in the United States—one very much in the spirit of the Constitution—would make it difficult to pass initiatives since opponents would only have to win twenty-five states to defeat a proposal, while proponents would have to win twenty-six states *and* a majority of the population.

There are organizations promoting a national initiative for the United States who try to address some of these problems in their proposal. These groups, including Philadelphia II and The Democracy Foundation, have proposed a constitutional amendment that would allow qualification of initiative proposals with conventional (paper) petitions, Internet signatures, or public opinion polls. The latter methods would lower qualification costs and allow citizens to vote on a wide range of constitutional and statutory measures. They propose to collect signatures equal to half of all registered U.S. voters in order to amend the Constitution with their Democracy Amendment.

CONCLUSIONS

Experience from American states and many established democratic nations illustrate that direct democracy has much to offer. It comes in many forms, and each provides a different way to enhance how citizens are incorporated into the polity. As such, it offers a way to strengthen the link between citizens and their government, and to enhance the legitimacy of democratic governments. There is even evidence, from the United States and Switzerland, that, if only at a minimal level, experience with direct democracy builds better democratic citizens.

This said, we must acknowledge that direct democracy is pretty unpopular both among professional political scientists and also the American media that covers politics. Part of this, we assume, comes from many American observers having a passing familiarity with the west coast experience with ballot initiatives. Disdain for this form of direct democracy comes from legitimate fears about how minorities are treated, but also from many observers annoyed with the "professionalization" of initiative campaigns. Objections are also based on personal disagreements with general policy outcomes associated with the process, or with a sense that electoral majorities must have been stupid to have approved such policies.[34]

As we note above, antiminority initiatives are checked by courts. As for other concerns, we note that initiative politics, just like *candidate* politics, football, journalism, charity fundraising, the Olympics, higher education, and many other parts of life have become more professionalized. There may be more to mourn about professionalization of Olympic hockey than about professionalization of politics. At least the former was the realm of amateurs in the past. We suggest that direct democracy be considered based on the merits of the process, and not based on objections to the people and policies that are currently associated with it. Direct democracy is something that citizens expect, and it is something that they get in most well-functioning democracies. The west coast initiative process has its faults—but it is only one form of direct democracy that could be considered for the United States.

NOTES

1. There is substantial debate about how far popular sovereignty extends in the United States. For example, if all sovereignty lies with "the people," and not the Constitution, then can a majority of citizens who agree on new political arrangements be bound by any pre-existing constitutional rules? See Akhil Amar, "Popular Sovereignty and Constitutional Amendment," paper prepared for the National Initiative for Democracy Conference, Williamsburg, VA, <http://ni4d.us/library.htm#articles>; Akhil Amar, "Of Sovereignty and Federalism," *Yale Law Journal* 96 (1987); Akhil Amar, "The Central Meaning of a Republican Government: Popular Sovereignty, Majority Rule, and the Denominator Problem," *Columbia University Law Review* 749 (1994); Richard D. Parker, "The 'First Principle' of Popular Sovereignty: Politics without End," paper prepared for the National Initiative for Democracy Conference, 2002, Williamsburg, VA <http://ni4d.us/library.htm#articles>.
2. Russell Dalton, Wilhelm Burklin, and Andrew Drummond, "Public Attitudes toward Direct Democracy," *Journal of Democracy* (October 2001): 141–153. See Matthew Mendelshon and Andrew Parkin, eds., *Referendum Democracy: Citizens, Elites, and Deliberation in Referendum Campaigns* (London: Palgrave, 2001); and David Butler and Austin Ranney, eds., *Referendums around the World: The Growing Use of Direct Democracy* (Washington, D.C.: AEI Press, 1994). Recent examples include votes on various treaties associated with European integration. See, for example, Andres Todal Jenssen and Ola Listaug, "Voters Decisions in the Nordic EU Referendums of 1994," in *Referendum Democracy*, ed. Matthew Mendelson and Andrew Parkin (New York: Palgrave, 2001); and Simon Hug, "Referendums on European Integration: Do Institutions Matter in the Voter's Decision?" *Comparative Political Studies* 33 (2000): 3–36. Other examples include votes on divorce in Ireland and Italy, abortion in Ireland, on Spain joining

NATO, nuclear power in Sweden in 1980, and Senate reform in France in 1969. See Shaun Bowler and Todd Donovan, "Popular Control of Referendum Agendas," in *Referendum Democracy*, ed. Matthew Mendelson and Andrew Parkin (New York: Palgrave, 2001).

3. Howard Ernst, "The Historic Role of Narrow-Material Interests in Initiative Politics," in *Dangerous Democracy: The Battle over Ballot Initiatives in America*, ed. Larry Sabato, Bruce Larson, and Howard Ernst (Lanham, MD: Rowman and Littlefield, 2001).

4. The following discussion is largely taken from Charles Price and Charles Bell, *California Government Today: Politics of Reform*, 5th ed. (Ft. Worth, TX: International Thomason Publishers, 1995). For more detailed discussion, see California Ballot Initiative Process, produced by the Secretary of State's office <http://www.ss.ca.gov/elections/elections.htm>.

5. Australians have voted on dozens of national matters, and most recently rejected a constitutional proposal to switch from a monarchy to a republic in 1999. See Brian Galligan, "Amending Constitutions through the Referendum Device," in *Referendum Democracy*, ed. Matthew Mendelson and Andrew Parkin (New York: Palgrave, 2001). On the 1992 Canadian referendum, see Richard Johnston et al., *The Challenge of Direct Democracy* (Montreal: McGill-Queens University Press, 1996).

6. The 1999 New Zealand Election study found that 65 percent agreed that referendums were "good things." Fifty-five percent gave this response in a 2000 Canadian poll. Only 1 percent in New Zealand and only 8 percent in Canada agreed that referendums were "bad things." The NZ data is available at <http://www.nzes.org>. The authors thank Matthew Mendelshon of Queens University for placing this question on his Canadian poll. Use of direct democracy in each nation is discussed in S. Bowler, T. Donovan, and J. Karp, "When Might Institutions Change? Elite Support for Direct Democracy in Three Nations," *Political Research Quarterly* (December 2002).

7. On Europe, see Russell Dalton, Wilhelm Burkin, and Andrew Drummond, "Public Opinion and Direct Democracy," *Journal of Democracy* 12, no. 4 (2001): 141–153. Of those who were familiar with the Swiss system, over 66 percent of respondents in most nations agreed it should be considered for their own nation.

8. John Hibbing and Elizabeth Theiss-Morse, *Congress as Public Enemy* (New York: Cambridge University Press, 1995). They find that only 24 percent of Americans approved of Congress as "the collection of members" but that 88 percent supported Congress "the permanent institution" (p. 106). Approval (of members of Congress) increased dramatically after September 11, 2001, but declined subsequently. See Brian Gaines, "Where's the Rally? Approval and Trust of Government since September 11," *PS: Political Science and Politics* (September 2002).

9. On trends in use of initiatives in the United States, see David Magleby, "Direct Legislation in the American States," in *Referendums around the World*, ed. David Butler and Austin Ranney (Washington, D.C.: American Enterprise Institute). See also S. Bowler, T. Donovan, and C. Tolbert, eds., *Citizens as Legislators: Direct Democracy in the American States* (Columbus, OH: Ohio State University Press, 1998).

10. Washington data are from the author's statewide polls, conducted by Applied Research Northwest in 1999. California data are from a 1996 Field/California Poll (F9604). The authors thank Janine Parry for placing initiative questions on the 2000 Arkansas Poll. In these polls, respondents were asked if they thought referendums "were good things, bad things, or neither good nor bad?" Only 3 percent in Washington, 7 percent in California, and 2 percent in Arkansas agreed that they were "bad things."

11. In 1987, a Gallup-conducted poll for Thomas Cronin found that 58 percent of respondents supported a national *advisory* initiative process, with 48 percent supporting a national "referendum." A 2001 poll found 57 percent of Americans approved of a national initiative similar to that used in the states. Two-thirds of respondents agreed that voters would be more likely to produce laws "in the public interest" than legislators. Extensive poll data on national initiatives and referendum may be found on the IRI Web site <http://www.iandrinstitute.org>.

12. These statements are based on the author's survey of legislators from California, Washington, and Oregon, and voter opinion polls from California and Washington. See S. Bowler, T. Donovan, M. Neiman, and J. Peel, "Institutional Threat and Partisan Outcomes: Legislative Candidates' Attitudes toward Direct Democracy," *State Politics and Policy Quarterly* 1, no. 4 (2001): 364–379.

13. Bruce Cain and Kenneth P. Miller, "The Populist Legacy: Initiatives and the Undermining of Representative Government," in Larry Sabato, Bruce Larson, and Howard Ernst, eds., 2001.

14. David S. Broder, *Democracy Derailed: Initiative Campaigns and the Power of Money* (New York: Harcourt, 2000). Hans Linde, former Justice of the Oregon State Supreme Court, also uses the republican government argument against the expansion of direct democracy. See Hans Linde, "On Reconstructing Republican Government," *Oklahoma City University Law Review* 19 (1994): 193.

15. William T. Mayton, "Direct Democracy: Federalism and the Guarantee Clause," paper presented at the National Initiative for Democracy Conference, 2002 <http://www.ni4d.us. library>.

16. *Kadderly v. City of Portland* (1903); Also see *Pacific States Telephone and Telegraph v. Oregon* (1909).

17. Natelson, 2000.

18. Elisabeth Gerber, *Populist Paradox: Interest Group Influence and the Promise of Direct Legislation* (Princeton, NJ: Princeton University Press, 1999), p. 164.

19. The figures are from Gerber, 1999, whose book remains the best study of interest groups and the initiative process. See also Elisabeth Gerber, Arthur Lupia, M. McCubbins, and D. R. Keiwiet, *Stealing the Initiative: How State Government Responds to Direct Democracy* (Upper Saddle River, NJ: Prentice Hall, 2001). Our own research, using different methods, produced similar results. See T. Donovan, et al., Chapter 4 in *Citizens as Legislators*, ed. S. Bowler, T. Donovan, and C. Tolbert (Athens, OH: Ohio University Press, 1998).

20. Arthur Lupia, "Shortcuts versus Encyclopedias: Information and Voting Behavior in the California Insurance Reform Elections," *American Political Science Review* 88 (1994): 63–76; S. Bowler and T. Donovan, *Demanding Choices: Opinion, Voting, and Direct Democracy* (Ann Arbor, MI: University of Michigan Press, 1998); Elisabeth Gerber and Arthur Lupia, "Campaign Competition and Policy Responsiveness in Direct Legislation Elections, *Political Behavior.* 17 (1995): 287–306; Elisabeth Gerber, *The Populist Paradox;* Elisabeth Gerber, Arthur Lupia, M. McCubbins, and D. R. Keiwiet, *Stealing the Initiative.*

21. Bruce Cain, "Voting Rights and Democratic Theory: Toward a Color-Blind Society," in *Controversies in Minority Voting*, ed. B. Grofman and C. Davidson (Washington, D.C.: Brookings, 1992).

22. Bruno S. Frey and Lorenz Gotte, "Does the Popular Vote Destroy Minority Rights?" *American Journal of Political Science* 42 (1999): 1343–1348; Todd Donovan and Shaun Bowler, "Direct Democracy and Minority Rights," *American Journal of Political Science* 43 (1998):1020–1025.

23. Zoltan Hajnal, Elisabeth Gerber, and Hugh Louch, "Minorities and Direct Legislation: Evidence from California Ballot Propositions," *Journal of Politics* 64 (2002): 154–177.

24. Thomas Romer and Howard Rosenthal, "Political Resource Allocation, Controlled Agendas, and the Status Quo," *Public Choice* 32 (1979): 27–44; Elisabeth Gerber, "Legislative Responsiveness to the Threat of Popular Initiatives," *American Journal of Political Science* 40 (1996): 99–128.

25. Elisabeth Gerber, 1996; Gerber, 1999; Gerber and Hug, 2001; see also John Matsusaka, "Fiscal Effects of the Voter Initiative: Evidence from the Last 30 Years," *Journal of Political Economy;* John Matsusaka, "Problems with a Methodology Used to Evaluate the Voter Initiative," *Journal of Politics* 63 (2001): 1250–1256. Conversely, see Edward L. Lascher, Jr., Michael Hagen, and Steven Rochlin, "Gun behind the Door? Ballot Initiatives, State Politics, and Public Opinion," *Journal of Politics* 58 (1996): 760–775; Michael Hagen, Edward L. Lasher, Jr., John F. Camorbreco, "Response to Matsusaka," *Journal of Politics* 63 (2001): 1257–1263.

26. On term limits and tax limitations, see Caroline Tolbert, "Governance Policies," in S. Bowler, T. Donovan, and C. Tolbert, eds., 1998. On campaign finance regulations, see John Pippen, Shaun Bowler, and Todd Donovan, "Election Reform and Direct Democracy: The Case of Campaign Finance Reform," *American Politics Research* 30 (2002): 559–582.

27. Todd Donovan and Shaun Bowler, 1998; Peter Schrag, *Paradise Lost: California's Experience, America's Future* (New York: New Press, 1998). Also see David S. Broder, *Democracy Derailed: Initiative Campaigns and the Power of Money* (New York: Harcourt, 2000).

28. On turnout, see C. J. Tolbert, Grummel, and D. Smith, "The Effects of Ballot Initiatives on Voter Turnout in the American States," *American Politics Research* 29, no. 6 (2001): 625–648; Mark Smith, "The Contingent Effects of Ballot Initiatives and Candidate Races on Turnout," *American Journal of Political Science* 45 (2001): 700–706. On knowledge, see Mark Smith, "Ballot Initiatives and Democratic Citizenship," *Journal of Politics* 64 (2002): 892–903. On engagement, see S. Bowler and T. Donovan, *British Journal of Political Science.*

29. Bruno Frey and Alois Stutzer, "Happiness, Economy, and Institutions," Institute for Empirical Research in Economics, Working paper No. 15, 1999.

30. J. Parkinson, "Who Knows Best? The Creation of the Citizen-Initiated Referendum in New Zealand," *Government and Opposition* 6, no. 3 (2001): 403–421.

31. Philip L. Dubois and Floyd Feeney, *Lawmaking by Initiative: Issues, Options, and Comparisons* (New York: Agathon, 1998), p. 56.

32. On Switzerland, see W. Linder, *Swiss Democracy* (New York: St Martin's Press, 1994), p. 100. On referendums more generally, see D. Butler and A. Ranney, 1994, pp. 62–63; Dubois and Feeney, 1998. For studies of these issues in the United States, see Bowler, Donovan, and Tolbert, 1998; Bowler and Donovan, 1998.

33. Ronald D. Allen, "The National Initiative Proposal: A Preliminary Analysis, *University of Nebraska Law Review* 58 (1979): 965.

34. The most recent example of criticism of the initiative process and spirited defense of representative—or as it is sometimes confusingly known, republican government, is by David Broder, 2000. See also Peter Schrag's thoughtful critique emphasizing California's experience. Republican government more typically means the absence of a monarch.

8

CAMPAIGN FINANCE

A well-functioning democracy requires that candidates for office be able to communicate with voters, and that voters are able to obtain information about candidates who seek office. Without communication and information, voters cannot make well-informed choices in an election. Ideally, voters would know something about who the actual source of information was during a campaign, so as to evaluate its credibility. In a perfect world, incumbents and challengers would also be on a level playing field when they compete to get their messages out to voters. But communication on a mass scale is not cheap. Elections cost money. One key question for any democracy, then, is how should elections be financed? Should the burden fall on individual candidates, on political parties, or on the government? Should campaign spending be limited? The answer to these question present a number of dilemmas: If campaign expenditures increase the levels of information that voters have about candidates, does lower spending mean the public might be less informed? If candidates and parties assume the burden of financing their own campaigns, do campaign donors end up having a privileged place in the political system?

WHY IS THE PUBLIC CYNICAL ABOUT CAMPAIGN FINANCE?

In Chapter 2, we described some of the reasons that people don't trust government. In the last few decades, a growing proportion of the American public has come to believe that government is run on behalf of narrow, special interests, and not for the benefit of everyone. A majority of American citizens believe that public officials don't care about them, that their representatives lack integrity, and that politicians will say anything and do anything to get elected.

We have argued that some of this discontent may result from election procedures that leave many citizens feeling underrepresented, and from election rules that produce candidates that many voters simply dislike. But that is only part of the problem. Large majorities of Americans believe that the system used to finance political campaigns is either unethical or corrupt, and that it skews representation to favor the interests of wealthy donors over the interests of the average citizen. Table 8.1 displays the results of various polls indicating Americans' distaste for their campaign finance system. If these data are any indication, part of the cynicism about politics we see in America may be due to the fact that citizens see their representatives as "on the take." As noted in the chapter on presidential nominations, Americans also believe that large donors, rather than voters, have the most influence in the selection of presidential candidates.

This cynicism about the role of money in politics is understandable if we consider some facts associated with campaign finance in the United States. We saw in Chapter 3 that congressional races and other elections are rarely competitive, in part because incumbents receive the vast majority of campaign contributions. Campaign spending, furthermore, is rising each year. Spending by congressional candidates rose by 36 percent from 1998 to 2000. Parties collected almost twice as much "soft money" in 2000 as in 1996.[1] Federal candidates spent over $1 billion in the 2000 election cycle, while the Democratic and Republican parties spent an additional $1.1 billion. This means

TABLE 8.1   AMERICAN ATTITUDES ABOUT CAMPAIGN FINANCE

DO YOU THINK MANY PUBLIC OFFICIALS MAKE OR CHANGE POLICY DECISIONS AS A DIRECT RESULT OF MONEY THEY RECEIVE FROM MAJOR CAMPAIGN CONTRIBUTORS?

Yes	73%
No	13
Don't know	15

Source: CBS News poll, conducted January 15–17, 2002.

DO YOU THINK POLITICIANS DO SPECIAL FAVORS FOR PEOPLE AND GROUPS WHO GIVE THEM CAMPAIGN CONTRIBUTIONS?

Yes, happens a lot	80%
Yes, happens sometimes	13
No	6

Source: TNS Intersearch, Horsham, PA, March 22–25, 2001.

HOW WOULD YOU DESCRIBE THE CURRENT WAY IN WHICH CANDIDATES FOR FEDERAL OFFICE RAISE MONEY FOR THEIR CAMPAIGNS?

Corrupt	31%
Unethical, but not corrupt	46
Nothing seriously wrong	15

Source: CNN/Time poll (Yankelovich & Harris), March 21–22, 2001.

that candidates are spending more and more time chasing contributions for themselves, for PACs they control, and for their parties. One study found that 43 percent of U.S. House candidates, and 55 percent of candidates for statewide office report spending at least 25 percent of their time simply raising money for their elections.[2]

Scholars are somewhat divided about whether there is a systematic relationship between contributions and how politicians vote on bills. A number of studies find an empirical link between contributions and votes, while others find weak effects or no relationship. Since contributors tend to give to people who sympathize with their plight in the first place, it is somewhat difficult to tease out the causal relationship between contributions and votes. Nevertheless, it is clear that money affects how representatives behave, and that the public is aware of this fact. Studies have identified links between interest group donations and victory in legislative races, between contributions and legislative assistance for contributors, and between contributions and interest group access to legislators.[3]

There is also strong anecdotal evidence that contributions buy government positions (ambassadors), key amendments to legislation, presidential pardons (i.e., Marc Rich), narrowly targeted expenditures, and tax cuts (ADM and Ethanol); and that contributions to key committee chairs go hand-in-hand with winning major government contracts (Lockheed, Global Crossings, etc.). Money clearly buys access and can block action. The *New York Times* reported that the Bush Energy Department consulted with sixty-four energy corporations and industry trade groups in 2001 (and just one environmental group) when considering new rules for how (or if) the Clean Air Act would be enforced. Industry representatives at the meetings contributed $8.4 million to federal candidates from 1999–2001.[4] Another *Times* report noted that eighteen of the top twenty-five energy industry contributors advised Vice President Cheney's secretive national energy task force in 2001.[5] Some argue that this sort of interest-groups influence, in the long run, weakens the national economy by providing narrowly targeted benefits to specific firms and industries at the expense of the general public.[6]

CAMPAIGN FINANCE IN AMERICA

HARD MONEY

There are many ways for money to help elect or defeat candidates in the United States, including direct *hard* money spending, and indirect *soft* money spending. In 1974, Congress responded to fundraising scandals associated with Richard Nixon's 1972 presidential reelection campaign by amending the Federal Election Campaign Act. The amendments placed limits on what groups, candidates, and parties could spend in federal (but not state or local) elections, and set up an independent agency, the Federal Election Commission

(FEC), to enforce the law. The law required that individuals or groups who give money to federal candidates, or spend money on behalf of candidates, make public what they were spending. Corporations, unions, and foreign nationals were banned from making *direct* contributions to candidates. In 1976 the U.S. Supreme Court ruled in *Buckley v. Valeo* that limits on expenditures violated First Amendment protections of free speech, unless they were combined with voluntary acceptance of public campaign funds. However, the Court maintained limitations on contributions.

Corporations, unions, and other interest groups can contribute to federal candidates indirectly, through Political Action Committees (PACs) they set up to raise funds from individuals via voluntary contributions. The 1974 amendments limited PAC contributions to $5,000 per candidate per election, and limited individuals to $1,000 per candidate, per election. Individuals could also give $5,000 to any PAC, and PACs could also give $5,000 to other PACs. Individuals and PACs could also give $20,000 to a national party committee. The 1974 law placed no limits on the total funds that a PAC can give in a year, but individuals were limited to $25,000 (to candidates, PACs, or parties). As of 1998, there were 1,700 corporate PACs registered with FEC, 900 "nonconnected" PACs, 800 "trade/membership/health" PACs, and about 370 union PACs. Money raised from PACs, parties, and individuals under limits established by the FECA came to be known as "hard money."

Figure 8.1 illustrates the levels of hard money raised by congressional candidates from 1984 to 2002. In the 2000 election cycle, federal candidates

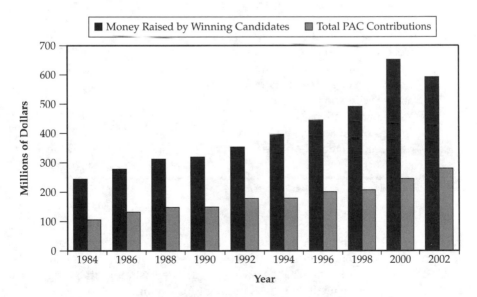

FIGURE 8.1   CANDIDATE FUNDRAISING IN CONGRESSIONAL ELECTIONS

Source: Federal Election Commission, various reports.

TABLE 8.2   TOP "HARD MONEY" PAC CONTRIBUTORS, 1999–2000

Democrats

International Brotherhood of Electrical Workers	$2,536,525
American Federation of St/Cnty/Mun Employees	2,457,974
Teamsters Union	2,369,595
Association of Trial Lawyers of America	2,301,000
Machinists/Aerospace Workers Union	2,164,138
United Auto Workers	2,125,050
Laborers Union	2,037,700
United Food & Commercial Workers Union	1,694,152
Service Employees International Union	1,653,524
National Education Association	1,634,875
American Federation of Teachers	1,571,655
Carpenters & Joiners Union	1,563,300
Communications Workers of America	1,462,945
National Association of Realtors	1,390,743
Ironworkers Union	1,326,700

Republicans

National Association of Realtors	$2,026,698
National Auto Dealers Association	1,687,700
National Beer Wholesalers Association	1,478,500
National Rifle Association	1,333,074
National Association of Home Builders	1,182,199
United Parcel Service	1,139,195
Verizon Communications	1,125,933
Associated Builders & Contractors	1,073,750
American Bankers Association	1,067,636
American Medical Association	1,059,869
National Federation of Independent Business	977,867
SBC Communications	898,625
Americans for a Republican Majority	847,391
Credit Union National Association	777,568
FedEx Corp	765,580

Source: Opensecrets.org, based on FEC records.

raised over $1 billion in hard money alone, mostly from individual contributors giving $1,000 per candidate. PACs contributed about one-third of all funds to U.S. House candidates in 2000, however, with the vast majority going to incumbents. Table 8.2 lists the top hard money PAC donors for Republicans and Democrats in the 2000 election cycle.

SOFT MONEY

Soft money refers to funds raised and spent on federal election contests that fall outside of the hard money federal expenditure and contribution limits. A once little-noticed footnote in the Court's *Buckley* decision, plus a 1979 amendment to the FECA and subsequent Federal Election Commission rulings, all set the stage for a revolution in how elections would be financed by the year 2000.

In 1979, Congress altered limits on fundraising by amending the FECA to allow state and local party committees to raise and spend unlimited amounts on certain "party building" activities (get-out-the-vote drives in support of the party's nominees and the production of campaign materials). FEC rulings eventually allowed nearly unlimited individual, union, and corporate contributions directly to parties. Thus by the 1990s, if someone wanted to give $100,000 or more to influence elections, they could do so in a single contribution if it went to a party committee. Nearly 1,000 organizations gave over $100,000 apiece to party committees in 2000. Table 8.3 (on page 158) lists the top twenty-five soft-money contributors from 1999–2000. Although party soft money was, ostensibly, to be spent on grass-roots party building activities, the Brennen Center estimates that only eight cents per dollar of party soft money is spent on such things. The largest chunk goes to finance televised campaign ads attacking or promoting candidates.[7]

In *Buckley*, the Court distinguished between individuals and groups that expressly advocate the election or defeat of a candidate, and those that did not. Groups that did not use words such as "vote for" or "vote against" in their commercials could avoid contribution limits and disclosure related to their "independent" campaign spending on behalf of a federal candidate. This distinction was not noticed much in 1976, but by 1996, a few "noncandidate" groups—parties, corporations, unions, and interest groups—began taking full advantage of it to broadcast "issue ads" attacking or promoting candidates. One study found about thirty groups (in addition to the parties) used the soft-money, issue-ad strategy in the 1996 election. By 2000, there were at least 125 groups using unregulated independent issue ads to affect federal elections.

Although parties still must disclose how they raise and spend their soft money, other groups need not. FECA rules designed to disclose who was paying for campaigns were eviscerated in the 1990s by the use of groups incorporated under Section 527 of the IRS code. When someone seeking to help a candidate established a nonprofit, noncandidate "educational" Section 527 group, donors to the group could enjoy tax deductions while avoiding contribution limitations and disclosure requirements. By establishing a Section 527 organization, individuals, corporations, unions, foreign nationals, or anyone could contribute unlimited amounts of untraceable money to a group that would technically campaign independent of the candidate, but on his behalf. In 2000 many groups used Section 527 organizations and similar front

TABLE 8.3   TOP SOFT MONEY CONTRIBUTORS, 1999–2000

ORGANIZATION	TOTAL	TO DEMS	TO REPUBS
Am. Fed St/Cnty/Mun Employees	$5,949,000	$5,949,000	$0
AT&T	4,398,920	1,776,269	2,622,651
Service Employees Int. Union	4,288,096	4,257,696	30,400
Bank of America	3,147,824	3,005,047	142,555
Carpenters & Joiners Union	2,873,500	2,873,500	0
Comm. Workers of America	2,405,000	2,405,000	0
Freddie Mac	2,398,250	1,025,000	1,373,250
Philip Morris	2,383,453	296,641	2,086,812
Microsoft Corp.	2,316,926	996,792	1,318,384
United Food & Comm. Workers	2,146,450	2,146,450	0
Global Crossing	2,083,195	1,161,652	921,543
SBC Communications	1,860,853	876,621	984,232
Bristol-Myers Squibb	1,740,951	213,250	1,527,701
Intl. Bhood of Elect Workers	1,730,000	1,730,000	0
Enron Corp.	1,671,555	532,565	1,138,990
American Fed. of Teachers	1,657,000	1,657,000	0
MGM Mirage	1,563,086	713,086	850,000
Slim-Fast Foods	1,563,000	1,543,000	20,000
Pfizer Inc.	1,558,817	160,000	1,398,817
Citigroup Inc.	1,511,014	763,806	747,208
Saban Entertainment	1,496,000	1,496,000	0
National Rifle Assn.	1,489,222	0	1,489,222
Verizon Communications	1,473,451	573,800	899,651
Williams & Bailey	1,365,000	1,365,000	0
FedEx Corp.	1,327,600	475,478	852,122

Source: Opensecrets.org, based on FEC records.

organizations to hide their true identity from viewers, while spending tens of millions on ads that directly promoted or attacked candidates.

In recent federal elections, issue ads produced by parties, groups, or Section 527 organizations have not been subject to many laws that regulate campaign finance—because, in theory, they advocate issues and are not attempts to determine election outcomes. In practice, there are no noticeable differences between ads produced by a candidates' campaign and issue ads produced by noncandidate groups that broadcast during an election. The volume of issue ads can sometimes overwhelm candidate ads. In seventeen of the most competitive U.S. House races in 2000, "outside" spending during the campaign (issue-ads funded by parties, Section 527 organizations, and other groups) exceeded spending of candidates by 2:1.[8]

Estimates place levels of spending on sham issue ads in 2000 at over $500 million, up from $150 million in 1996.[9] The vast majority of spending was by parties. Known groups such as the AFL-CIO, the Business Roundtable, U.S. Chamber of Commerce, Planned Parenthood were also major players funding unregulated issue ads during the campaign season. Other groups spending millions on ads had innocuous sounding names like Citizens for Better Medicare (financed by the pharmaceutical industry), Americans for Equality (the NAACP), American Family Voices (AFSCME), and Americans for Job Security (a conservative group funded by insurance firms and other businesses). Citizens for Better Medicare spent $25 million between Super Tuesday (March 7th) and the November election—praising Republicans and attacking Democrats who backed prescription drug legislation that the pharmaceutical industry opposed. The ads did not mention that they were paid for by the pharmaceutical industry.

Another Section 527 organization from 2000 was Republicans for Clean Air—a group that appeared out of nowhere to run $2.5 million in TV ads in Ohio, New York, and California immediately prior to the March 7 Republican primaries.[10] As we note in Chapter 6, John McCain had been building momentum against George W. Bush going into the March 7 primaries. The Republicans for Clean Air ads attacked McCain's environmental record, while praising Bush's. The Sierra Club and the League of Conservation Voters assailed the commercial's accuracy. Postelection research determined that Sam Wyly, a prominent Texas Republican from the energy industry who was a major contributor to Bush's Texas gubernatorial campaigns, financed the ads. The group was created by Wyly and a political consultant who worked with the Republican congressional leadership.[11]

The role of soft money thus exploded in the 1990s, and came to rival hard money as a source of campaign funds. During the 2000 election, both parties set new records in soft-money fundraising. The Democrats and Republicans collected nearly $500 million in soft money in 2000. Republicans collected $250 million—up 81 percent since 1996, while Democrats raised $245 million—up 98 percent from 1996. Most of this money was transferred to state party committees to spend on federal election activities in the states. State parties also raised about $600 million of their own soft money in 2000.[12] The 2000 presidential election was the first in history in which the parties spent more on TV ads than candidates did.[13] Given lax disclosure requirements, it is difficult to know how much was spent during the election by other nonparty groups.

Corporations and unions can increase the size and effect of their contributions by giving both hard and soft money. The American Federation of State, County, and Municipal Employees (AFSCME), for example, gave $2.58 million in hard PAC contributions in 2000, plus another $5.95 million in soft money, nearly all to Democrats. Corporations like Enron and Federal Express also get more bang for their bucks by giving both hard and soft money. In

2000, FedEx gave $1.175 million in hard PAC money ($765 to Republicans) and $1.327 million in soft money (mostly to Republicans).[14]

DIRTY MONEY AND DIRTY POLITICS

The top-twenty-five soft-money donor list reads as a "who's who" of unions and corporations that seek—and often receive—favorable treatment from Congress and presidential administrations. In 2000, leading donors included: no. 19, Pfizer—a pharmaceutical firm that reported $1 billion in profits in 1998, but paid no income tax. Pfizer actually received a $100 million refund as a result of tax credits their lobbyists secured from Congress. Joining them in the top tier of contributors is another pharmaceutical company that enjoys similar industry-specific tax advantages—Bristol-Meyer Squibb, no. 13. Both firms also lobby to limit consumer access to generic drugs. Such drugs cut into their profit margins on brand-name pharmaceuticals.[15]

In 2002, the Eli Lilly corporation contributed more money than any other pharmaceutical firm—$1.6 million in PAC and soft money, with 80 percent going to Republicans. Lilly managed to get a "rider" amendment onto the 2002 Homeland Security bill that protected it against lawsuits resulting from a vaccine (thimerosal) alleged to have caused autism in children. No one in Congress admitted to authoring the narrowly tailored amendment to the bill, which President Bush signed into law. Lilly had spent over $3 million on elections between 2000 and 2002. Bush's Budget Director (Mitchell Daniels Jr.) served on Lilly's Board of Directors, and Bush appointed the company's CEO to advise him on domestic security matters months before signing the bill.[16]

Microsoft (no. 9) increased donations to both parties in 2000 after losing a federal antitrust trial. After the 2000 election, the new Bush Justice Department pulled back on its antitrust actions against the firm. Microsoft was joined on the top-ten list by another major firm seeking to limit its exposure in the judicial arena (Philip Morris, no. 8).

A (once) relatively unknown telecommunications firm, Global Crossings, ranked eleventh on the list of contributors: Incorporated in Bermuda in order to avoid U.S. taxes, it gave nearly $3 million in hard and (mostly) soft money to federal candidates in 2000. It then won a $137 million Pentagon contract (with options of $450 million more) in July 2001. AT&T (no. 2 on the list) noted that Global never had the security standards to be eligible to bid on the contract, but the government changed rules about who could bid in order for Global to be eligible for the contract. Global's influence was further enhanced in other ways. They hired a senator's wife (for $2.5 million over six months), and a former secretary of defense (William Cohen) as lobbyists, donated $1 million to President Clinton's library fund (while Clinton was in office), and gave stock opportunities to President Bush (the elder) and to the head of the DNC (Terry McAuliffe) worth $14 million and $18 million, respectively. The company filed for bankruptcy in early 2002, but remained a candidate for the Pentagon contract.[17]

Global ranks with other telecommunications firms (including no. 2 AT&T, no. 12 S.B.C., no. 23 Verizon, no. 47 Bell South, no. 60 Quest, no. 66 World-Com/MCI, and no. 115 Sprint) who contributed over $32 million to candidates, parties, and candidate-controlled PACs between 1999 and 2001. The telecoms sought to influence regulations that structure how they will share billions of dollars in profits from supplying Internet access, cable TV, standard telephone, high speed data access, and various wireless services.[18] On a key vote that advanced regulations favorable to the "baby bells" at the expense of consumers and long-distance carriers, members of Congress voting "yes" received an average of $14,700 from the baby bells—compared to $2,200 from long-distance firms. Those voting "no" received more from long-distance firms. Contributions were a better predictor of the floor vote than party affiliation.[19]

Public opinion data in Table 8.1 (on page 153), and survey data presented in Chapter 2, suggest that the vast majority of Americans believe that public policy is made to serve the interests of these large donors, rather than the general public. Enron (no. 15), the failed energy giant, reveals much about what campaign contributions can buy. By late 2001, Enron was suspected of manipulating energy prices, disclosing false information about its business dealings, lying to investors about earnings, defrauding consumers, forcing employees to hold onto worthless stock (while executives cashed theirs in), and defrauding shareholders. These activities precipitated the firm's eventual bankruptcy and may end up costing shareholders and consumers well over $100 billion, but they produced tremendous wealth for some Enron executives.

Before its collapse, Enron contributed aggressively to candidates from both parties to promote deregulation of energy and broadband markets that it controlled, and energy projects it had interests in (see Table 8.4 on page 162). In the 2000 election cycle alone, Enron gave $1.671 million in soft money (68 percent to Republicans) and $280 million in PAC funds to federal candidates (69 percent to Republicans). From 1990 to 2000, Enron gave more than $9 million to candidates and parties (mostly Republican), while reporting another $8,700,000 in lobbying expenses between 1997 and 2001. Arthur Anderson, the accounting firm that helped Enron hide its pyramid-scheme financing from investors, gave $5,000,000 to candidates during the same period, and reported an additional $9,500,000 in lobbying.[20]

In retrospect, it seems that the contributions paid off. State and federal statutes and regulations were changed to give Enron tremendous leverage over energy supply, production, distribution, and long-term contracts. The company was able to manufacture an energy "crisis" in western states by reducing transmission capacity at critical moments and then forcing local power users into long-term contracts at inflated rates.[21] Enron and other large contributors, including Arthur Anderson, also succeeded in getting regulations

TABLE 8.4   BUYING LAX REGULATIONS, 1990–2001

Arthur Anderson

Soft money contributions	$2,622,800
Contributions to PACs	650,000
Contribution to individual candidates	1,947,000
Contributions in Texas	10,000
Anderson contribution totals	5,229,800
Anderson lobbying spending (1997–2001 only)	9,500,000
Anderson total	$14,729,800

Enron

Soft money contributions	$3,567,200
Contributions to PACs	1,146,700
Contributions to individual candidates	1,237,000
Bush/Cheney Inaugural Fund	300,000
Republican Convention contributions	1,000,000
Bush recount fund	10,000
Contributions in Texas elections	312,000
Other state-level contributions	1,500,000
Enron contribution totals	9,072,900
Enron lobbying spending (1997–2001 only)	8,500,000
Enron total	$17,572,900
Total reported political spending	**$32,302,700**

Source: Opensecrets.org, based on FEC records.

on accounting firms weakened, and securities laws passed that made it difficult to collect damages from firms like Enron and Anderson.[22] Enron, although bankrupt and under investigation by members of Congress whose campaigns they financed, stood to collect $254 million in tax credits as a result of a bill Congress passed in 2000.

Although the size of these contributions might seem large to citizens, and even to candidates, they pale in comparison to what is at stake. Federal laws, regulations, and purchasing decisions affect how billions of dollars in business will flow to a relatively small number of firms. Microsoft has billions in profits each year that could be affected by Justice Department actions. In 2000 Lockheed (no. 37 in soft money) won a $200 billion contract to build the next generation of military aircraft, edging out Boeing (no. 72), while spending $10 million lobbying Congress and the Clinton administration. Lockheed contributed much more to key congressional committee members than Boeing, and to committee chairs involved with weapons procurement. When the stakes are this high, a few million dollars might not seem like much to the donor.[23]

American elected officials are not passive recipients of all this cash. The average member of Congress must actively raise funds for her party's accounts and her personal campaign accounts—something that is absent in European nations discussed below. As noted above, the typical representatives here spend a substantial amount of time in the pursuit of campaign cash. One congressional leader, Republican Whip Tom Delay, was sued in 2000 (by rival Democrats) for racketeering, due to his aggressive pursuit of contributions and suspicious association with untraceable Section 527 organizations.[24] Delay, know around Capitol Hill as "the Hammer," had made it known that he would not deal favorably with lobbyists who failed to contribute to Republican causes, and that he would look askance at lobbyists who gave money to Democrats.

This kind of behavior—like any other of the behaviors we recount in this book—is not confined to one party, in this case, the Republicans. Some credit former Democratic Whip Tony Coelho for being among the first to adopt this technique in dealing with special interests. As with all the examples throughout this book, we should underscore that we see both main parties deserving of credit and blame.

CAMPAIGN FINANCE AND PARTICIPATORY INEQUALITY

For our purposes, the issue is not whether campaign contributions make the difference when it comes to setting public policy. The main point is that reasonable people—including many contributors and millions of American citizens—believe that it does. The power of large contributions by interested groups, as it is perceived by the general public, distances citizens from their government. The problem is made worse by the fact that most Americans are not in a position to give very much money—their voice is their vote, not their checkbook.

As Schlozman, Brady, and Verba point out, contributing money has become an important form of political participation in the United States. About one-fourth of citizens contribute some money to political campaigns. However, in 1988 the top 9 percent of income earners gave over half of all contributions—even though they cast just about 10 percent of all votes. The 56 percent of Americans in the two lowest income brackets cast 46 percent of all votes (many poor citizens fail to vote), but gave just 16 percent of all contributions.[25] Given the explosion of $100,000-plus soft money contributions since 1988, and a growing wealth gap between the rich and poor, this form of participatory inequality has probably grown even more pronounced. If voting and contributing are some of the primary forms of participation, a key question is whether voter-cum-donors, or just plain old voters, are represented equally. The discussion above suggests that they are not. It is no surprise, then, that 72 percent of Americans wanted stricter campaign finance laws adopted as of 2002.[26]

REFORMING CAMPAIGN FINANCE:
CAN CAMPAIGNS BE RUN WITH "CLEAN" MONEY?

The underlying concern about money and politics is the same overseas as in the United States. The question of "Who pays, and what are they getting for their money?" is one that preoccupies other democracies too. Campaign finance rules used in these nations, and in some American states, may offer some guidance about how campaigns might be financed without raising expectations that major donors receive favorable treatment from elected officials.[27]

MODES OF CAMPAIGN FINANCE IN OTHER NATIONS

Most advanced European democracies reflect a context for campaign finance that is entirely different from the United States. The need for campaign funds from large donors is reduced in several ways. First, parties have mass membership bases that provide "clean" contribution funds from individual members that American parties do not have. Second, state subsidies provide an additional source of funds. Third, the largest campaign expense—TV—is provided at greatly reduced cost in some of these nations. Fourth, elected officials often cannot solicit, or accept, personal campaign contributions from the interests that lobby them. Finally, since there are few limits on how party organizations raise money, and since candidates do not raise their own funds, there is little need for outside groups to establish bogus "independent" campaign organizations to launder money.

Parties are much more central features on the political landscape outside the United States. As a consequence, politics overseas is far less centered on candidates and far more focused on political parties. This is especially true for European countries where the electoral system only allows voters to cast a ballot for parties and not for individual candidates. Under list-PR, for example, voters cannot choose an individual candidate but must cast a ballot for a party and then the party decides which individual party member goes to the legislature. In the United States, campaigning and organizing activities, especially during elections, are centered on individuals. In Europe, the focus is much more on the party. Individual candidates, then, are largely irrelevant so far as European politics is concerned. Parties raise money in this context, not individual candidates. This means that donor access to representatives is, nominally, one step removed from the direct relations that exist in the United States.

Two other points follow from this. First, outside the United States, parties often gain an important portion of their finances from individual members. Citizens pay a fee to join the party. The amount of the fee varies. For Britain's Conservative party it is 15 pounds ($22) each year; for the Dutch PvdA the fee is income based, on a progressive scale from around f.30 ($50) a year to a maximum of 2 percent of gross annual income. Second, European parties are more or less permanent features of the landscape. Party activities go on between elections and so parties need money to pay the bills between elections; rent and salary and operating expenses all need to be found. American national parties have only recently began to resemble (but not yet match) European parties as the main players in financing national elections.

With this preface in mind, there are three broad areas to discuss in relation to campaign finance in Europe and other nations—the degree to which governments provide public subsidies to parties, the presence of limits on spending and contributions, and the question of transparency.

PUBLIC SUBSIDY: THE CASE FOR IT

One of the concerns about private money is that legislators and parties may be bought by *special* interests. Not only does this seem untoward on the face of it, it is especially troublesome given that parties are so important to democratic politics. As the Neill report on *Standards in Public Life* in Great Britain put it

> Political parties are essential to democracy. Needless to say, they are not always popular. They emphasize conflict rather than co-operation. They are associated with vehement controversy. They can appear self-serving. Nevertheless, no modern democracy can exist without them. In Edmund Burke's words, "Parties must ever exist in a free country."[28]

The criticisms in this quotation, with the emphasis on conflict rather than cooperation, may sound more persuasive than the idea that parties are essential. Yet, among other things, parties help to organize elections, recruit candidates to office, and give coherence to public policy. They help tie citizens to the political system by giving them a "party identification" that gives them an identity and a rooted interest in politics itself. Even in supposedly nonpartisan elections, something very much like parties form, and have to, in order to make the electoral process—any electoral process—function.[29] Given the importance of political parties to the functioning of democratic politics, how should they raise funds sufficient to enable them to perform their important tasks? Many nations provide some form of public subsidy to parties in order to guarantee that they need not solicit campaign funds, and to help insure that elections are conducted with clean money. In U.S. federal elections, public subsidies are provided directly to the national parties for presidential elections, only partly in cash payments for campaigning, as well as some subsidies for the conventions that are inextricably part of the campaigns. The argument in favor of public support is that it will help parties (and legislators) perform the functions that are important to democratic politics—rather than spending time raising money. Public subsidies also help to reduce a party's dependence on large contributors or lobby groups. Furthermore, subsidies will help promote equality among parties. Public money

helps small parties express their opinions on the political stage, and so helps
to level the political playing field.

The most prominent forms of subsidy are direct cash payments funded by
taxes. But other subsidies exist that may not be so obvious. For example, nearly all national legislatures allow their members to send material to constituents. Keeping constituents informed is part and parcel of being a
representative, but it is also a means of campaigning. The *frank*—as the practice of publicly funded legislative mailings is known in America—is a subsi-
dized campaign tool, but one that is only available to incumbents.

A more obvious form of subsidy is to provide free TV and radio time to
political parties. Spending on TV ads is probably the largest expense associated with most federal elections in the United States. Many advanced democracies lower the costs of campaigns substantially by providing free TV time,
and by banning paid political advertising on TV. Australia and Italy allow
paid ads, but Australia also provides subsidies to underwrite campaign costs.
Paid TV ads are forbidden in Britain and Germany. Instead, parties are allot-
ted a fixed amount of airtime for which they are not charged. Larger parties
are given more time than smaller parties. The regulations against political advertising and the allocation of free air time thus amount to a public subsidy
to political parties. In New Zealand the subsidy is quite direct: Parties are
given money specifically in order to buy TV time.

Television stations in the top seventy-five U.S. media markets took in between $800 million to $1 billion in political ad revenue in the year 2000—
charging candidates much more than their standard ads rates. American
networks and local stations reduced their coverage of candidates in 2000, possibly increasing candidate demand for paid ads near election time.[30] In 2001,
the U.S. Senate approved a proposal by Robert Torecelli (D-N.Y.) that would
have made political TV ads cheaper to buy. American TV and radio station
owners immediately stepped up their contributions to key U.S. House members, and gave soft money to both party's congressional campaign committees,
while lobbying to defeat Torecelli's amendment. Broadcasters gave over $1.5
million to candidates and parties in 2001, and the House killed the Torecelli
proposal in February of 2002.[31]

The most noticeable form of campaign subsidy outside of the United
States is direct payment to a political party, usually tied to the party's vote
share. German parties, for example, receive a series of payments both directly and to the party-controlled research foundations. In order to receive
funds, a party has to attract at least 0.5 percent of the vote in a general election. After this point the public subsidy rises in line with every vote. Each
party receives DM1.3 (sixty cents) for every vote up to 5 million and after
that DM1 for every vote. Smaller parties are aided by giving more DM per
vote for the first 5 million votes. Like many nations, German parties have individual party members and also donors to a party, and the parties receive
matching funds of DM 0.5 for every DM in donations and subscriptions. Total

TABLE 8.5   STATE SUBSIDIES TO GERMAN PARTIES

PARTY	OWN INCOME (DUES, DONATIONS, AND MARKETING, IN MILLIONS OF DM 1999)	STATE SUBSIDY (IN MILLIONS OF DM 1999)	SUBSIDY AS A PROPORTION OF TOTAL INCOME IN PERCENT (COLUMN 3 AS PERCENT OF COLS 2 + 3)	VOTE SHARE (PARTY VOTE) 1998 ELECTIONS
SPD	212	93	30	40.9
CDU	182	79	30	28.4
CSU	45	17	27	6.7
Greens	34	16	32	6.7
FDP	32	14	30	6.2
Others (12 parties)	54	26	32	11.1
Total	559	245	30	

(1 DM = 50 cents approx.).

Source: <http://www.bundestag.de/htdocs_e/datab/finance/final_determ_gen.html>.

funding to all parties through this means is restricted to DM 245 million (approximately $120 million).

Several other nations such as Australia, Finland, Austria, France, Norway, and Sweden have similar subsidy schemes, although the schedule of rates and amount of subsidy varies. In Sweden, for example, all parties who receive votes over a 2.5 percent threshold receive cash—with additional bonuses for every seat won. In Australia the subsidy takes the form of a reimbursement for campaign expenditures. Although some subsidies, most notably those in Germany, are given with few restrictions, others come with strings attached. In Finland, for example, a certain portion of the subsidy must go to women's organizations.[32]

One area in which the distribution of public subsidy is explicitly equal is in referendum campaigns. Several nations give equal amounts of public subsidy to the "yes" and "no" sides of referendum campaigns. For example, Nordic countries provided millions of dollars in funding equally to both sides of the debate over their referendums on membership in the EU. In this way they ensure a minimum level of spending, even for new issues, and so allow voters access to some information.[33]

Depending on the nation, public financing of parties can form a substantial share of a party's regular campaign funds. Campaign related contributions to German parties, for example, account for roughly one-third of total party income when compared to membership dues and other payments (see Table 8.5). However, these figures greatly understate the amount of state subsidy. Additional money goes to the party caucuses and also to research foundations (*Stiftungen*) directed by each party. These research foundations conduct polling and other kinds of research helpful to parties; total state aid to these foundations runs to roughly DM200 million ($100 million). Once these sources of funds are added to the total, some estimates of the total contribution of state subsidies to German party coffers are around 70 percent.[34]

PUBLIC SUBSIDY: THE CASE AGAINST IT

There are several arguments against state subsidy. One is that parties will become more interested in maintaining their own access to state funds rather than being concerned for the public good. In effect, the parties will become creatures of, rather than controllers of, the state, and become remote from voters. After all, if parties can rely on a sizeable income from the state it has little need to rely on too many individual members and, hence, ties between parties and voters will be weakened even further. Parties will not be voluntary political associations but become agencies of the state. Matching schemes such as those in France and Germany—where some state funds are tied to individual memberships—do go some way toward addressing this point.

Second, the way in which subsidies are awarded depends on previous vote share: Past success at the polls leads to current subsidy, which can help lead to future success at the polls—In other words the vote rich get richer, the poor stay poor. New parties are thus not helped very much at all by subsidy schemes. In fact critics might argue that subsidy schemes simply advantage the status quo. The figures for Germany in Table 8.5 show that the bulk of campaign related financial support—77 percent—goes to the two major parties, the SPD and the CDU/CSU, although this is in proportion to their combined 76 percent vote share in the 1998 election. It would be hard to argue that the twelve smaller parties who, combined, received around 11 percent of the vote, should receive the bulk of funds. France's subsidy scheme allows new parties to receive state aid, provided they raise at least one million francs (approx. $250,000) from 10,000 people, at least 500 of whom must be elected representatives. Obviously this is a sizeable hurdle to clear but, in principle, it is a way for new parties to receive help early on in their political lives.

Third, the subsidy scheme does not, in and of itself, remove the need for parties to raise private money improperly—Germany provides an example of this. Despite its generous subsidy scheme, in the 1980s the Flick company provided envelopes of cash to the German CDU party. At stake were over $175 million in taxes that Flick sought to avoid. In the 1990s Helmut Kohl, the CDU's former party leader and former German chancellor acknowledged that clandestine bank accounts—some of them in foreign countries—existed and that he personally received about DM 2 million in donations not publicized in the party's statements of account. Millions of dollars in corrupt payments can thus take place in a political system in which public subsidy of political parties is among the most generous anywhere. Germany differs from the United States in that corporations and politicians can be prosecuted if caught doing these sorts of things.

LIMITS ON EXPENDITURES AND CONTRIBUTIONS

Explicit limits on campaign contributions or expenditures may help address some of the pitfalls of state subsidy. By placing a ceiling on total campaign expenditures, the spending arms race and the need to pursue private (or illegal) sources funds can be limited. The case for limits on expenditures is that they can help to make elections more competitive by leveling the playing field for parties of different sizes. Small parties cannot, then, be massively outspent and therefore be shouted down by larger ones. Similarly, limits on contributions address worries about elected officials being bought and paid for by wealthy donors.

There are two broad lines of argument against spending and contribution limits, however. First, that they amount to restrictions on freedom of speech. In the United States, mandatory limits on spending would probably require a constitutional amendment. Second, that they can be hard to police. As a retired British party official said, "Show me a limit and I'll show you how to get round it."[35]

As with public subsidies, experiences with spending and expenditure limits overseas vary, with some states imposing limits of one kind or another with varying degrees of success. Table 8.6 presents some comparisons of other nations campaign finance practices. In New Zealand, for three months prior to the election parties may spend a maximum of NZ$1million on advertising. Since monies for election broadcasts can only come from the public subsidy there is some ease in policing this limit. In Britain regulations limiting campaign expenditures were introduced in 2001, giving that country one of the most restrictive campaign environments in the modern world. National parties are limited to just under 20 million UK pounds (approximately $30 million) for

TABLE 8.6   CAMPAIGN FINANCE RULES IN SELECTED COUNTRIES

	LIMIT ON CONTRIBUTIONS	DISCLOSURE LAWS/ REGULATIONS	LIMIT ON EXPENDITURES	STATE SUBSIDY
UK	No	Yes	Yes	Yes
France (companies cannot donate)	No	Yes	Yes	Yes
Germany	No	Yes	No	Yes
Sweden	No	No	No	Yes
Canada	No	Yes	Yes	Yes
Australia	No	Yes	No	Yes
Denmark	No	Yes	No	Yes
New Zealand	No	Yes	Yes	Yes

Source: Neill Report, *Fifth Report of the Committee on Standards in Public Life*, Chairman, Lord Neill of Bladen, QC, "The Funding of Political Parties in the United Kingdom," Cm 4057-I HMSO, London.

each election period. Below this spending limit there are no limits on the donations an individual, firm, or labor union may make and donations above a
certain limit must be reported.

As can be seen from Table 8.6 none of these nations limit donations to
parties. Again, the ease with which limits may be circumvented—by donations "in kind" (e.g., of paper and office supplies instead of money) or by
straightforwardly untraceable cash donations—helps to explain why such
limits are not imposed. Tracking donations is probably one of the hardest
ways to try and regulate party expenditure. By and large, then, these nations
do not limit contributions to parties. Although it may seem somewhat odd,
given the importance of the soft money debate in the United States, European
polities tend to impose few restrictions on how their political parties finance
campaigns. Left-of-center parties thus rely on large infusions of cash from
trade unions, while right-of-center parties depend upon corporations.[36]

TRANSPARENCY

Given the difficulties of enforcing contribution expenditure limits, an alternative approach is to have greater transparency in contributions, that is, making
sure the public knows who is backing a party with money. As a Royal Commission on Canada's Electoral System and the Financing of Parties put it:

> Full disclosure of information on financial contributions and expenditures is
> an integral component of an electoral system that inspires public confidence.
> Essential to enhancing the integrity of the political system are the principles
> of transparency and public accountability. Full and timely disclosure re-
> quirements help remove suspicion about the financial activities of candidates
> and parties by opening the process to public scrutiny.[37]

As can be seen in Table 8.6, all of these European nations do have disclosure
regulations. In fact, the legal problems that German's former chancellor and
his CDU party face are associated with alleged attempts to avoid full disclo-
sures about who was funding the party. In the United States, such requirements can often be evaded quite easily. For the most part, disclosure laws in
these European nations often include regulatory incentives and not just legal
requirements. Up to a certain limit, for example, donations to German parties
are tax deductible, which requires that donors report their activity. Australia,
on the other hand, requires that all donations above AUS$1500 (US$750) be dis-
closed. As with any campaign finance regulation, there are ways around these
laws. Australian donors could give AUS$1499 without being subject to the
disclosure requirement.

The argument against transparency is largely rooted in concerns over privacy. What an individual chooses to do with his or her own money is surely
his or her own business. The ballot is secret, so why not make contributions

the same? This is especially the case if someone is likely to be hounded or harassed as a consequence of making a contribution. In the United States, groups as different as the NAACP and U.S. Term Limits have argued that disclosure of their donor lists would subject supporters to reprisals.

Other objections are more practical. One objection, for example, is that excessive administrative burdens may be imposed. For example, Canadian law requires disclosure for relatively small amounts, C$100 (approximately U.S.$75). Record keeping can become quite burdensome when thresholds are too small, although where to put the threshold beyond which a contribution should be reported is not clear.

A second practical problem comes in deciding when reporting of contributions should take place, and to whom they should be reported. The argument in favor of disclosure is that if voters know who is backing a party, then they are in a better position to judge it and vote accordingly. If transparency is to mean anything, then news of contributions needs to be given to voters before election day. This means that donor information has to be collated a few days before, which, in its turn, means donations need to be made a few days before that. Although this sounds quite feasible it does still leave the problem of what to do with donations made in, say, the last week or two of a campaign: Should they be accepted or not? In the United States, some state governments, most notably Washington and California, are establishing rapid updates of information about campaign donations available on the Internet, thus, all but very last-minute donations can be reported by the media.

EXPERIENCE WITH CAMPAIGN FINANCE
RULES IN THE AMERICAN STATES

Some elements of European-style campaign finance methods are used in the American states, but, lacking party-centered elections, no state has rules that closely match Europe. More commonly, states place various limits on contributions to parties or to candidates. The former are largely absent in Europe, while the latter are unneeded there.

Still, a number of American states have some provisions for public subsidies. Usually, these are payments directly to parties without any links to spending limits. A few states have tried to level the playing field recently by giving funds directly to candidates in exchange for their abiding by spending limitations. Three states have probably gone furthest in establishing "clean money" elections. Voters in Arizona, Maine, and Massachusetts recently approved public financing of statewide and legislative elections. (The Massachusetts program was to go into effect in 2002.) In Maine, any candidate who collects a certain number of $5 contributions is eligible for "fixed and equal campaign funds" from the state in exchange for forgoing all private contributions.[38] In 2000, Arizona and Maine conducted the first elections in the United States where legislative candidates were offered full voluntary public funding in exchange for spending limits. In Maine about one-half of those elected to the state senate and 29 percent of the lower house used public funds only.[39] Fifty-three percent of publicly funded candidates beat their privately funded opponents.[40] Connecticut's legislature passed a similar full-public funding bill, but the governor vetoed it. Vermont had similar legislation pending in 2002.

Vermont held its 2000 gubernatorial and lieutenant governor elections with a full public funding option. Minnesota provides a partial, voluntary public funding option to candidates for all state elected offices, with the program funded by a voluntary check-off on individual's state tax form. Candidates qualify for funds if they agree to limit spending. Party candidates receive some money after the primary, and all participating candidates receive funds after the election if they win at least 10 percent of the vote (5 percent for governor). Minnesota broadens the base of small donors by giving them a refund of $50 for the first $50 contributed to a candidate—this means that citizens direct which candidates get much of the public subsidies. With generous subsidies and reasonably high spending limits, over 90 percent of candidates have participated in the program since 1990. The amount a candidate receives from the state does not vary according to how much they raise privately—funds are fixed according to the level of office. Candidates qualify after raising a threshold amount in $50 increments from private donors ($1,500 for lower house, $3,000 for upper, $35,000 for governor). Parties can spend money on behalf of their candidates in Minnesota without limits.[41]

Reformers believe that contribution or spending limits, particularly in combination with public financing, will make American elections more competitive while limiting the public's suspicions of corruption. Opponents worry that they will reduce nonincumbent spending and further insulate incumbents. It is assumed that incumbents are more likely to have access to large networks of small (or large) donors. Incumbents may even be more advantaged since they start any contest with high levels of name recognition. This logic derives from congressional elections, where there are diminishing returns on spending for incumbents—those who are already well-known can't buy much more recognition. Challengers, in contrast, are often unknown and thus start from scratch, so they may get much more bang for their buck.[42] In elections where incumbents are relatively unknown, however, limits on spending might encourage competition, since incumbents and challengers start their campaigns in similar positions.[43]

There is anecdotal evidence that public funds can change the dynamics of elections. Nearly all partisan offices in the United States are won by Democrats or Republicans. In Minnesota, however, Jesse Ventura was elected governor in 1998 as a Reform Party candidate. Since the Democratic and Republican nominees decided to accept public funds, their spending was limited to about $2 million per candidate. Each major candidate received about

$600,000 in state money. As the Reform candidate, Ventura received $308,000 in public funds in exchange for spending no more than the $2 million limit.[44] Although he spent just under $800,000, without public subsidies Ventura could never have come so close to matching the major party candidates' spending.[45] A third party candidate in Vermont's 2000 gubernatorial contest received nearly 10 percent support.

Public funds may also mobilize candidates to challenge incumbents who might otherwise run unopposed. After Arizona's first legislative election with full public funding, there was a 60 percent increase in the number of candidates. Maine experienced a 40 percent increase in the number of contested legislative primaries in its first publicly funded elections. Most publicly funded candidates in Arizona said they could not have run without public financing.[46]

There is also empirical evidence that public subsidies "work" under certain conditions. A study of outcomes from gubernatorial elections in the United States from 1978 to 1997 found that spending limits create parity in candidate spending between Democrats and Republicans.[47] Furthermore, if public subsidies are provided to candidates and spending limits are set relatively high, parity may be achieved with above-average levels of campaign spending. However, the same study found that major party challengers end up raising less money than they would otherwise (compared to incumbents) in states with public financing if contribution limits are too restrictive.

CAMPAIGN FINANCE REFORM IN THE 107TH CONGRESS

After nearly a decade of attempts at overhauling federal campaign finance regulations, both houses of Congress passed bills that ban soft money national party spending on advertising in federal elections. As noted above, this has become one of the fastest growing areas of campaign expenditure. In March of 2002, the House passed the Shays-Meehan bill after Republican House leaders (Tom Delay, in particular) initially refused to bring the bill to the floor. A majority of House members signed a discharge petition in order to force a floor vote. Earlier, the Senate approved a similar version of reforms under the McCain-Feingold bill. President Bush signed the bill known as the Bipartisan Campaign Finance Reform Act (BCRA) into law in 2002.

Major provisions of the bill included requiring that national party organizations only collect donations in annual increments of $25,000 and a ban on so-called issue ads broadcast within sixty days of the November election (and thirty days of a primary) if they directly mention a federal candidate. Corporations and unions are explicitly banned from using monies from their treasuries to campaign. Anyone spending $10,000 on an ad that includes the "likeness" of a candidate must disclose their spending within twenty-four hours. The legislation also banned candidates and parties from soliciting donations to shell organizations (Section 527s, or 501(c) nonprofits), so that donations cannot be laundered through "leadership PACs" and "candidate PACs" as they were prior to 2002.

The bill increases slightly the amounts that could be given to parties as hard money. It also opened up the possibility that current soft-money donors might contribute to state parties in the future as a way to help a party and cultivate favor with it. Donors can give only $10,000 to state party committees and the money can't be transferred across states, but the legislation did not proscribe state parties from creating numerous new specialized committees to which donors could give $10,000 each. Nonetheless, state parties are banned from spending the money directly on advertising for federal candidates.

It is difficult to project what the effect of the law will be. Restrictions on party and group spending on issue ads were struck down by a lower court on First Amendment grounds. Others worry that the soft money ban will weaken parties, or that it will protect incumbents. A Brennen Center report dismisses these worries by noting that incumbent senators and House members were more likely to lose their elections before the "invention" of soft money. It also notes that parties rarely spent soft money on anything but TV ads, and, as Norman Ornstein and Thomas Mann suggest, these ads rarely mention the party. Although Democrats have pushed for the soft money ban and Republicans have fought it vigorously, some observers, like David Broder, believe the ban could hurt Democrats more in the short term than Republicans. As we note above, Democrats have been able to match GOP soft money, but they have not been able to raise as much in smaller hard money contributions from PACs and individuals.

If the law is upheld, it could have major consequences for how campaigns are conducted. For one thing, less money might be spent in elections, which could lead to less information reaching voters. Less tangible effects involve how public perceptions of politics might change. As the Brennen Center report noted, a ban on soft money would "preserve the integrity" of campaign finance laws that have long been evaded. This might reduce public cynicism about government. The odds of this seem low. Days before the new law took effect in November of 2002, major players from the Democratic and Republican parties established new groups to raise unlimited amounts of money for campaigns. If they can argue that these groups are truly independent of their parties, they may be able to completely evade the new law.

CONCLUSIONS

In debates about regulating campaign finance, it is important to remember what candidates and parties spend all their money on. Campaigns are attempts to inform and persuade voters, and to bring them to the polls.[48] Although many of us are annoyed at the tone of these campaigns, particularly the negative ads financed by soft money, there are solid reasons to think that campaign spending is a good thing for democracy. TV ads, campaign mailings, bumper stickers, and other forms of advertising that cost money, all contribute to a richer information environment for voters. Spending on these things makes the public aware that an election is taking place, makes them aware of who the candidates are, and of what the candidates stand for. Although the fundraising side of the campaign equation leads to perceptions of official corruption, it's worth remembering that there are virtues to the expenditure side.

It is clear that the system of financing most American elections provides tremendous advantages to incumbents. The incumbents' paramount advantage is that they can use the power of their office to raise money in quantities that deter almost any challenger. If challengers can somehow match incumbent spending, however, their campaign may be just as effective, even more so. A key question for the health of our polity, then, is whether we wish to maintain the current inequities, or provide some means for challengers to mount effective campaigns? One (of many) tricks to answering this lies in a related question: How can we level the playing field without decreasing the amount of information that campaigns transmit to voters?

A number of studies demonstrate that higher levels of spending are associated with more informed voting. Our own, earlier work found that voters were able to rely more on their political ideology and partisanship when deciding on ballot measures that had high levels of spending. Such effects were less likely when little money was spent.[49] Another study of spending in congressional elections found that voters knew more about candidate's issue positions and ideology in districts where there was more campaign spending.[50] Spending was particularly effective in generating awareness of challengers and of challenger positions on issues. As one study has it, "the effects of campaign spending lie more on the side of democratic boon, than democratic bane."[51]

The key, then, is to find a way to equalize spending while maintaining a rich information environment for voters. Most of the American campaign finance reform debate simply avoids this issue. Limiting soft money contributions to parties might do a bit to combat perceptions that elected officials are corrupt, but a ban on soft money will do little to make elections more competitive—and the lack of competitiveness, we believe, is a large component of public cynicism. Worse, limits on soft money might reduce the only information flow to voters that contains consistent, coordinated, and programmatic partisan appeals. Whatever reforms Congress adopts in the near term—soft money bans or contribution limits—members of Congress and incumbent politicians generally will continue to solicit money from interests that seek favorable treatment from them. They will continue to have tremendous advantages in raising money, compared to challengers.

NOTES

1. Based on FEC reports.
2. Paul Herrnson and Ronald Faucheux, *Campaign Assessment and Candidate Outreach Project*, 2000 <http://www.bsos.umd.edu/gvpt/herrnson/reporttime.html>. See also Ronald Dworkin, "The Curse of American Politics," *New York Review of Books* 43 (1996): 19.
3. For reviews, see Stacy Gordon, "All Votes Are Not Created Equal: Campaign Contributions and Critical Votes," *Journal of Politics* 63 (2001): 249–269; Wawro, "A Panel Probit Analysis of Campaign Contributions and Roll Call Votes, *American Journal of Political Science* 45 (2001): 563–579; Diana Evans, "Before the Roll Call: Interest Group Lobbying and Public Policy Outcomes in House Committees," *Political Research Quarterly* 49 (1996): 287–304; Richard L. Hall and Frank Wayman, "Buying Time: Moneyed Interests and the Mobilization of Bias in Congressional Committees," *American Political Science Review* 84 (1990): 797–820; David Austen Smith, "Campaign Contributions and Access," *American Political Science Review* 89 (1995): 566–581; Gregory Saltzman, "Congressional Voting on Labor Issues: The Role of PACs," *Industrial and Labor Relations Review* 40 (1987): 163–179.
4. Don Van Natta, Jr., "Energy Firms Were Heard on Clean Air Rules, a Critic Says," *New York Times*, 2 March 2002, A11.
5. *New York Times*, 1 March 2002.
6. Mancur Olsen, *The Rise and Decline of Nations* (New Haven, CT: Yale University Press, 1982).
7. Craig B. Homan, *Buying Time 2000: Television Advertising in the 2000 Federal Election* (New York: Brennan Center for Justice, 2001).
8. David Magleby, "Outside Money in the 2000 Presidential Primaries and Congressional General Elections," *PS: Political Science and Politics* (June 2001): 203–204. See also <http://www.byu.edu/outsidemoney>; David Magleby, *The Other Campaign: Soft Money and Issue Advocacy in the 2000 Congressional Elections* (Lanham, MD: Rowman and Littlefield, 2002).
9. David Magleby, *Dictum without Data: The Myth of Issue Advocacy and Party Building* (Brigham Young University: Center for the Study of Elections and Democracy, 2000). One report notes "$509 million dollars for issue advertising during the 1999–2000 election cycle." See Annenberg Public Policy Center, November 7, 2001 <http://www.appcpenn.org/issueads/estimate.htm>. This figure includes party (RNC, DNC, etc.) and nonparty independent expenditures. A Brennan Center report estimates that $100 million was spent by nonparty independent groups.
10. The Center for Public Integrity reported the buy at $2.5 million, while the Annenberg Public Policy Center reported it at $25 million.
11. See *Washington Post*, 2000, on links to GOP consultant. See The Clean Air Trust <http://www.cleanairtrust.org/villain.0300.html> for information on environmental organization responses. See Center for Public Integrity, 2001, "Stealth PACs Revealed: Interest Groups in the 2000 Election Overview, at <http://www.public-i.org/adwatch/overview.htm> for other details.
12. Federal election figures are from the FEC. Estimates of state party soft money come from the National Institute on Money in State Politics <http://www.followthemoney.org>.
13. Brennan Center press release, 4 February 2002.
14. Contribution reports are taken from the Center for Responsive Politics, compiled from FEC reports <http://www.opensecrets.org>.
15. Ralph Nader, *Crashing the Party* (New York: St. Martin's, 2002), p. 53.
16. Sherly Gay Stolberg, "Provision in New Security Law Helps Drug Giant Eli Lilly," *New York Times*, Friday, 29 November 2002.
17. Joseph Kahn, "Contract Offers Look at How Global Played Influence Game," *New York Times*, 28 February 2002, C1.
18. Jane Hardy, "Key Vote Due on Telecom Future," *Seattle Post-Intelligencer*, 26 February 2002, sec. B, p. 1.
19. Larry Makinson, "Money Talks in the Tauzin-Dingell Bill Contributions Correlate Strongly with Final Vote," Center for Responsive Politics Press Release, 28 February 2002, vol. 6, no. 44 <http://www.opensecrets.org/alerts/v6/alertv6_44.asp>.
20. In January of 2002, Enron admitted that it had been underreporting its actual lobbying expenses to the FEC. Spending and lobbying data from Center for Responsive Politics.
21. According to complaints filed by the attorneys general of Washington, Oregon, and California. See Christine Gregoire, "It's a Long Road to Truth about Enron," *Seattle Post-Intelligencer*, 26 February 2002, sec. B, p. B4.

22. Christine Gregoire, 2002.
23. Thomas Ferguson, *Golden-Rule: Investment Theory of Party Competition and the Logic of Money-Driven Political Systems* (Chicago, IL: University of Chicago Press, 1995).
24. Richard H. Dunham, "Singing with the Sopranos on Capitol Hill," *Business Week Online*, 8 May 2000 <http://www.businessweek.com/bwdaily/dnflash/may2000/nf00508d.htm>.
25. Data from Kay Schlozman, Henry Brady, and Sidney Verba, *Voice and Equality: Civic Voluntarism and American Politics* (Cambridge: Cambridge University Press, 1996).
26. Jeff M. Jones, "Seven in Ten Support New Campaign Finance Legislation but Few Doubt It Will Limit the Powers of Special Interests," Gallup News Service, 13 February 2002, *CNN/USA Today*/Gallup Poll.
27. We start from the premise that it is undesirable that a political party should be dependent for its financial survival on funds provided by a few well-endowed individuals, corporations, or organizations. The familiar maxim that he who pays the piper calls the tune is widely believed to operate in the sphere of politics. Whether or not the suspicion is justified, the ordinary voter is apt to suspect that a very large gift to a political party must be made with some specific object in view. The Committee on Standards in Public Life: The Funding of Political Parties in the United Kingdom, Neill Report, London: HMSO. 1998. CM 4057-I CM, 4057-II. At 4.3.
28. Neill Report, 1998: 2.1.
29. See R. Dalton and M. Wattenberg, eds., *Parties without Partisans* (Oxford, UK: Oxford University Press, 2000) for a recent review and evaluation of the importance of political parties across the Western world, including the United States. The title of their book comes from another quotation by Schattschenider to the effect that democratic politics are "unthinkable" without parties.
30. Alliance for Better Campaigns, *Gouging Democracy: How the Television Industry Profiteered on Campaign 2000* (Washington, D.C.: Alliance for Better Campaigns).
31. Holley Bailey, "The Ad Busters: Broadcasters and Campaign Finance Reform," Center for Responsive Politics Press Release, 13 February 2002, vol. 6, no. 41. <http://www.opensecrets.org/alerts/v6/alertv6_41.asp>.
32. Jon Pierre, Lars Svåsand, and Anders Widfeldt, "State Subsidies to Political Parties: Confronting Rhetoric with Reality," *West European Politics* 23, no. 3 (2000): 1–24.
33. See Jahn et al., "The Actors and the Campaign," in *To Join or Not to Join: Three Nordic Referendums on Membership in the EU*, ed. Anders Jenssen et al. (Oslo, Norway: Scandinavian University Press, 1998).
34. See Pierre et al., 2000.
35. Neill Report, 1998, p. 119.
36. While all parties may benefit from not having to engage in an endless fundraising "arms race" it may not be accidental that the introduction of Britain's first national spending limits was passed by a left wing (Labour) government. The Labour party is traditionally outspent by its right wing rivals. Limiting the expenditure of all parties is thus one way of making sure the expenditure gap does not grow too great.
37. The Lortie Commission, *Final Report: Reforming Electoral Democracy*, The Lortie Commission, 1 (1991): 421–422.
38. "Maine's Clean Election Act" <http://www.newrules.org>. The threshold is 50 contributions for house, 150 for senate, and 2,500 for governor.
39. Elizabeth Daniel, "Public Financing: Making it Work," *National Voter*, League of Women Voters (June–July 2001): 8–13.
40. "Maine's Clean Election Act" <http://www.newrules.org>.
41. Information on Minnesota's law is from Peter Wattson, Senate Counsel, State of Minnesota, "Minnesota's Campaign Finance Law" <http://www.senate.leg.state.mn.us>.
42. Gary Jacobson, *The Politics of Congressional Elections* (New York: Harper Collins, 1992).
43. David Samuels, "Incumbents and Challengers on a Level Playing Field: Assessing the Impact of Campaign Finance in Brazil," *Journal of Politics* 63 (2001): 569–584.
44. Stephen Frank and Steven Wagner, *We Shocked the World: A Case Study of Jesse Ventura's Election as Governor* (Fort Worth, TX: Harcourt Brace, 1999). Ventura received less because fewer taxpayers check off the option to direct funds to the Reform Party's public account.
45. Frank and Wagner, 1999.
46. Daniel, 2001.
47. Donald A. Gross, Robert K Goidel, and Todd Shields, "State Campaign Finance Regulations and Electoral Competition," *American Politics Research* 30 (2002): 143–165.

48. There is literature arguing that spending on negative ads can decrease voter participation. See Stephen Ansolabehere and Shanto Iyengar, *Going Negative: How Political Advertisements Shrink and Polarize the Electorate* (New York: Free Press, 1997).

49. Bowler and Donovan, 1998; Gerber and Lupia, 1995, make a similar case. In contrast, other studies find that voters learn about candidates from TV ads. See Craig Brians and Martin P. Wattenberg, "Campaign Issue Knowledge and Salience: Comparing Reception from TV Commercials, TV News, and Newspapers," *American Journal of Political Science* 40 (1996): 172–193.

50. John J. Coleman and Paul E. Manna, "Congressional Campaign Spending and the Quality of Democracy," *Journal of Politics* 62 (2000): 757–789. Also see Bradley Smith, "Faulty Assumptions and Undemocratic Consequences of Campaign Finance Reform," *Yale Law Journal* 105 (1996): 1049–1091. Smith was appointed chair of the Federal Election Commission by George W. Bush.

51. Coleman and Manna, 2000.

9

THE MECHANICS OF RUNNING ELECTIONS

If we put aside the question of which electoral system we should use to translate votes into representation (i.e., proportional representation, winner-take-all districts, AV, etc.) the simple act of counting votes can be quite complicated and, sometimes, controversial under any system. Holding an election involves a series of bureaucratic tasks of organizing polling places, printing ballot papers, and checking that only the truly eligible people get to have their votes counted. A national election is a mammoth undertaking. As the National Commission on Federal Election Reform (chaired by Jimmy Carter and Gerald Ford) noted, a national election means 100 million voters go to 190,000 local polling places and come in contact with 1.4 million poll workers. It would be astounding, therefore, if there were absolutely no problems at all with that plumbing. Like plumbing, no one gives much thought to actual systems of conducting elections until they go wrong.

The 2000 U.S. presidential election saw the plumbing go wrong in a spectacularly bad way and prompted a wide variety of reactions and hurried examinations of that plumbing system. Florida highlighted the fact that, in any election, many votes go uncounted and numerous people who are registered are unable to vote. Table 9.1 (on page 180) illustrates the estimated number of votes that were "lost" in the 2000 presidential election as a result of the way American elections are conducted. As many as 6 million people did not have their votes counted in 2000 due to machine errors, difficulty with the registration process, or the fact that they could not find their polling place or didn't have time to wait in line. A fraction of these voters were in Florida, but the race was close enough there that these errors affected the result.

Not surprisingly, several commissions subsequently studied the question of what to do about the electoral process and, largely in light of their work, the House and Senate passed a bill in 2002 seeking to amend and upgrade the organization of elections. The National Commission on Federal Election Reform, the National Council of State Legislature (NCSL) Task Force, as well as a range of state commissions and task forces (see list at the end of

TABLE 9.1   ESTIMATED VOTES "LOST"
IN THE 2000 PRESIDENTIAL ELECTION

Faulty equipment/confusing ballots	2 million
Registration process	3 million
Polling place operations	1 million

Source: Report of the Caltech/MIT Voting Project. These are the high-end estimates
from the report.

this chapter) were jolted into life by the embarrassment and upset caused by
the 2000 election.[1] Some had begun to work before the election since many of
the problems seen in Florida were not restricted to that state but were simply
examples of general problems associated with election administration. Other
reports—including the CalTech/MIT project—were initiated in response to
events in Florida.

The various reports and commissions investigating the conduct of American elections identify the same basic issues. The question, put simply, is this:
How can we provide for fair elections in which all valid votes are counted properly and accurately and ensure that people who are not supposed to vote do not
have their votes counted. Further, if there are problems (recounts, registered
voters not appearing on lists sent to polling places), we need clear rules for sort-
ing these problems out—rules that are established ahead of the election.

The NCSL report—perhaps the best of them—presents the goals of election administration as follows:

Voting is the voluntary act of a single individual expressing his or her belief
in a representative democracy.

A.   Every eligible voter should have the opportunity to vote.
B.   Every vote must count.
C.   Voting should be a simple, convenient, and user-friendly process that
     encourages each citizen to express his or her choices.
D.   Voters deserve open, barrier-free access to the polls.
E.   Voting systems should be chosen to allow voters to clearly and easily
     express their vote; and accurately record such votes.
F.   States that use different voting systems in different jurisdictions should
     strive to minimize any disparate impacts of those systems.

While voting should be individual and private, procedures for counting
and challenging votes should be open, transparent, and easily documented to
ensure public confidence in the results.

A.   Rules regarding post-election challenges should be easily interpreted
     and available prior to the election.

B. The processes for counting and recounting ballots in an election must be governed by uniform standards.
C. States should clearly define what constitutes a vote.

It is widely accepted by the writers of these reports that not having rules in place to ensure these things threatens the legitimacy of the political system itself. If voters cannot trust the authorities to count their vote, and count it fairly, the very purpose of elections is undermined. Aside from indecision over who was to be elected in Florida, the various miscounts, recounts, and undercounts threatened public confidence in the system of elections. These issues turn out to be harder problems to address than it might seem at first sight.

In the discussion below, we focus on three broad topics: administration of voter records, the equipment used in voting, and new methods of voting outside of traditional polling places. Through all of these issues runs the central defining characteristic of the U.S. electoral process. In Mann's phrase, "[a]uthority over the administration of federal elections is widely dispersed among [county] governments." In practice this means there are wide disparities in the way elections are conducted not only between states but within them too. Much of the burden for administering and conducting elections means, in effect, that there are 3,066 different ways of conducting federal elections in the United States, one for each county. We can demonstrate the variety of electoral experience simply by noting differences in registration procedures.

VOTER REGISTRATION

The underlying principle of registration sounds innocuous, even trite: In an election we should count the votes of people properly allowed to vote (e.g., citizens over eighteen) and not count the votes of people who may have voted but should not (e.g., noncitizens and everyone under the age of eighteen). Voter registration means keeping a record of who is and who is not allowed to vote.

REGISTERING TO VOTE

The very act of deciding on how easy it should be to register to vote sparks political debate. Procedures for registering to vote vary across states quite considerably. For example, six states (Idaho, Maine, Minnesota, New Hampshire, Wisconsin, and Wyoming) have same-day registration, whereby any qualified resident of the state can go to the polls on election day, register, and vote. No other states allow this. All others—except North Dakota, which has no registration process—require that a citizen submit a registration form some time before an election. For Alabama the registration has to be done at least ten days before an election; for California fifteen days, for Colorado twenty-nine days, for Michigan thirty days.

This relatively simple difference in registration procedures is not without consequence. Supporters of same-day registration argue that it leads to increased voter turnout. In North Dakota and the six states with same-day registration, turnout is 10 percent to 17 percent higher than the national average. Minnesota estimates that election day registrations account for five to ten percent of voter turnout. The candidates who would benefit most from such rules are those who mobilize new voters and those who pull infrequent participants out to the polls (e.g., Jesse Ventura). Some argue that ease of registration may present opportunities for voter fraud (depending on the kinds of ID required to vote), as well as additional administrative costs. If polling areas also become registration areas then there will be a need for additional poll workers and equipment.

RECORD KEEPING

It sounds simple enough but there exists considerable variation even in the very basic administrative process of keeping the list of who is properly eligible to vote. States and counties differ in how easy or hard it is to register to vote, and how registration records are kept. Twenty-seven states have a computerized system for storing voter registration data, although not all are truly centralized. Some link county or municipal systems, others do not. Of those state systems that are computerized, not all are on-line. Computerized and on-line registration allows better record keeping and allows local polling place workers to verify the registration status of voters. Such systems may also help people who move within a state to keep their registration current more easily. Similarly, computerized systems make it easier to remove duplicate registrations. But the ease and convenience of computerized or on-line registration comes with high start-up and maintenance costs. It cost Michigan $7.6 million to develop a voter database in 1995, and an annual appropriation of $1.4 million is needed to keep it up-to-date.

Using a centralized database requires developing a system for uniquely identifying each voter. This is most easily done with a social security number, but not all states can use those. Furthermore, many citizens are opposed to using their social security numbers due to privacy concerns. Although computerized lists of registration data would help a basic problem of record keeping, it is not always seen as an immediate or obvious solution. Notwithstanding these objections, several reports, most notably the National Commission report, advocated the use of uniform statewide registration and record-keeping procedures. In 2002, the U.S. House and Senate both voted to establish a national record-keeping standard by requiring all states to maintain statewide computerized lists of registered voters. First-time voters, moreover, would be required to show some form of identification when they vote.

National standards of record keeping might have provided some legal recourse to address abuses that occurred in Florida between May 1999 and

November 2000, when Florida's Republican Secretary of State hired a private firm to conduct an illegal purge of thousands of eligible voters prior to election day. Nearly 3 percent of the state's African American voters—who vote overwhelmingly for Democrats—were ordered to be removed from voter registration lists that county officials sent to local precincts. The U.S. Civil Rights Commission estimates that 8,000 voters—far more than Bush's official 537-vote margin of victory—were wrongly removed from the voter rolls. When they arrived at their polling places on election day, they were not allowed to vote since they were not on the printed list of eligible voters.[2]

PROVISIONAL VOTING

Provisional voting essentially allows people to cast a vote subject to their registration being validated at a later date. After all, records of who is eligible to vote do not necessarily rely on the most up-to-date technologies. Someone could arrive at a polling place and be legally allowed to vote, yet the record keeping may not have caught up and so she or he may not appear on the electoral roll. This was a major issue in Florida in the 2000 election—many legally registered would-be voters were turned away from their polling places. Should such people be allowed to vote or not? And if so, should their votes be counted? Again, rules have traditionally varied across states. As of 2002, twenty states and the District of Columbia allowed such voters to cast a specially marked ballot. The most common term for this ballot is *provisional ballot*; other terms include *challenge, emergency, special,* and *affidavit* ballot. These special ballots are separated from other ballots and are counted later. California does not count a provisional ballot unless an election official can verify the voter's right to vote, or unless ordered by a state superior court. Connecticut counts such ballots only if an election is contested. If there is a contest, a Board of Admissions decides whether to count a challenged ballot.

How consequential are these differences in registration and provisional voting procedures? It seems certain that liberal registration and voting rules would mean that more people would have their votes counted, but does that really amount to much in the bigger scheme of things? The Caltech/MIT report on voting provides some empirical evidence that can be used to answer this. Its authors estimate that between 1.5 and 3 million votes were lost in the 2000 presidential election due to "registration mix-ups" and due to difficulties that prevented voters from registering or proving that they were registered.[3] Aside from potential partisan advantages that may be gained from changing voting rules, this is a sizeable number of people to be excluded from voting due to the barriers created by bureaucratic procedures. If participation is seen as a good thing in and of itself, then clearly trying to address problems of registration to include several million more people is a good aim.

But there are also partisan questions: Which sorts of voters are likely to benefit from easier registration and voting laws: Democrats or Republicans?

The best guess seems to be that Democrats would have the edge since their voters are more likely to include people who rent and who thus fall off the voter records as they move more frequently. Republicans seem to expect that simplified registration rules would benefit Democrats, and have led congressional fights against national standards that would liberalize voter registration. But, again, the effects of relaxing registration laws are likely to be felt unequally across states since some states already have easy registration laws.

Mann notes the partisan tone to debates over registration laws, with Republicans generally being more concerned about possible fraud. This was evident in the debate over adoption of the 1993 "motor voter" registration law—which allowed voters to register at public offices such as a state Department of Motor Vehicles. Both parties, however, could be said to be quite concerned about partisan advantages to be gained from changing registration procedures, since registration rules operate like any of the election rules we have talked about—they shape who wins and loses. Senate Democrats and Republicans did unite to support the Help America Vote Act of 2002, which required that by 2004 all states must develop some kind of system that allows provisional voting for those who are left off the official registration lists.[4] Republicans gave support to the measure only after being promised that first-time voters who registered by mail would be required to show identification when they vote.[5]

WHAT ELSE WENT WRONG IN FLORIDA: VOTING TECHNOLOGY

Some of these kinds of questions also arise in discussions of the technology of voting; that is, in the machinery used to count votes. The actual technology of voting varies both within and between states. Depending upon the county one lives in, votes may be cast by pencil and paper, by electronic touch-screen voting, or by a whole series of mechanical and electronic devices of various vintages.

This is one area where different rules about seemingly innocuous features—the machines and procedures that should be used to count votes—can have a serious effect on the result of an election. The Cal Tech/MIT report estimated the impact of different vote-counting techniques. Table 9.2 lists the estimated error rates associated with various types of voting equipment. Paper ballots, when counted manually, may have the lowest average number of spoiled, uncounted, and unmarked ballots. This requires a hand count, however, which is slow and expensive.

Machine-read punch cards, while allowing faster counts, are most susceptible to errors in the form of "overvotes" (that is, a vote being rejected because multiple votes are read for a single office). Punch card ballot systems, one of the most widely used voting technologies in the United States (and

TABLE 9.2   AVERAGE RESIDUAL VOTE BY MACHINE TYPE
IN U.S. COUNTIES, 1988–2000 PRESIDENTIAL ELECTIONS

MACHINE TYPE	AVERAGE RACE
Punch Card—"DataVote"	3.2%
Direct Recording Electronic	3.0
Punch Card—"VotoMatic"	2.9
Average	2.6
Optical Scan	2.3
Paper Ballot	2.0
Lever Machine	1.6

Source: Caltech/MIT Voting Project, February 2001.

Florida), routinely discard 2 percent to 5 percent of ballots.[6] In contrast, lever machines and Direct Recording Electronic machines (DRE, which can use a touchscreen) produce fewer overvotes because they do not permit voters to cast more than one vote per office. Lever and DRE systems, however, eliminate the actual ballot, since voters interact with a machine rather than a piece of paper. This makes it difficult for voters to double-check the votes they cast—which increases errors—and also leaves election officials with no original record of the voter's intent in the event of a recount.

The Caltech/MIT study reported that 1.5 to 2 million votes were lost in the 2000 election by virtue of errors in voting technology alone. They identified the "residual vote" as an indicator of the accuracy of various counting methods. The residual vote rate (see Table 9.2) is defined as the fraction of total ballots cast for which no presidential preference was counted. Some voters—quite legitimately—may not feel like voting for a presidential candidate. It is unlikely, however, that variation in residual voting across different counting methods has anything to do with the voters' willingness to vote for a presidential candidate. Differences, then, are probably the result of how the machines function.

Table 9.2 illustrates that all counting technologies have their flaws. Students know that not all Scantron answers will be recorded if the bubble is not completely filled in, and also know that hole punchers do not always make a clean hole in the paper. It is apparent, then, that voting systems based on hole punches and Scantrons make similar mistakes and consequently may leave ballots uncounted. Different technologies seem to produce different levels of residual voting, however. Paper ballots (of the sort that are hand counted), lever machines, and optically scanned ballots produce lower residual vote rates than punch cards and DRE machines.

The Caltech/MIT report came out strongly in favor of using newer vote-counting technologies, especially optically scanned ballots. Optical scanners will not register multiple votes for an office, and allow the voters the opportunity to correct their errors before they insert their completed ballot paper into a machine to be counted. These systems were in use in many parts of the United States by 2000, but it will cost several billion dollars to upgrade all U.S. counties to optical scan technology. After 2000, Palm Beach, Florida, spent $14 million to replace their aging punch card machines with optical scanners. In 2002, the Congress appropriated over $2 billion to assist states in upgrading their voting machines. It also required that by 2006 states install machines that provide voters the opportunity to verify their choices and correct errors before their ballot is cast.

The actual technology of voting shapes whether or not someone's voice is heard in the electoral process. One of the broader areas of agreement across a range of reports studying voting in the United States is that—at least within states—there should be developed a standardized set of rules governing registration and also the act of voting. When Congress finally passed legislation in 2002 directed at reforming voting practices, they set minimal federal standards for the conduct of elections, but they gave states substantial latitude in deciding how to comply with the new federal standards. It is difficult to project what the effects of new federal standards and new voting equipment will be. Some suspect that Democrats will benefit since their voters would be more likely to need provisional ballots, and, as in Florida, the older, faulty punch card vote machines are often still used in less affluent and urban counties that house large concentrations of Democrats. Or, put differently, if adequate technology and provisional balloting were used throughout Florida in 2000, Al Gore would most likely have won the state with several thousand votes to spare.[7]

A little noticed aspect of the debates about modernizing America's voting machines is that the adoption of new technologies can open the door for the use of new election systems. One barrier to the use of cumulative voting, alternative voting (or instant runoff voting), and other election systems is that standard American punch card machines are often ill-equipped for processing ballots needed for these systems. State and local governments replacing their old voting equipment can request that companies bidding for their contracts provide equipment designed to process these ballots, as well as standard ballots.[8]

If new vote-counting machinery is used under the present winner-take-all election systems, the adoption of new technologies will probably have only marginal effects on the political system. Accuracy matters in extremely close elections. Election results will be more accurate, but we don't expect that increased accuracy will have a substantial effect on the competitiveness of American elections nor on the structure of the party system. By extension, better accuracy in vote counting—while a laudable goal—will probably not have a noticeable effect on the public's high levels of cynicism about politics. As we demonstrate in previous chapters, this cynicism predated the

Florida election crisis of 2000. Most American legislative elections are so un-competitive that increased accuracy in vote-counting technology will be un-necessary. It is a bit like using a laser-beam rather than a ribbon to judge who crosses the finish line first in a race with just one runner. One method will produce a more accurate estimate of the winner's time, but the same winner will be determined either way.

VOTING FROM HOME AND ABROAD

Other recent technological changes, however, may offer the promise of alter-ing the composition of the electorate. Voting by mail, or via the Internet, may make it easier for millions of people to cast their ballots. Both are technolog-ical fixes that address barriers to participation associated with the costs and inconvenience of the vote act. Like the use of new voting equipment, these re-forms may not alter how citizens perceive the effectiveness of their vote—but by reducing the inconvenience associated with voting, they may bring new voters to the polls and thus have a noticeable effect on election outcomes.

Being allowed to vote by mail—possibly weeks before the election date, or being allowed to click on the Web and vote, are both ways in which the costs of voting are reduced. Assuming appropriate registration, voters can use these technologies to vote at a time convenient to them. They can, for ex-ample, complete a mail ballot in stages before mailing it in. The states of Ore-gon and Washington have widespread use of mail-in ballots, and other states have adopted rules that make "absentee" voting by mail relatively easy. No state has yet to use the Internet on such a scale but both proposals are worth examining in some detail.

VOTE BY MAIL

In 2000, only about 14 percent of Americans voted outside of traditional polling places. However, the Pacific Northwest leads the nation in the con-duct of elections entirely via mail, with most voters in Oregon and Wash-ington voting by mail. In 1996 Oregon conducted a vote-by-mail election for the U.S. Senate. Washington also conducted a state-wide vote-by-mail refer-endum on financing a football stadium in 1997. In 1998, Oregon's voters ap-proved an initiative to allow that all future elections in the state be conducted by mail. In the 2000 election, Oregon was the first state to hold an all-mail bal-lot election for president. Instead of using traditional polling places where voters go to cast ballots on election day, a ballot was automatically mailed to each registered voter. Oregonians could either return the ballot by mail or drop off the ballot at a designated site. The state of Washington also allows voters to register as "permanent absentee," in order to vote by mail. By 2000, over half of all votes cast in state and federal elections in Washington were by mail. In order to save money, some Washington counties have adopted the Oregon model and conduct all of their balloting by mail.

The general argument in favor of vote-by-mail is that it will increase turnout and lower the costs of conducting elections. In 2000, eighty percent of Oregon's registered voters returned ballots. Although high by national standards, this is near Oregon's historic norm for presidential election turnout. One of the few empirical studies of voting by mail in Oregon concluded that turnout does increase under voting by mail, but the effect is most pronounced for lower order elections (local races and primaries) where interest and turnout has often been quite low. Still, this does not mean that increased turnout produces an major change in the composition of the electorate. As Karp and Banducci—authors of the study—put it:

> Voting only by mail is likely to increase turnout among those who are already predisposed to vote such as those with higher socio-economic status . . . the expanded pool of voters will be limited most likely to those already inclined to vote but [who] find it inconvenient to go to the polling place.

Another study of voting by mail in Oregon reached similar conclusions. "Vote-by-mail" voters tend to resemble traditional polling place voters more than nonvoters, except that they were older, less partisan, and more urban than traditional voters. They also found that the vote-by-mail electorate differed just slightly from nonvoters, being better educated and more interested in politics. Echoing Karp and Banducci, they concluded that vote-by-mail enhances participation of those predisposed to vote "who, on certain polling-place election days, find that family or school responsibilities, temporary illness, or other 'emergencies' prevent them from participating." Thus, this electoral reform "may provide a permanent surge in turnout without any substantial shift in relative two-party strength or overall information level of the electorate."[9]

Against the argument that mail voting improves turnout are several counterarguments. First is that voting by mail takes the social aspects of voting away from voters. One of the appeals, and possibly one of the motivations to vote, is that voters get to meet their neighbors in the polling station as they collectively make a choice. This social aspect of voting is clearly lacking if voters vote by mail. Others argue that early voting by mail breaks federal law, which requires federal elections to be held on the first Tuesday of November. In April of 2002, however, the U.S. Supreme Court declined to hear a challenge to a 9th Circuit Court of Appeals decision that held that early voting was permissible since ballots were not counted until election day.[10]

A more serious concern, perhaps, is that voting by mail, and in fact any kind of early voting, means that last-minute revelations or campaign events cannot influence voters. In Oregon and Washington, ballots are mailed three weeks prior to election day (or the last day for ballots to be postmarked). About one-third of voters complete and return their ballots immediately after receiving them, which means their decisions cannot be affected by events that occur in the last two weeks of the campaign. Mail voting also adds to the time that election officials need to finalize their vote counts, since they must wait days after the election to be sure that all ballots with valid postmarks work through the postal system and are processed.

Another concern is that voting at home, by mail or via the Internet, can generate fraud and mistakes. It is easy to see how voting at home presents risks that might be absent in the privacy of the polling place. For example, spouses and roommates could complete ballots, or possibly exercise undue influence on how other residents cast their votes. There has been little systematic evidence of this to date.

Vote-by-mail may also increase the error rate in voting if punch card ballots are used. When punch cards are completed at home, the voter has no device to attach the card to a list of candidates. This means they must locate specific numbered chads on the card and use a paper clip, pen, or something similar, to punch them out. They have no easy way to correct errors. Ballots that can be marked with a pen or pencil, and then scanned, reduce the danger of errors.

Much of the recent criticism of vote-by-mail and early absentee mail voting may be based on observations from the 2000 Florida presidential election. In fact, the Caltech/MIT report recommends restricting or abolishing on-demand absentee voting by mail. Their perspective is probably affected by error rates associated with punch cards, and the fact that local officials in Florida presided over the counting of hundreds of illegal absentee ballots with votes for George W. Bush that arrived after election day.[11] One problem with damning voting-by-mail with this perspective, however, is that similar reasoning could be used to critique any voting method by which local officials have substantial discretion in processing ballots.

INTERNET VOTING

Many states have explored using the Internet for elections. Most proponents of Internet voting argue that such a system would increase voter participation and, in the long term, reduce the costs of elections. As of 2002, no state conducted any elections via the Internet, although Arizonans had the option to cast their ballots in the 2000 Democratic presidential primary using the Internet. A plurality (41 percent) decided to vote at home, on-line, while 36 percent voted by mail, 14 percent voted with traditional ballots in polling places, and 5 percent voted by Internet at polling places. There are reasons to expect that many Americans who do not vote would do so if they could vote on-line. A survey from Arizona found that six of ten nonvoters reported they would vote if they could do so via the Internet.[12] A national (ABC News) poll found that 42 percent of Americans would vote on-line if allowed to, with support greatest among the young.

In 2002 the United Kingdom experimented with Internet voting in local elections. In the UK case, the appeal is held to be especially strong among younger voters. In an interview with the *Guardian* newspaper, a leading member of the UK government described the traditional system of voting—going to the polling booth to mark crosses on ballots with a pencil—as "astonishingly quaint." He went on:

> I suspect for anybody under 40, polling day is the only point in the year when they actually see a pencil stub, and that's probably why it's tied to a piece of string, because it's so rare and they might pocket it as a souvenir.[13]

Despite the enthusiasm of some politicians, especially those trying a little too hard to connect to a younger generation of voters, a number of task forces and special committees that have been formed to study the potential of Internet voting have found that today's technology may not yet handle secure voting over the Internet. This is true even for the UK, where the independent and nonpartisan Electoral Reform Society echoed concerns from the California Internet Voting Task Force.

The California task force found that, although the Internet would allow increased access to many potential voters, technological threats to security, integrity, and secrecy of ballots exist. Viruses or hackers, for example, could corrupt the results. Moreover, when voting takes place over the Internet, for those who do not live alone, as through the U.S. Postal Service, the privacy and security of the voting booth may be lost. Internet voting, then, does not seem a likely choice for widespread adoption any time soon. Many do believe, however, that some forms of on-line voting will be a reality eventually. Even if "remote" Internet voting from home is not widely adopted soon, "polling place Internet voting" offers new opportunities for administering elections while retaining the privacy of the voting booth. The Secretary of State of Washington, the National Science Foundation, and others, moreover, have developed secure systems for digital signatures that may resolve some concerns about the potential for fraud associated with Internet voting.

As with vote-by-mail, we expect that any increase in turnout associated with wide-spread use of Internet voting would probably be limited to those voters who are occasionally inconvenienced on election day, and to those in higher socio-economic groups who are already predisposed to vote. Nonetheless, as with vote-by-mail, Internet voting could produce a marginal increase in turnout for lower-level elections. Some worry that any such increase in participation will "exacerbate the current class bias in American elections."[14] Although this may in fact be true, it seems an odd justification for resisting an innovation that increases overall participation. This reasoning would have us pursuing election procedures that *reduce* participation of groups until someone's view of a representative electorate is produced.

A NATIONAL HOLIDAY?

Much of the discussion of registration laws, new voting technologies, and voting from home hinge on the argument that lack of turnout at election time results from logistic burdens and aspects of daily life that make voting too bothersome for many people. The Carter-Ford National Commission on Electoral Reform (2001) suggested that one way to address this would be to make election day a national holiday, as it is in Germany. The idea is that if people are given a day off from work expressly in order to vote, then it should be much easier for people to vote. Thomas Mann, author of the Brookings Institute report of elections, presents a similar idea by suggesting that longer polling place hours might also help ease the burden of voting.

CONCLUSIONS

To the extent that problems with American elections are not just a function of the amount of money or kind of technology supplied to local election officials, but are related to underlying issues of who feels represented and who does not, then it seems that many problems associated with American elections are likely to continue despite the adoption of new technologies. Investing money in technology may solve some of the problems seen in Florida, but not all of them. It is true that by making registration and voting less bothersome, more people will vote. However, there are other structural reasons why many people do not vote, or do not feel represented even when they do. Technology will help tackle the question of who a vote has been cast for, but it probably will not do much to address the cynicism about politics and elections that we discussed in earlier chapters. As we have demonstrated, the public's disenchantment with electoral politics predates the 2000 election in Florida.

For the most part, the changes and reforms discussed in this chapter—while often drawing broad agreement across both parties—are relatively narrowly drawn. This in itself suggests that the political consequences of these kinds of reforms are likely to be of limited importance. The main ground for disagreement is over the question of whether federal standards should take authority over elections away from state officials.

Even if most or all of these changes take place—voters still need a reason to turn out and vote. In the UK, government attention to voting by Internet was prompted at least in part by the low (59 percent) turnout in the 2001 General Election. Yet turnout *should* have been low at this election. All pre-election polls put the incumbent—Prime Minister Tony Blair—ahead by a very wide margin and his challenger was generally held to be noticeably less than charismatic. In contests that are such foregone conclusions it is hard to fault voters for staying at home.

Similarly in the United States: If politicians and the political system are, as we saw in Chapter 2, held in such low regard, and if policies and contests seem so little relevant to ordinary people, it is likely that turnout will remain low. Vote-by-mail or by Internet may be "the" solution, if the problem is that voting is too burdensome for many voters. Moreover, if there are inequalities in the barriers posed to people then there is not just a problem of low turnout but of the integrity of the system, as in Florida. That is, if the cost of going to the polls is a major barrier to people taking part in politics—if it involves taking too much time off work or finding too many bits of paper—then these reforms will increase turnout and participation in varying measure. But if low turnout and low participation rates are not really caused by the cost of physically voting but because of a lack of interest in politics, a lack of competitive elections, and feelings of low efficacy, then these reforms will have very little effect in the long run.

ELECTION-RELATED REPORTS

California Internet Voting Task Force report, January 18, 2000
http://www.ss.ca.gov/executive/ivote/

Reports from the California Secretary of State on election reform
http://www.ss.ca.gov/elections/elections_er.htm

Caltech/MIT Voting Technology Report: Voting—What Is, What Could Be, July 2001
http://www.vote.caltech.edu/

Building Consensus on Election Reform: A Report of the Constitution Project's Forum on Election Reform, August 2001
http://www.constitutionproject.org/eri/CP_ERreport.pdf

Revitalizing Democracy in Florida: The Governor's Select Task Force on Election Procedures, Standards and Technology, March 1, 2001
http://www.collinscenter.org/info-url2660/info-url_list.htm?cat=FINAL percent20REPORT

The 2000 Election: A Wake-Up Call for Reform and Change, issued by the Georgia Secretary of State, February 2, 2001
http://www.sos.state.ga.us/pressrel/2000_election_report.htm

Iowa's Election 2000: Facts, Findings, and Our Future, March 12, 2001
http://www.sos.state.ia.us/elections/elect_info.html

Report of the Special Committee on Voting Systems & Election Procedures in Maryland, February 2001
http://www.sos.state.md.us/sos/admin/html/elect-repo.html

Making Every Vote Count: Report of Secretary of State Matt Blunt to the People of Missouri and the Blunt Commission to Review Election Statutes, January 29, 2001
http://mosl.sos.state.mo.us/sos-elec/bluntcommission/mevc-report.pdf

National Association of Counties National Commission on Election Standards and Reform, May 2001
http://www.naco.org/programs/infotech/elections/reportindex.cfm

National Association of Secretary of States State-by-State Election Reform Best Practices Report, August 1, 2001
http://www.nass.org/reports/reform_report.htm

Report of the National Workshop on Internet Voting, sponsored by the National Science
Foundation, March 6, 2001
http://www.internetpolicy.org/research/e_voting_report.pdf

Ohio Elections Summit Report
http://www.state.oh.us/sos/ESpg1.htm

Report of the Oregon Elections Task Force, February 6, 2001
http://www.sos.state.or.us/elections/other.info/task.pdf

*U.S. Commission On Civil Rights: Voting Irregularities in Florida During the 2000 Presidential
Election,* June 8, 2001
http://www.usccr.gov

U.S. Commission On Civil Rights: U.S. Commission On Civil Rights Dissenting Opinion
http://www.manhattan-institute.org/html/final_dissent.htm

Wingspread Conference on Election Reform—On April 10–12, 2001
http://www.ncsl.org/programs/legman/elect/taskfc/wings.htm

Voting in America: Final Report of the NCSL Elections Reform Task Force

NOTES

1. There is a large degree of overlap between these reports, both in terms of the nature of the
   problems to be addressed and the kinds of solutions offered. Again, this is not so surprising,
   as the work of one commission was often informed or strongly influenced by the work of preceding ones. The NCSL Task Force report is the most comprehensive, in part because it can
   refer back to several previous commissions and studies. It is also one of the most thorough
   and contains much useful information on differences in state practices.
2. Greg Pabst, "The Great Florida Ex-Con Game: How the 'Felon' Voter-Purge Was Itself Felo-
   nious," *Harper's Magazine,* March 2001.
3. One source of this figure is that 7.4 percent of respondents to the U.S. Census Current Population Survey who were registered voters but did not vote reported that they did not vote
   because of registration problems. There are roughly 40 million registered voters who do not
   vote nationwide.
     Overall, the report estimates that between 4 to 6 million votes were lost in 2000 as a result
   of registration failures, errors in counting, and errors at polling places.
4. Robert Pearl, "Senate Passes Bill to Clean up Nation's Voting Systems," *New York Times,* 12
   April 2002, A22.
5. Edward Walsh, "Election Reform Passes Senate," *Washington Post,* 2002, A10.
6. Woods and Hancock, 2000, on APSA Web site.
7. Gore would likely have picked up thousands of more votes in the 2000 Florida election contest if optical scanners were used in place of the infamous "butterfly ballots." See Jonathan
   Wand et al., "The Butterfly Did It: The Aberrant Vote for Buchanan in Palm Beach County,
   Florida," *American Political Science Review* 95 (2001): 793–810; Burt Monroe, "Did Votes Intended for Gore Go to Buchanan?" manuscript, Indiana University, 2000.
8. For example, the nation of Ireland recently received bids from major voting equipment man-
   ufacturers for a contract to supply machines that process that nation's Single Transferable Vote
   and Instant Runoff Voting ballots. Vancouver, Washington, San Francisco, California, and
   Cambridge, Massachusetts demonstrate that the technology exists for mass processing of
   such ballots.
9. Pricilla Southwell and Justin Burchett, "Does Changing the Rules Change the Players? Vote-
   by-Mail and the Composition of the Electorate," *Social Science Quarterly* 81(2000): 837–845, see
   page 844.
10. *New York Times,* 16 April 2002.

11. David Barstow and Don Van Natta, Jr., "How Bush Took Florida: Mining the Overseas Absentee Vote," *New York Times* 15 July 2001; Kosuke Imai and Gary King, "Did Illegally Counted Overseas Absentee Ballots Decide the 2000 U.S. Presidential Election?" *Perspectives on Politics*, forthcoming.
12. Rocky Mountain Poll, Behavior Research Center, Phoenix, AZ, November 24, 2000.
13. Comments of Robin Cook, leader of the House, *Guardian* 7 (January 2002).
14. Michael Alvarez and Jonathan Nagler, "The Likely Consequences of Internet Voting for Political Representation," paper prepared for the Internet Voting and Democracy Symposium, Loyola Law School, 2000, Los Angeles, CA, page 28; see also Caroline Tolbert and R. McNeal, "The Democratic Divide: Exploring Citizen Attitudes about the Internet and Political Participation," paper presented at the Western Political Science Association, 2002, Long Beach, CA.

10

CONCLUSIONS

We began this book by demonstrating that many Americans feel disconnected with their government. We observe high levels of cynicism about the value of elections, low levels of voter participation, and, among many citizens, a general sense that they are not well represented in the political process. Approval of American political institutions did go up dramatically (albeit briefly) after the terrorist attacks of September 11, 2001, but it remains to be seen what this reflected, given that trust in government and Congress soon returned to previous levels. Whatever the case, it is unlikely that war or response to the threat of terrorism can remain a healthy way to sustain support for democratic institutions. As we evaluated various electoral reforms here, we have considered how they might provide such support for our institutions.

Of course there is no easy way to assess which reforms might provide an opportunity for a structural shift in the ways that citizens are engaged with electoral politics. In fact, there is probably no "magic bullet" reform to be selected from the menu that we considered. It is unlikely that any single institutional fix can create a dramatically more energized citizenry. From the start we have argued that electoral institutions "matter" in the sense that they structure who wins and loses, who sets the political agenda, and who has influence over elected officials. That being said, institutions, particularly electoral institutions, are only part of the equation. Aggregate levels of social affluence and education, the relative distances between economic strata, the broad fabric of voluntary associations and private institutions that form civil society, frictions and displacements created by structural changes in the macroeconomy—all of these things are likely to affect how citizens relate to their government.

Electoral institutions matter in important ways, but often on the margins. Nevertheless, the effects of changes in some of these institutions, as we have discussed, can be substantial. Many of these proposed reforms, furthermore, are things that can be changed far more easily than these broader social factors. Put differently, it is easier to pass statutes or constitutional amendments about how elections will be conducted and about how votes will translate into representation than it is to alter levels of affluence, education, or macro-economic forces. If an electoral reform produces a major, long-run change in the nature of who is represented, and thus, changes the nature of the demands that governments finds it prudent to address, these social and economic features may also change. But this is getting beyond the focus of our concern— which is discussing how election rules might be changed to make more people think that elections matter.

A MENU, BUT DON'T ORDER EVERYTHING

We hope that readers come away from this book with a sense of some items on various electoral reform groups' agendas at the start of the twenty-first century. We have considered a relatively long list of these items: term limits, various PR and semi-PR systems for Congress, increasing the size of Congress, direct election of the president, new versions of the electoral college, a national initiative, different nomination and primary systems, and publicly funded election campaigns. This is only a fragment of the range of reforms that exist in the realm of discussion. Most of the things we have considered, however, also exist in the realm of practice—either at the state level in the United States, or in other established democratic nations. As we have seen, this gives us some empirical basis for conjecture about how the proposal would affect things if adopted.

It is important to stress that each reform proposal was considered in isolation from the others. Some of our primary concerns about the effects of reforms are whether they will make elections more competitive and make election results more representative of people's preferences. Some proposals might do this, but their effects may be conditioned, muted, or possibly reversed, depending on whether or not other institutional features are changed or held constant. The list we have considered can be thought of as a menu from a restaurant, or even a large food court. Some items may go well together while others clash—one would probably not order sushi with a hot fudge sauce.

For example, open primaries let independents and partisans pick general election candidates and thus may cause general election choices to be more representative of the mass public's preferences in some situations (see Chapter 6). At the same time, "Instant Runoff Voting" (the Alternative Vote) is expected to give general election voters a better way to express their "sincere" preferences for a wider range of parties or candidates (see Chapter 5).

Although each of these reforms may sound good, they might conflict with each other—and open primaries may also conflict with the logic of proportional representation (see Chapter 4). That is, open primaries could pull every party's nominee closer to the political center. This might be of value if many people in the center feel unrepresented in two-candidate, winner-take-all contests. When there are only two credible choices, parties may present voters with candidates that represent distinct extremes of the political spectrum, and thus leave many in the center without a choice they sincerely support. However, multiparty, multicandidate contests conducted under IRV or PR are supposed to allow voters to express their sincere support for three or more parties that have a chance of winning (or of affecting who wins without causing a least preferred party to win). Under this context, voter choices may be maximized by allowing parties to present a wide range of distinct proposals to voters. Open primaries could blur the range of such choices, which could defeat the logic of multiparty politics.

The effects of other reforms we have considered may also be muted by structural features of elections such as the partisan composition of single-member districts and, thus, have little effect on competitiveness. Term limits (Chapter 4) and campaign finance reforms (Chapter 8), as examples, seem to offer less promise for increasing the competitiveness of congressional elections than the use of multimember districts. Term limits may bring "new blood" into Congress once every few election cycles, and campaign finance reforms (such as public financing) may alter incumbent advantages in some close seats,[1] but neither reform addresses the fact that every ten years U.S. House seats are being designed to be increasingly safe for one or the other major party.[2] Term limits would change the face of a representative and cause an occasional primary election to be contested but, in a safe seat, this would probably have no effect on making the general election any more relevant to voters. Recall that most U.S. House seats are safe seats, regardless of whether an incumbent is running or not.

This raises another point about the trade-offs and interdependencies among these proposals. Lacking any major reform that increases the competitiveness of general elections (such as PR, instant runoff voting, independent redistricting commissions, etc.), the only real action for voters is in the primaries. If this is the case, then should primary elections be made more competitive—if only occasionally via term limits? If nothing is done to make general elections more competitive and more relevant to voters, should primary contests be opened to all voters? The answers to such questions depend not just on an assessment of an individual reform proposal, but requires some consideration of the structural features of U.S. elections.

PROSPECTS FOR ELECTORAL REFORM IN THE UNITED STATES

Since there are new winners and losers under any substantive electoral reform, the adoption of most of the major reforms we have considered would certainly be contentious. Politically, we expect that there is a low probability that reforms producing major structural changes—such as Proportional

Representation—would ever be adopted in the near term at the national level. Even if one could establish that a particular change in electoral rules would make the political system a "better place," in terms of Pareto optimality, or however defined, there is still the fact that many incumbents have little interest in undoing rules that set the terms for their ascent to office.

Nonetheless, many of the things we considered in previous chapters—most notably PR—have reasonably well-organized supporters in the United States who continue to promote their cause (See Table 10.1). With effective

TABLE 10.1   A SELECTION OF ELECTORAL REFORM GROUPS ACTIVE IN U.S., CIRCA 2003

GROUP	MAJOR ISSUES	ADDRESS	URL
U.S. Term Limits	Term limits	10 G St., NE Suite 410 Washington, D.C. 20002	www.termlimits.org
Center for Voting and Democracy	Proportional representation, fair representation	6930 Carroll Ave. Suite 610 Takoma Park, Maryland 20912	www.fairvote.org
Philadelphia II/ The Democracy Foundation	National citizens' initiative process	1600 N Oak St., #1412, Arlington, Virginia 22209	www.ni4d.org
Brennan Center for Justice	Campaign finance, ballot access, primary voting, voting rights	161 Avenue of the Americas 12th Floor New York, NY 10013	www.brennancenter.org
Initiative and Referendum Institute	Initiative process	1825 I St., NW Suite 400 Washington, D.C. 20006	www.iandrinstitute.org
Center for Responsive Politics	Campaign finance reform	1101 14th St., NW Suite 1030 Washington, D.C. 20005-5635	www.opensecrets.org
Ballot Access News	Minor party ballot access	Box 470296 San Francisco, CA 94147	www.ballot-access.org
Fairness and Accuracy in Reporting (FAIR)	First amendment, presidential debates	112 W. 27th St. New York, NY 10001	www.fair.org/index.html
League of Women Voters	Direct election of the president, open meetings	1730 M St., NW Suite 1000 Washington, D.C. 20036-4508	www.lwv.org

advocates and broad popular support, major electoral reforms have been adopted in other established democracies despite opposition from incumbents and political insiders. In the 1990s, electoral reform advocates and citizens in Italy, Japan, and New Zealand forced their nations' governments to introduce fundamental changes in how their elections were conducted.

For those who wish to see structural changes in how American democracy operates, there are additional reasons for optimism. During the period of time that this book was being written (2001–2002), electoral reform advocates were able to claim several important achievements. During this time alone, the president signed legislation banning some forms of soft money, and both houses of Congress passed legislation setting new federal standards for voter registration and the conduct of elections. Republican party officials gave serious consideration to introducing dramatic changes to the calendar structuring selection for delegates to their 2004 presidential nominating convention. In San Francisco, the citizens' initiative was used to adopt "instant runoff voting," although the same proposal failed in Alaska. Advocates of direct democracy, furthermore, were heartened by the fact that the New York state senate approved a bill in 2002 (supported by the governor) that would bring the citizen initiative process to New York. This same year, the Philadelphia II group launched a campaign to promote a national initiative for the United States.

The twentieth century also offers examples of sustained interest in electoral reforms that produced many changes to the process of elections and the nature of representation. Direct election of U.S. senators, expansion of voting rights, and state adoption of provisions for initiatives and referendum are all examples of reform efforts that produced results in the early decades of that century. The rapid diffusion of legislative term limits across many states in the 1990s stands as a more recent example of a reform movement that successfully changed election rules—against the wishes of many incumbent elected officials.

There were also near misses. Responding to the close fight and crowded field of the 1948 presidential election, Congress considered a constitutional amendment to award a state's electoral college votes in proportion to the popular vote the candidate received in the state. A 1950 Senate vote on this amendment received 64 votes in favor, and 27 against—which was 3 more than required for the two-thirds majority needed to amend the Constitution. The House, however, voted the proposal down. In 1969, the House approved a constitutional amendment to replace the electoral college with direct election of the president on a vote of 338 to 70, but the idea received only 51 votes in the Senate ten years later.[3]

Our point here is not that these reform efforts reflect some movement toward a logical, coherent democratic vision, or that they even reflect a trend toward greater (or "better") democratic practices. Rather, these examples simply make the point that change is possible. Political institutions generally, and electoral rules specifically, are more fluid than many might expect.

Change—albeit often incremental—can come despite decades of resistance by elected officials. A "crisis" election result (Florida 2000), a critical scandal (Enron), a few seats swinging to change the composition of Congress, a successful ballot initiative campaign in a key state—any of these things, if well-timed, may provide the final push needed to force the adoption of a particular electoral reform. Put another way, these reformers are keeping their flames burning, waiting for the right crisis that will define their reform as "the" solution to a problem that needs fixing.

BARRIERS TO ADOPTION OF REFORMS

Of course, reform is by no means inevitable. In previous eras, major electoral reforms were championed by relatively large-scale insurgent political and social movements that linked electoral reforms to their broader political agendas. For the Populists and Progressives, electoral reforms were tools to advance major substantive goals such as fighting monopolies and large corporate trusts, and redistributing income. Populists and Progressives, furthermore, had well-known, visible governors and U.S. senators who promoted their reform ideas. Senator William Jennings Bryant of Nebraska, Senator George Buckalew of Pennsylvania, Senator George Norris of Nebraska, Governor Hiram Johnson of California, and Governor William S. U'Ren of Oregon were a few well-known elected officials who championed major electoral reforms.

Progressive Era reforms, moreover, were often adopted only after many seemingly disparate social movements—suffragettes, prohibitionists, labor activists, and farmers—built coalitions dedicated to changing the nature of elections and representative democracy. Each may have had their own different substantive policy goals, but they were brought together as a political force after realizing that their substantive agendas would be better advanced under different electoral arrangements. The civil rights movement, as another example, was not just about "fixing" the voting process—it involved extending basic political rights to a well-defined group of people. The goal was to get the vote, and then to use the vote for specific political ends that would help African Americans.

Today, however, conditions are different. Serious problems do exist with our electoral system. As of 2002, America's congressional elections are about as uncompetitive as at any point in the modern era.[4] As we have seen in previous chapters, there are many proposals that would probably make elections more competitive and make election results more reflective of what people want when they cast their ballots. But this does not mean that the wide-spread adoption of electoral reforms are imminent. Many of the more modest proposals such as publicly funded campaigns or improved electoral machinery—in some form or another—may continue to be diffused from innovative states and become used more widely. However, none of the reform proposals discussed in this book are being advanced by major social movements that are making vocal arguments about how their substantive concerns would be better addressed if the United States were to adopt, say, proportional representation or a national initiative process. Without the weight of such movements, we don't expect major structural changes to occur soon.

NOTES

1. As we discussed in Chapter 8, there are reasons to expect that some finance reforms, such as spending limits, may actually harm challengers more than incumbents in some situations, and thus make elections no more competitive.
2. "How to Rig an Election," *Economist* 25, April 2002.
3. Lawrence D. Longley and Neal R. Pierce, *The Electoral College Primer 2000* (New Haven, CT: Yale University Press, 1999).
4. *The Economist* 25, April 2002.

INDEX